*Intimate Conflict*

SUNY Series, The Margins of Literature
*Edited by Mihai I. Spariosu*

# *Intimate Conflict*

## *Contradiction in Literary and Philosophical Discourse*

A Collection of Essays by Diverse Hands

Edited by
Brian G. Caraher

STATE UNIVERSITY OF NEW YORK PRESS

Published by
State University of New York Press, Albany

© 1992 State University of New York

All rights reserved

Printed in the United States of America

No part of this book may be used or reproduced
in any manner whatsoever without written permission
except in the case of brief quotations embodied in critical articles and
reviews.

For information, address State University of New York
Press, State University Plaza, Albany, N.Y., 12246

Production by Cathleen Collins
Marketing by Bernadette LaManna

Library of Congress Cataloging in Publication Data

Intimate conflict : contradiction in literary and philosophical
    discourse : a collection of essays by diverse hands / edited and
    introduced by Brian G. Caraher.
        p.   cm.
    Includes bibliographical references and index.
    ISBN 0-7914-1026-9 (pbk.) — ISBN 0-7914-1025-0
    1. Contradiction in literature.  2. Discourse analysis.
    3. Philosophy—Language.   I. Caraher, Brian.
PN56.C676I57   1992
809'.91—dc20                                                91-30059
                                                                CIP

10  9  8  7  6  5  4  3  2  1

For Irving Massey,
with much thanks and affection

Such dim-conceived glories of the brain
    Bring round the heart an indescribable feud;
So do these wonders a most dizzy pain,
    That mingles Grecian grandeur with the rude
Wasting of old Time—with a billowy main,
    A sun, a shadow of a magnitude.

        John Keats, "On Seeing the Elgin Marbles"

# Contents

|   | Contributors | ix |
|---|---|---|
|   | Acknowledgments | xi |
| 1 | *Introduction: Intimate Conflict*<br>Brian G. Caraher | 1 |
| 2 | *Strife and Contradiction in Hesiod*<br>Henry W. Johnstone, Jr. | 35 |
| 3 | *Plato's Masterplot: Idealization, Contradiction, and the Transformation of Rhetorical Ethos*<br>Charles Altieri | 39 |
| 4 | *The Mechanics of Creation: Non-Contradiction and Natural Necessity in* Paradise Lost<br>Mili N. Clark | 75 |
| 5 | *Money of the Mind: Dialectic and Monetary Form in Kant and Hegel*<br>Marc Shell | 127 |
| 6 | *Metaphor as Contradiction: A Grammar and Epistemology of Poetic Metaphor*<br>Brian G. Caraher | 155 |
| 7 | *Contradiction and Repression: Paradox in Fictional Narration*<br>Richard Kuhns | 181 |
|   | Index | 199 |

## Contributors

CHARLES ALTIERI is Professor of English at the University of Washington at Seattle and the author of numerous articles and book contributions in literary criticism and theory, classical literature, and modern and contemporary poetry and poetics. His books include *Enlarging the Temple, Act and Quality, Self and Sensibility in Contemporary American Poetry, Painterly Abstraction in Modernist American Poetry*, and *Canons and Consequences*.

BRIAN G. CARAHER is Associate Professor of English at Indiana University and an Associate Editor of *Works and Days*. He teaches literary theory, history of criticism and critical theory, and modern British and Anglo-Irish literature. He has published numerous essays and book contributions in literary theory, poetics, and poetry, as well as *Wordsworth's "Slumber" and the Problematics of Reading*. *The Joyce of Reading* is forthcoming.

MILI N. CLARK is Associate Professor of English at the State University of New York at Buffalo where she is a former associate chair and director of undergraduate studies. She is currently working on the aesthetics of taste in Milton.

HENRY W. JOHNSTONE, JR. is Professor Emeritus of Philosophy at the Pennsylvania State University at University Park. He is the founding editor of *Philosophy and Rhetoric* and is associated with the renascence of *The Journal of Speculative Thought*. Among his influential contributions to philosophy are *Philosophy and Argument* and *The Problem of the Self*.

RICHARD KUHNS is Professor of Philosophy at Columbia University and has written extensively on the connections between philosophy and literature. He has published *The House, the City, the Judge: the Growth of Moral Awareness in the Oresteia; Structures of Experience: Essays on the Affinity between Philosophy and Literature; Psychoanalytic Theory of Art;* and most recently, *Tragedy: Contradiction and Repression*.

MARC SHELL is John D. and Catherine T. MacArthur Prize Fellow for 1990–95 and Professor of Comparative Literature and English and American Literature and Language at Harvard University. His books include *The Economy of Literature; Money, Language, and Thought; The End of Kinship; Children of the Earth; Elizabeth's Glass;* and *Art & Money* (forthcoming).

# Acknowledgments

My thanks go to Irving Massey for first suggesting to me the idea of this collection and teaching me to appreciate the ways of contradiction. I thank all my contributors not only for their marvelous work but for their extraordinary patience with an Odyssean project that has taken some years to bring home to safe haven. I also wish to thank the anonymous readers for SUNY Press who provided some fine critique and solid suggestions for the collection, and Richard Kuhns and Irving Massey for their sound advice regarding the introduction and title essay. I also wish to acknowledge a half-year's sabbatical leave that Indiana University provided me in 1990, during which the final version of this text was edited and assembled.

I also wish to acknowledge the editors of *English Literary Renaissance* and *Philosophy and Rhetoric*, who have kindly given permission to use essays that originally appeared in their pages. Mili N. Clark's essay on Milton and mine on poetic metaphor reflect considerable revision and expansion over the earlier articles. Mili Clark's original essay appeared in *ELR* 7 (1977): 207–242, and the earlier version of my contribution was first published in *Philosophy and Rhetoric* 14(1981): 69–88. I also gratefully acknowledge the kind permission of the University of California Press to use a chapter that originally appeared in Marc Shell's *Money, Language, and Thought: Literary and Philosophical Economies from the Medieval to the Modern Era* (1982). I also gratefully acknowledge the kind permission of the University of Chicago Press to use a shorter version of a chapter that appears in Richard Kuhns's *Tragedy: Contradiction and Repression* (1991).

# 1

# *Introduction: Intimate Conflict*

## Brian G. Caraher

The topic of contradiction in discourse cannot be rendered as simply as an appeal to a textbook derivation of the principle of non-contradiction or the law of excluded middle.[1] This selection of essays by diverse hands in the fields of literary studies, comparative literature, aesthetics, and philosophy sets out to demonstrate just how rich and productive the notion of contradiction in discourse can be. The unifying focus centers on the pivotal role of contradiction in both literary and philosophical discourse and analysis. It is a notion that has arisen in various configurations in the work of modern literary theorists and philosophers, but it has not received any extended or systematic treatment. This volume would fill that need.

The main idea pursued throughout this introduction and the six essays is that contradiction should be taken as a basic literary and philosophical concept and that as such it indicates the conflicted and conflictual nature of philosophical thinking, aesthetic experience, and literary language. Contradiction does not cancel, undermine, or paralyze cognition and discourse but, instead, helps to constitute these activities in intriguing and sometimes disturbing perplexity. In Aristotelian and later analytic and symbolic logics, contradiction poses a problem for systematic thought and discourse. Its treatment through the law of excluded middle, for instance, is often a fundamental strategy in generating and codifying the rules of rational discourse. The efforts of the contributors to this volume revolve around the contention that the impulse to secure and guarantee non-contradiction in discourse may not be much more pivotal than the generative function of contradiction itself. Contradiction, in other words, occasions inescapable and necessary discursive conflict in literature and philosophy, and such conflict constitutes fundamental strategies of thought within the twin disciplines.

It is very difficult for either finely trained intellects or the ordinarily opinionated to get much beyond the view that logical, verbal, and argumentative contradictions seriously disable discourse of any kind. The detection of contradictions in discourse characteristically seems a primary gesture in the disputation and rejection of claims to speak the truth regarding some area of experience and knowledge. In his *Tractatus Logico-Philosophicus* Ludwig Wittgenstein presents a powerful instance of this sort of view. For example, Wittgenstein regards tautologies and contradictions as the two "limiting cases" of the truth-functionality of logical propositions. In propositions 4.462 and 4.464 he puts his case succinctly:

> Tautologies and contradictions are not pictures of reality. They do not represent any possible situations. For the former admit *all* possible situations, and the latter *none*.
> A tautology's truth is certain, a proposition's possible, a contradiction's impossible.[2]

Contradictions do not give us "pictures of reality"; their truth is "impossible" to determine. Within the early Wittgenstein's model of logical language as a mirror of the world, contradiction is "the outer limit" at which the possibility of true statements or pictures of the world vanishes (*TLP*, pp. 71, 75, 79; 4.466, 5.101, 5.143). The visual, spatialized, and pictorial qualities of Wittgenstein's representational or correspondence theory of logical language and truth, however, promote an intellectually austere regard for the kind of propositions that can speak the truth of things. Analytic statements that allow one to model or picture facts and certain sorts of relations among them demand acceptable representations of things in the world. Contradictions cannot render possible states of fact and merely confuse clear lines of analytic representation. As Wittgenstein asserts: "It is impossible to represent in language anything that 'contradicts logic' as it is in geometry to represent by its co-ordinates a figure that contradicts the laws of space, or to give the co-ordinates of a point that does not exist" (*TLP*, p. 19; 3.032). However, the Dutch artist M. C. Escher has gained considerable notoriety for his numerous graphic representations of contradictions that can be displayed within the field of analytic geometry and visual perspective. For instance, Escher's *Ascending and Descending* (1960) and *Waterfall* (1961) (see figures 1 and 2) represent visual loops that defy the logic of "the laws of space" or depict "co-ordinates of a point that does not exist." Escher's art models a visual manner of representation that allows contradiction of logical and analytic forms of rendering the truth of things. Moreover, Escher's work permits intimate conflict among world-pictures, world-models, and our ways of rendering things visible, representable, indeed *possible*. Escher invents a visual language that lets us see the

Introduction 3

*Figure 1.* Ascending and Descending, *by M. C. Escher (lithograph, 1960). Reproduced with the kind permission of Cordon Art, Baarn, Holland and the Collection Haags Gemeentemuseum, The Hague, Holland.*

laws of visual logic, spatial relationships, and analytic geometry speaking against themselves in figurations that generate rather than vacate possibility. The austerity of the early Wittgenstein's propositions regarding the impossible truth-claims of contradictions would

*Figure 2.* Waterfall, *by M. C. Escher (lithograph, 1961). Reproduced with the kind permission of Cordon Art, Baarn, Holland and the Collection Haags Gemeentemuseum, The Hague, Holland.*

strive to delimit and circumscribe the instructive possibilities of contradiction for discourse.

In juxtaposing Escher's lithographs and Wittgenstein's propositions, I want to suggest the possibilities of contradiction as a discursively generative element. Jacques Derrida has noted the embeddedness of contradiction in metaphysics and the history of philosophy in the Eurocentric West; contradiction is philosophy's "speculative, teleological, and eschatological horizon."[3] Derrida also intimates that contradiction might well be the "repressed" of philosophy.[4] With regard to various forms of discourse—artistic, literary, and philosophical—contradictions allow models or "pictures of reality" to speak against themselves in a manner that does not necessarily render them truth-functionally impossible, silent, or nonsensical. Contradictions can speak the possibility, even the truth, of things in ways that our models of austere representation cannot completely repress.

## *Truth in Painting: Rendering Contradiction*

One of the few generally available and frequently acknowledged texts that actually already addresses contradiction in both literary and philosophical discourse is Martin Heidegger's lengthy essay entitled "The Origin of the Work of Art."[5] This difficult piece of writing sets out to think through the elemental features and originary scene of the work of art, and Heidegger's thought and language bear ample traces of the poetical character of his mode of philosophical thinking and his paradoxical propensity toward mysticism.[6] Besides his tendency to intertwine literary and philosophical discourse, Heidegger further transgresses conventional disciplinary boundaries by contending that truth happens in the work of art—and, what is more, happens in and through a state approximating nothing less than contradiction.

Truth can be said to happen in the work of art, according to Heidegger, in and through strife, struggle, and conflict—that is, the opposition of intimate opponents who belong to one another. Truth, when thought through in the sense of the Greek word *aletheia*, involves "the unconcealedness of beings" (OWA, p. 51). Such unconcealment is possible in a work only because the work opens up a place in which the truth of things that are can show itself. In other words, "[t]he work as work sets up a world. The work holds open the Open of the world" (OWA, p. 45). Heidegger also calls the Open or the open place "a clearing" or "a lighting" (pp. 53–54). Truth, then, is lit up or illuminated in the Open, the clearing of what is. Heidegger's two examples—or better yet, emblems—of this unconcealment of things in the Open of truth are the so-called peasant shoes rendered by Vincent Van Gogh in the painting called *The Shoes* and the idea of the ancient Greek temple that houses its god within. Both works of art create an open place in which the unconcealment of the truth of beings—peasant shoes, the god of a region and a people—can come into the open and be seen as calling up and centering a world. There is at the same time, however, a countermovement to this movement of unconcealment, clearing, or lighting. Heidegger explains that there must always be a countermovement of concealment that affords continuous opposition to unconcealment and whose contrary resistance guarantees the very possibility of seeing truth unconcealed in the clearing. For Heidegger these countermovements of concealment and unconcealment constitute an "essential striving" in which the "opponents," though opposed to one another in an inescapable and contrary struggle, do not consume themselves but instead "raise each other into the self-assertion of their natures" (OWA, p. 49). One opponent is the world, that which is brought into the open place of unconcealment in and through the truth of its beings; the other is the earth, the spontaneously self-secluding and perpetually concealing support of the world. The attempt to bring truth to happen in the work of art, for Heidegger, finds its origin in the essential and perpetual struggle between two opposites. World must not usurp earth, nor earth world. The intimate conflict between them must be maintained for truth to happen in the work:

> Truth is present only as the conflict between lighting and concealing in the opposition of world and earth. Truth wills to be established in the work as this conflict of world and earth. The conflict is not to be resolved in a being brought forth for the purpose, nor is it to be merely housed there; the conflict, on the contrary, is started by it. This being must therefore contain within itself the essential traits of conflict. In the strife the unity of world and earth is won (OWA, pp. 62–63).

Strife—continuous contradiction of opposites that belong to one another—instigates the work of art and discloses perpetual conflict at the origin of the work of art.

Heidegger's idealized evocation of the originary scene of the work of art, however abstract and generalized, does serve to open up the topic of contradiction in art, poetry, and philosophical discourse. The exacting concentration upon the work of art and the conflictual intimacy at its origin carry Heidegger's highly generalized thought into a peculiarly intense dwelling upon implications of his exemplary works of art. Indeed, Heidegger's choice of examples is not arbitrary or neutral; his examples and his use of them intimately shape his conception of the work of art in general. The heavily worn shoes isolated and set in repose in Van Gogh's painting summon up for Heidegger the image and the type of the hardworking, quiet, peasant woman and the intimate opposition between her rural world and the earth that always supports it:

> From the dark opening of the worn insides of the shoes the toilsome tread of the worker stares forth. In the stiffly rugged heaviness of the shoes there is the accumulated tenacity of her slow trudge through the far-spreading and ever-uniform furrows of the field swept by a raw wind. On the leather lie the dampness and richness of the soil. Under the soles slides the loneliness of the field-path as evening falls. In the shoes vibrates the silent call of the earth, its quiet gift of the ripening grain and its unexplained self-refusal in the fallow desolation of the wintry field. This equipment is pervaded by uncomplaining anxiety as to the certainty of bread, the wordless joy of having once more withstood want, the trembling before the impending childbed and shivering at the surrounding menace of death. This equipment belongs to the *earth*, and it is protected in the *world* of the peasant woman. From out of this protected belonging the equipment itself rises to its resting-within-itself. (OWA, pp. 33–34)

This passage, perhaps the most evocative in Heidegger's essay, maintains a partial rendering of the painting. From the painting's silence and still repose Heidegger constructs a world of types, familiar images, characteristic actions, and the generalized narrative of rural existence frequently harbored by those who can view it at a peaceful and sedentary remove. Nevertheless, Heidegger's narrative, his rendering of the truth of the painting for himself as poetical philosopher and as philosophical poet of art, speaks a significant and useful truth about the intimate conflict at the origin of the work of art.

This painting speaks the truth about the elemental and originary conflict of world and earth because Heidegger himself gives it a voice with which to speak. Heidegger insists upon transferring the function of voice to the work itself: it speaks, and it speaks its truth subtly yet generally for those who attend carefully upon it. However, it is Heidegger's typological and narrative constructions that give voice to a work whose world would recede into muteness and opaque self-refusal without him. Heidegger wants to tell the story of a "primal conflict" between dialectical opposites, opponents who belong to one another elementally (OWA, p. 55). Indeed, he rehearses an originary struggle in which his presuppositions and convictions about the work of art are heard speaking to him from the open place of the work that his own efforts at rendering have brought into the clear light of articulation. Contradiction (as the etymology of the word suggests, *a speaking against*) doubly shapes Heidegger's sense of the origin of the work of art. The work involves a contrary struggle between world and earth and between unconcealment and concealment, but it does so because Heidegger reads his tale of contradiction into that place from which he wants the tale to speak authoritatively to him and against other possible renderings of the origin of art. Indeed his second major example—"a Greek temple" that "simply stands there in the middle of the rock-cleft valley"—exists primarily as an idea or ideal of the work of art; it scarcely has being other than in the idealized evocation that Heidegger's own words and conceptions will allow it (OWA, pp. 41–42). The point is that Heidegger hearkens to the intimate struggle taking place within a work of art because of the contradiction at work in his own self-concealing and self-refusing stance before it. His philosophy of art engages in a hermeneutic circle, yet more important than this fact is the fact that he resists confronting this hermeneutic dilemma as the scene of an originary contradiction. The work speaks of a world in intimate conflict with a self-concealing earth only because a self-concealing world of concerns on the part of its spectator engages it in order to generate an open place where the truth of the struggle between concealment and unconcealment can be spoken to the spectator from outside himself. The work of art speaks for, in place of, and against the world of concerns of the interpreter who would render it. That is, Heidegger contradicts—speaks against—himself in order to hear the work of art speak to him about an originary intimate conflict.

In *The Truth in Painting*, Jacques Derrida performs an elaborate deconstruction of Heidegger's "The Origin of the Work of Art."[7] Derrida's performance dwells at enormous length upon Heidegger's reading of Van Gogh's *The Shoes* and a counter-reading of the painting mounted against Heidegger by Meyer Schapiro (*TP*, pp. 255–382). Derrida writes against the "truthful," referential, and indicatively assured identifications that Heidegger and Schapiro make in their different renderings of Van Gogh's painting. Derrida questions how Heidegger can know the shoes are, for one thing, a pair and, furthermore, a pair of shoes belonging to a rural, female peasant. Derrida also questions Schapiro's presumption that the shoes belong to one another as a pair and his aesthetic conviction that the shoes point back to the artist—that is, they are the shoes of a city-dwelling, male and self-reflexive artist. These two contrasting appropriations render the shoes the property of some person, some ghostly presence clearly outside the texture of the painting. Derrida calls each of these renderings in its own way a "hallucinatory projection" motivated by a different "ideology" of identification (*TP*, pp. 366–68). Instead, Derrida insists that "the shoes are there in painting, they are *there for* . . . painting at work. Not in order to be reattached to the feet of somebody or other, in the painting or outside it, but there *for-painting* (and vice versa)" (*TP*, p. 372). Derrida's clever, critically astute, yet painfully taxing performance[8] does coincide with my point about the circularity of Heidegger's rendering of *The Shoes*. Heidegger presumes to speak for and about the truth in Van Gogh's painting without questioning how that truth is a projection as well as the project of his own world of concerns.

Does this conclusion now leave us perpetually in a "strange loop" in which our presuppositions and convictions precondition our renderings of paintings and our projections of the truth of things? Perhaps not, especially if we are willing to attend to the state of contradiction that we place ourselves in when we search for the truth of things in "the things themselves." The position and role of the spectator of art is pivotal, constitutive, constructive, and deconstructive. To truncate the fully creative activities of receiving, interpreting, judging, assessing, classifying, rejecting, reorganizing, reviewing, critiquing, historicizing, discarding, discovering, or appraising works of art leaves them without human agents and social matrices. Works do not work without those who know how or desire to learn how to work them. Heidegger himself senses that "we are moving in a circle" when we try to infer the nature and origin of art from the work, the thing itself (OWA, p. 18). He insists on this route, however, even later on when he senses the "circle" closing "again" and briefly muses whether his path toward the truth in art involves "the empty sophistry of a conceptual game, or is it—an abyss?" (OWA, p. 50). Remaining open to how we read our preconceptions into the very appearances of things may be the only path toward avoiding conceptual games and bridging the abyss created by trying to think the truth of things in themselves.[9] We render "the truth of things" such as works of art by implicitly contradicting the fact that it is predominantly our own preconceptions and world of concerns that we render. Two further examples of reading "the truth in painting" may help clarify things here as well as indicate a way to regard contradiction as a fundamentally formative activity in the discourse of art.

In his ingenious and wonderfully suggestive book *Gödel, Escher, Bach*, Douglas Hofstadter employs the notion of "strange loops" to explain the nature of pattern and paradox in mathematics and logic.[10] Against the work on logical and mathematical systems by Bertrand Russell and Alfred North Whitehead, Hofstadter pits the now legendary insight of Kurt Gödel—namely, that logico-mathematical efforts to prove the systematic consistency of mathematical systems ultimately disclose incompleteness, contradiction, and undecidable propositions (*GEB*, pp. 15–24). "Strange loops," moreover, can be those moments of illusion or those recognitions of paradox and contradiction that happen when, "by moving upwards (or downwards) through the levels of some hierarchical system, we unexpectedly find ourselves right back where we started" (*GEB*, p. 10). That is to say, in proceeding through the normal and supposedly well-mapped terrain of logico-mathemathical reasoning, thought suddenly circles back to itself at its own point of origin. Purportedly systematic structures of logical reasoning disclose gaps, incompletions, outright contradictions, level-entangling puzzles, and undecidable paradoxes. Almost invariably these strange loops implicate self-reference—that is, a proposition becomes trapped in an endless circle of autoreferentiality (*GEB*, pp. 21–23). Hofstadter transfers the notion of strange loops or meta-systemic paradoxes from the fields of logic and mathematics to those of music (Bach) and visual representation (Escher). Strange loops may help to explain the systematic incompletion of logico-mathematical systems of reasoning, but they afford only an extremely clever analogy for the sort of contradictions that drawing and painting render.

Take, for instance, the two lithographs by M. C. Escher that Hofstadter discusses at some length at the outset of his book and then circles back to in his concluding pages (*GEB*, pp. 10–15, 716). *Waterfall* (1961) and *Ascending and Descending* (1960) both create illusions of strange visual loops. In the first, water circulates in the figure of a sharply angular **B**, even though the loop of circulation involves what appears to be a two-story drop from a height well above a millwheel toward which the water falls. Nevertheless, the fallen water circulates in a trough that empties once again at the top of the waterfall. In the other lithograph, two columns of hooded monks walk in opposite directions on a single staircase whose four right angles strangely loop the staircase into an endless grid of mutual ascension and descension. Hofstadter contends that Escher constructs a "chain of levels" that the viewer gets trapped within; the viewer expects and perceives certain levels of visual stability in the drawings, but then gets taken up in an endlessly circulating loop that appears to "represent[] an endless process in a finite way" (*GEB*, pp. 15, 97–99). The viewer, in other words, is repeatedly thrown back in frustration as well as in fascination with the endless self-referring loop that circulates not only through the work but also through his or her attempts to process the work consistently, completely, and without contradicting established frames of visual understanding. Yet this account of paradoxical and self-referring circularity in Escher's work approximates, in the words of Heidegger, a "conceptual game."[11] Hofstadter does not question the appearance of his presupposition of an endless self-referring and paradoxical circularity in Escher's works of art. He transfers as an explanation of the truth of things in Escher's drawings what is perhaps best seen as analogy: the phenomenon of strange loops in logico-mathematical systems. Is the "system" of painting or lithography or of visual understanding of two-dimensional spatial representations *equivalent* to that of formal and symbolic systems in logical and mathematical reasoning? If not, then we need to see the notion of strange loops as an analogy that the practice of painting can play with in certain quite fascinating ways.

Escher's two drawings indeed can be said to work for their viewers because they pit two different and mutually contradictory visual perspectives against one another within one and the same work. The perspective of two-dimensionality makes possible the angular **B**-shaped figure that forms the looping pathway of the circulating water. The flat two-dimensionality of the lithographic surface supports this shape much as this page supports the letters upon it, but the flat surface of the drawing also supports a three-dimensional perspective that Escher painstakingly cultivates throughout the foreground and, in the case of *Waterfall*, the more faintly traced background. The practices of Western visual arts, at least since the Renaissance, have honed the skills necessary to construct, both from the artist's as well as the spectator's position, the illusion of three-dimensional spaces from what is fundamentally a two-dimensional surface. Thus, it is from the sudden and unexpected contradiction of these two visual perspectives within one and the same visual field that the illusion of paradoxical circularity arises. The viewer is alternately propelled into two mutually contradictory subject-positions in viewing Escher's *Waterfall* or *Ascending and Descending*, just as Escher had to negotiate the conventions and expectations of these two perspectives in contriving the works. Now, additionally, these two drawings present the visual image of a loop that cannot be negotiated from the perspective of three-dimensionality yet is clearly constructable from a two-dimensional perspective. However, there is no single, formal, consistent, and complete system of painting—at least in the way that logical reasoning has been codified—in which a strange loop can occur as an undecidable proposition. Contradiction in drawing and painting can bear analogy with strange loops in systematic symbolic reasoning, yet perhaps more productive is the recognition that Escher's work contrives to place its viewers in a state of visual contradiction in order to draw them toward the fundamental contradiction set to work in the visual representation of three-dimensional space in a two-dimensional surface. Much like the case of Heidegger before *The Shoes* of Van Gogh, the intimate conflict set to work in the field of visual representation must be put into play by the viewer who contradicts himself or herself by trying to render the work as it is through his or her own preconceptions. The viewer stands within the discernible and unavoidable circle of practices that constitutes the field of visual representation. The immense value of Escher's work is to summon attention time and again to those preconceptions that enable us to structure that field in mutually contradictory ways.

A second and final example of how painting renders contradiction as a fundamentally formative activity in the discourse of art involves attending to a miniature painting by Paul Klee entitled *Child Consecrated to Suffering (Woe)* (1935) (see figure 3). This work (housed in the permanent collection of the Albright-Knox Art Gallery in Buffalo, New York) can serve as a visual analogue of the linguistic and literary examples that I dwell upon in my essay, "Metaphor as Contradiction." Though this miniature by Klee is one of my personal favorites, it is not one of his best-known works. There seems a strangeness and self-refusing gracefulness about it, and its childlike evocation all but belies the full maturity of the artist with which it happens to coincide. The miniature was painted in the wake of Klee's "decisive trip" to Egypt in the winter of 1928–1929 and his exploration of the ancient cities, temples, and tombs of that long-enduring land of the living and the dead.[12] By 1935 Klee was undergoing the first symptoms of what proved within five years to be a fatal illness, and his career and fortunes were suffering under assault by the Gestapo for purported

*Figure 3.* Child Consecrated to Suffering *(oil and watercolor, 1935). Reproduced with the kind permission of the Albright-Knox Art Gallery, Buffalo, New York.*

"decadence" in art.[13] Although these biographical facts do not explain the work, they can help contextualize it.

The viewer seems immediately drawn to a stark visual contradiction between the fine specificity of the representational image of a child's face and the highly stylized iconic treatment through which the visage is rendered. Indeed, the image collects and displays various symbols of endurance and consecration. One can recognize various hieroglyphs from the Egyptian *Book of the Dead*: the icons or hieroglyphs for 'bread' and 'spirit' help constitute both eyes of the child. In the texts of the ancient Egyptians they symbolize, in turn, life or endurance and seeing or knowing. The child's nose is rendered through the Egyptian hieroglyph for 'hands', and these iconic hands hold up and offer the child's eyes and the letter *W* (*das Weh*, Woe) in an act of consecrating human life and suffering—something like the manner in which the sun-disk of Ra is often imaged in the *Book of the Dead* held aloft by a pair of arms in an act of adoration and consecration.[14] The centrally located letter *W*—the initial letter of the German words for water (*Wasser*), knowing and knowledge (*wissen* and *Wissenschaft*), and consecrating and consecration (*weihen* and *Weihe*)—helps shape the image of this strange, tearful, precociously wise, and scarcely ancient face.

The collection of these letters, icons, and symbols does not appear to be random and fortuitous. The arrangement of the iconic elements revivifies them once more as visual metaphors that have an immediately arresting impact. The gathering and blending of Egyptian, German, and other graphic signs in order to compose all the features of the child's face creates not only symbolic resonances with the title of the painting but also a texture of vital metaphors through which both the face and its symbolic glyphs may be glimpsed simultaneously. In other words, the painting does not read allegorically. The face is not simply the substrate or vehicle for the allegorical and symbolic content of its title and extra-referential contexts, nor vice versa. Both the iconic elements and the face both enable one another to appear together, somewhat in the manner that Heidegger describes earth and world enabling one another to come into being in the painting by Van Gogh. The child's face in Klee's miniature is wholly dependent upon the arrangement of letters and hieroglyphs in order to be seen by the viewer at all, yet these same iconic elements are drawn together and given space to resonate symbolically by the contours and features of an arresting human face. A strange and compelling reciprocity emerges between the face and its symbols, but that reciprocity is founded upon a visual contradiction experienced by the viewer in position before the painting. A long-suffering yet childlike face seems present before the viewer of the painting. However, that seemingly familiar and recognizably natural visage of a human being is rendered solely by means of highly stylized iconic elements—elements, moreover, that viewers might generally link with strange texts and indecipherable writing rather than with the familiar and visibly immediate image of being human. Contradiction blesses the knowing of this painting; knowledge of suffering and endurance consecrates the face of the child that the viewer renders through visual and intimate conflict.

In this essay I have attempted to show that there is a sense in which contradiction yields creative or generative activity: it produces rather than disables constructive discourse in the philosophy and criticism of the visual arts. Indeed, contradiction *renders*: it *draws* things intimately together—restores or gives things back to one another—even as it *separates* or divides things from one another in mutual difference. If there is to be "truth in painting," then contradiction may render it—the contradiction in which the viewer places himself or herself in attempting to render sense and the intimate conflict that such a position composes for the viewer to disclose.[15]

## *Discourse on Contradiction: Rendering the Senses of a Word*

A history of the role of contradiction in discourse might be a useful, though perhaps impossible, project. Except for a handful of diverse figures—Heraclitus, Zeno, Hegel, Marx, and Engels—it would likely be a sketchy, speculative, and pseudo-historical effort. Instead, I will offer a compact delimitation of four primary senses or uses of the term *contradiction* and briefly connect each one to a manifest strand of discursive practice. These four strands can weave a provisional background for the six essays that follow, but more than anything else they articulate prominent senses of the word *contradiction* as it has been used within Western thought. The notion of contradiction as 'intimate conflict' constitutes a fifth sense of the word that I would like to place in discursive circulation. However, it is not and never would be thinkable without the other uses of the term *contradiction*. They collectively yield a set of 'family resemblances' (to borrow a concept from the later Wittgenstein) among themselves and thereby mutually support and help define the discursive space each sense inhabits. The sense of contradiction as intimate conflict—as a conflicted yet generative principle of artistic, literary, and philosophical discourse— that I have worked to establish in the foregoing section of this essay maintains crucial resemblances among its better-known siblings. Briefly drawing the profiles of these more familiar senses should help to delineate what is similar yet what is divergent with regard to the fifth sense.

First, the term *contradiction* is used both in logic and in ordinary language to name a statement in opposition to another statement—that is, it names the state or situation of denial or negation. Generally, a pair of sentences or a pair of sub-sentential or multi-sentential utterances offer contrary truth-claims, and a choice must be made between the two claims if discourse is to proceed. This basic, standard sense of 'contradiction' links up strongly with a major strand of thought in philosophy and logic—namely, the preoccupation with contraries, oppositions and antinomies as the constitutive structures of reality, cognition, language, and thought. Contrariety forms a fundamental concern in the thought of such pre-Socratic philosophers as Anaximander and Empedocles. Contraries and oppositional structures form the core of Aristotle's criticism of his predecessors and help to constitute his own work in cosmology, ontology, the categories of thought and language, the nature of the soul and the senses, and his studies in ethics and teleology of human conduct.[16] Aristotelian contrariety has left a strong imprint on Thomistic thought, but such concern for oppositions is easily recognizable in (as well as fundamental to) Kant's critical philosophy and the work of such modern thinkers as F. H. Bradley, Bertrand Russell, C. K. Ogden, and Jean Piaget.[17] Perhaps the least acknowledged but most consulted achievement within this strand of thought about the nature of contrariety is Roget's *Thesaurus of English Words and Phrases*: the thesaurus is a masterpiece of mapping the lexicon of ordinary language along strictly antinomic lines.[18] Even the standard practice in dictionaries of clarifying a particular meaning for a word through providing synonyms and antonyms reflects the habit of antinomic and oppositional thought. Moreover, at least one literary scholar has shown that a thematic concern for negating affirmations can be traced through numerous Renaissance, Enlightenment, and Modern literary authors and philosophers.[19] In this initial sense of 'contradiction', two competing truth-claims are rendered recognizable. The antinomic or oppositional structure of language and logic supports this recognition and provides a clear and categorical calculus (or thesaurus) for decision. All six of the following essays subsume this basic sense of contradiction, but it is especially important for the conceptual articulations of the essays by Henry Johnstone, Charles Altieri, and Mili Clark.

A second sense of the word *contradiction* involves a use-meaning as easily recognizable as the first sense. 'Contradiction' names that condition in which a sentence or an utterance contradicts, negates, or speaks against itself. A single statement—rather than two counterposed ones—makes two apparent and mutually negating truth-claims. For this sense of 'contradiction', such related notions as 'paradox', 'lie', 'nonsense', 'doublespeak', and 'undecidability' supply a host of synonyms. The paradoxical fragments of Heraclitus of Ephesus and the famous paradoxes of Zeno of Elea are the quintessential examples of this sense of 'contradiction' among the ancient Greeks.[20] Heraclitus' paradox that one cannot step into the same river twice and Zeno's argument that the infinite divisibility of bodies in motion brings one to postulate a lack of motion still have recognizable circulation. The Alice books of Lewis Carroll, and even Douglas Hofstadter's work today, play endlessly with the contradictory possibilities engendered by the paradoxes of ordinary language, logic, and other systems of symbolic thought.[21]

Besides these clever and playful purveyors of paradox, however, there exists the complex heritage of mystical and mystico-religious thought that pivots upon the recognition of paradoxes and contradictions as the means to truth or as truths themselves.[22] Christian religious poetry and the strange and numerous by-ways of European mystical thought must be recognized here, though the poetry of Saint John of the Cross and T. S. Eliot's *Four Quartets* may be cited as two highly refined, intellectually intense examples. For instance, Eliot concludes "East Coker" with these words steeped in paradox:

We must be still and still moving
Into another intensity
For a further union, a deeper communion
Through the dark cold and the empty desolation,
The wave cry, the wind cry, the vast waters
Of the petrel and the porpoise. In the end is my beginning.[23]

In general, this heritage of thought articulates in numerous permutations the belief or claim that opposites coincide, that contraries belong together in ineffable unity.[24]

G. W. F. Hegel posits contradiction and the coincidence of opposites at the center of his thought on consciousness and the structure of reality and logic. Hegel's notions of contradiction and supersession in *The Phenomenology of Mind* and his claim in *Science of Logic* that opposite determinations resolve themselves into a single ground—namely, "the unity of reflection"—represent major idealist conceptions strongly linked to the paradox of the coincidence of opposites.[25] Furthermore, in modern American literary criticism, Cleanth Brooks develops a sense of contradiction as paradox. Brooks contends that the structure of poetry in English exhibits discordant and contrary elements that are welded together in the imaginative unity of the poem itself.[26] For this second major sense of contradiction, then, the notion of paradox emerges as a highly flexible concept for thinking about contraries not as negating one another but as inhering in some sort of metaphysical singleness or organic unity. This sense of contradiction, moreover, is engaged to varying degrees by Marc Shell and myself in the essays that follow.

A third standard sense of the term *contradiction* seems a good deal less clear than the first two, and this condition may be directly attributable to the fact that contradiction in this supplemental sense focuses less upon the play of contrariety and paradox in propositions and utterances and far more on inconsistencies and discrepancies within complex acts and historical and psychological events. Here 'contradiction' demarcates a human condition involving purposes and ends in which things tend nevertheless to be contrary to each other. That is to say, inconsistencies and discrepancies in human motivation and activity become apparent and are clearly not random or merely capricious. The materialist critiques of Hegelian idealism carried out by Karl Marx and Friedrich Engels recover a sense of contradiction as a historical and material reality in the actions of human beings, classes, and socioeconomic states of organization. Historical and material contradictions manifest highly consequential inconsistencies and inequalities in the progressive development of humankind's historical reality.[27] Sigmund Freud's work on the psychology and interpretation of dreams also circles continuously about the notion of contradictory motivations that are set to work and discoverable within dreams, slips of the tongue, and various other "means of condensation and compromise-formation."[28] Such studies by Marx, Engels and Freud disclose contrary and discrepant situations in several realms of complex human behavior and tend to point out the numerous devious, insistent and costly ironies that bedevil desires and action in the world.

Indeed irony in its ancient Greek sense of dissembling or simulated ignorance characterizes well this third sense of contradiction.[29] Human individuals as well as social aggregates engage in ongoing, self-repressive and self-deceptive ironies. The master decoder of the contradictions and repressed, deceptive ironies of philosophical discourse today, of course, must be seen in the figure of Jacques Derrida. His notorious deconstructions of the occluded contradictions found in the mastertexts of Western philosophy expose relentlessly their discrepant and inconsistent presuppositions and truth-claims.[30] Contradiction in this third sense, in the eyes of major Continental thinkers of the modern age, helps comprise the dreamwork of the psyche, the community, and some of the most profound idealizations of psyches and communities. Richard Kuhns' essay most clearly engages this sense of contradiction, but it operates as well within the conceptual preoccupations of the essays by Altieri, Clark, and Caraher.

The fourth sense of the word places the recognition of a contrary, paradoxical, or ironic state of affairs directly within a conception of human nature. Often in ordinary usage a person may be referred to as "a contradiction," indicating the belief that such a person contains or is composed of contradictory elements that are irremediably active. This casual ordinary usage, moreover, is reflected in a wide-ranging series of literary and philosophical meditations that construct, explore, and even offer consolation concerning the contradictory nature of humankind in general. St. Augustine's *Confessions* and the *Confessions* of Jean-Jacques Rousseau offer two famous instances of thinkers exploring their own contradictory natures and inclinations while generalizing their predicaments as exemplary of the fate of human nature. While in a more conventionally philosophical vein, René Descartes, Blaise Pascal, Søren Kierkegaard, and Paul Ricoeur have all written prominently and influentially on the flawed and fallible condition endemic to human nature. This condition they link directly to the instability, duality, and contradiction disclosed at the fundament of human being and destiny.[31] It is, of course, no accident that the thought of all four of these authors receives immense shaping and authoritative power in conjunction with a Christian teleology of the soul.

However, a contemporary work much along the lines of such explorations of the contradictions that radically shape the nature and teleology of being human but without marked religious affiliation or implication is *The Problem of the Self* by Henry W. Johnstone, Jr.[32] Johnstone explores speculatively, pragmatically and linguistically the interconnections among the concepts of person, self, and contradiction. His persuasive claim is that contradiction is not merely a logical concept but a pragmatic one—one that encompasses the inconsistencies and errors, the flaws and failings, of individual persons by evoking a flexible sense of selfhood capable of bringing contrary actions and tendencies into more conscious alignment. This conception of the self is not transcendent or ineffable. Rather the self is an ongoing problem and project of consciousness striving to accept the responsibility and burden of living in its constitutive state of contradiction. For Henry Johnstone, the self is literally "a contradiction"; contradiction structures the person's projection as a self. This fourth sense of the word *contradiction* seems best engaged in the essays by Altieri, Clark, and Kuhns, where contradiction within the intellectual project of a character is strongly in evidence.

Four manifold senses of the word *contradiction* have been at play in discourse: contrariety, paradox, irony, and the contradictory self.

These four senses will be taken up explicitly, explored aggressively, and rearticulated productively as the contributions to this collection move toward rendering an additional sense of contradiction.

## *Contradiction in Discourse: Rendering a Narrative of Essays on Contradiction*

Some introductory words about the essays themselves would seem in order. Each of the following essays can stand as an excellent contribution to literary critical and philosophical thought. Each one constructs a richly textured inquiry into major texts and central problems in the canons of Western literary and philosophical development. All six essays, furthermore, are historically contexted investigations that are also attuned to the contemporary implications and ramifications of their historical inquiries. Numerous connections will emerge in reading these essays in the order in which they are assembled. This particular order does underscore a strong chronological pattern that runs through the arrangement. However, there are conceptual patterns and developments that unfold over the course of the essays and that go well beyond the tracing of a historical chronology. I shall specify only a handful of such patterns here and trust that attentive readers may pursue the motifs of lack, deception, calculation, crisis, tragic flaw, creative authority, self-generation, and iconoclasm that can and do emerge.

Hesiod, Plato, Aristotle, Aquinas, Milton, Kant, Hegel, Wordsworth, Melville, Marx, Freud, Russell, and I. A. Richards (among others) come under discussion. In addition to these figures and some of their central texts, the notion of contradiction plays significantly throughout and is related to questions of logic, ethics, religious doctrine, monetary thinking, repression, dialectic, fictional narration, creative intention, poetic form, metaphor, irony, deconstruction, aesthetics, and the teleology of literary criticism. What centers this multifaceted discussion is precisely how the notion of contradiction—beyond the four senses that I have outlined—comprises a major generative strategy within literary and philosophical discourse. In general, a move from a ternary (or three-termed) model of contradiction, thought, and action to a predominantly binary model will be traceable. Also, a clear development from the attempt to manage contradiction as a logical, ethical, and metaphysical problem to a recognition of experience and thought within contradiction will emerge. That is to say, the role of the ironist and the function of irony—both intimately connected with the recognition of contradiction—appear progressively to be the fundamental rhetorical ethos and rhetorical mode of the writer, the literary theorist, or the philosopher who lives with an understanding of the constitutive nature of contradiction.

Henry Johnstone's brief, conceptually precise essay commences the collection through examination of one of the earliest texts of Western literary culture. The *Theogony* of Hesiod offers a brief, provocative passage implicitly espousing a generative role for contradiction. Johnstone delimits the classic sense of contradiction at the outset of his piece, and he characterizes the concern for contradiction as "typically Western." His allusion to his own work in *The Problem of the Self* indicates the possibility of a binary model of contradiction, but this option is not taken up by Hesiod or, for that matter, by other pre-Socratic thinkers or writers. As Johnstone elucidates it, Hesiod constructs a passage about strife breaking out among the immortals. This strife among the Olympian gods yields evidence of a problem without clear resolution. Indeed, this sort of irresolvable conflict turns upon mutually "competing truth-claims"; someone among the gods has apparently lied, but the liar and his falsehood are yet inseparable from what appears true. Moreover, "strife arising from competing truth-claims" must be clearly counterposed to "the principle of non-contradiction" because the latter offers neither force nor principle for selection in a contest of conflicting claims. The force of Johnstone's essay resides in his careful demonstration of a sense in which strife or contradiction is itself vital and empowering. Hesiod poses a situation in which truth-claims are in irremediable competition and the principle of non-contradiction cannot afford the rule for choice or the law of exclusion. Johnstone, in other words, succinctly makes a case for the textual existence and philological and philosophical viability of contradiction in one of the founding texts of Western literary and philosophical thought.

Henry Johnstone's essay opens up a reflective space for considering contradiction as a way to describe situations in which truth-claims are in competition with one another. Charles Altieri's richly articulated essay on "Plato's Masterplot" makes the most of this reflective space. In his essay, Altieri engages a perspective on Plato and Socrates that he began to develop in "Plato's Performative Sublime and the Ends of Reading," but the half dozen pages in this earlier essay on the role of contradiction in Plato's Socratic dialogues only hint at the fullness and dexterity of his reading in this new essay.[33] Altieri sees contradiction as pivotal to Plato's masterplot for philosophy. He contends that Plato makes character and ideals central to philosophy. The self-evasions and contradictory self-displays of sophistic rhetoric as well as the lack of ironic self-questioning in epic narrative need to be overcome, and character and idealization provide the medium and the means for reconstructive sublimation. This masterplot installs *ethos* squarely within philosophical thought, yet it also summons attention to the productive and provocative function of contradiction in instituting the terms and course of that thought.

Altieri begins his investigation by looking into Sigmund Freud's *Dora: Fragment of an Analysis of a Case of Hysteria* (1905). Freud's analysis curiously reveals his own attempt at analytic mastery producing self-evasions and contradictions. His desire for *logos*—"the authority of a descriptive science with general rules"—wars with *ethos*—"the authority of an exemplary reader of particular cases." This modern ethical and philosophical dilemma has a pretext in the *Dora* of classical Greek thought—namely, Plato's *Phaedrus*. In the *Phaedrus*, though, Plato finds a way to manage contradiction. Plato's dramatized struggle with self-evasive and "sophistic notions of ethos" becomes "the basis for a new philosophical version of ethos." In other words, Plato recognizes that "cultural frameworks establish contradictions." These contradictions constitute dilemmas of and for coherence within a cultural framework, but they also motivate self-reinvention. Altieri appeals to Robert Nozick's principle of self-subsumption and views the activity of subsumption as a fundamental principle and project of the self. The self-subsuming self handles contradictions, and self-subsumption is thereby an "original constitutive act" of a person. (These notions, by the way, closely resemble those unfolded by Henry Johnstone in *The Problem of the Self*.) Moreover, Altieri argues that Plato's way of projecting contradictions in his dialogues creates the needed space for the activity of self-subsumption. Indeed, Plato's dramatism itself constitutes a form of idealizing self-subsumption in which "one can expose and explore one's own motives in the discourse" and "can articulate specific psychological and affective powers which underlie claims to resolve contradictions." Plato can engage in the kind of self-display and self-subsumption that eludes and bedevils Freud. Altieri contends that "the self-irony of Socrates' desires" in the *Phaedrus* as well as Plato's dramatic counterpointing of philosophical and rhetorical lovers—indeed philosophy and rhetoric as contrasting modes of evoking the character of desire—show the way toward grounding and assessing philosophical idealizations. Such idealizations focus upon a character's way of life and do so within a general cultural grammar or framework of rational practices, including the ongoing project of overcoming or subsuming one's own evasions and contradictions.

Altieri goes on to trace "Plato's struggle with contradictions inherent in public life and in the roles one can play as a critic of that life." Four dialogues receive extended treatment—*Gorgias, Phaedrus, Symposium, Republic*—though the public and philosophical role of Socrates always dwells in the foreground. Altieri sees Socrates as an increasingly more self-ironic and playful character. Socrates performs, ever more deftly, the process of self-reflection that leads the self through potentially paralyzing contradictions toward distinctly empowering idealizations. Altieri beautifully phrases the nature of this process:

> Philosophy may not provide truths, but it articulates a dramatically appropriate world of contradictions, suppressed by other orientations, as its means to testing and projecting new identities.

Even so, one must concede "Socrates' awareness of division." There is no absolute and unavoidable necessity to face up to one's contradictions and to search for and create coherence among one's desires. There is always room for sophistry, for failure, and for tragedy. However, for Altieri the power of Plato's performance provides "the model we still need" for the philosophical subsumption of our motive contradictions. "The minimal lesson of Plato," Altieri concludes, "is a sense of the contradictions we must explicitly face in our efforts to produce self-subsuming states."

Mili Clark's essay, "The Mechanics of Creation," also portrays an extended attempt to manage contradictions, an attempt on the part of Milton and Milton's God to handle the contradictions that plague the physics and metaphysics of *Paradise Lost*. Clark offers a philosophically attuned reading of the conceptual complexities implicit in Milton's epic myth of the creation. She focuses upon the powerful "contradiction in concept" that the mythic structure of Milton's poem is at continual pains to overcome or to subsume—namely, the statement by God that man is "sufficient to have stood, though free to fall" (*Paradise Lost*, III.99). The human and cultural context of Platonic self-subsumption stands projected on a divine and cosmic scale. Clark carefully articulates the contradiction between sufficiency to stand with God and freedom to fall from grace that plays through the fate of the angels as well as of Adam and Eve and is "repeated in the continuing myth of man's historical adventure." This contradiction yields an enduring dilemma for Milton's God: the physics or mechanics of creation propagates sin naturally, from parents to children, from generation to generation; but the propagation of virtue, of saving grace, of goodness, cannot occur biologically or naturally. God must perennially "reconstitute man's sufficiency to stand and the freedom of his will to respond to grace at just those moments in history when sin has brought mankind to the point where righteousness is on the brink of extinction." God must accordingly face the enduring contradiction at the seams of his creation: "After the Fall, nature and grace are in conflict. History is the perpetuation of the central contradiction in the myth of *Paradise Lost*." The solution of Milton's God is to interfere with nature from without and institute the law of non-contradiction. However, this solution reveals a contradiction within God—namely, "that he is two Gods: the God who is self-sufficient and without need of other beings and the God who creates other beings because he needs them to realize his perfection." This divine contradiction resides at the core of the Christian conception of God, and Milton employs "the principle of non-contradiction, or law of excluded middle," to manage logical contradictions between God's omnipotent freedom and the possibility of his being compelled to create by necessity. Milton strives to show that God acts always and everywhere in consonance with his other attributes. Non-contradiction, then, is the principle that guarantees against God's subservience to necessity as well as rules against or excludes any sense of his arbitrariness or irrationality. The principle of "non-contradiction locks together in perfect harmony and order attributes which in a lesser being than God could conflict with one another to the point of mutual repulsion."

God's creatures, however, have no intrinsic access to or possession of the principle of non-contradiction. Instead, his "creatures can contradict themselves; this is what 'free to fall' means." The principle of non-contradiction is "possessed exclusively by God" in Milton's cosmology, but it affords the needed "third term which mediates the oppositions of sufficiency and falling." In clear outline, then, we have a classic, ternary model of contradiction; a third term or principle mediates the opposed demands of two ideas or premises and guarantees that there will be no competition between the two as to their truth-claims. However, God's creatures are ordered by and through "natural necessity," an inherited and generative structure of deficiency and self-contradiction. They do not have, without the gift of grace, a third term by which to mediate the contradictions attendant upon their being. God's creation thus involves his own rather ironic 'fall' from solitariness and self-sufficiency into the necessity to provide for his world of fallible and fallen beings. God precipitates his own continuous fall into contradiction and the perpetual need for the principle of non-contradiction "to hold himself together internally." Ultimately there is no final solution to the contradiction that shapes God's creativity as well as God's creatures. Milton's "tactic," according to Mili Clark, "is to call attention repeatedly to the contradiction as the source of energy which fuels the creative activity, divine and human."

In the essays by Johnstone, Altieri, and Clark, then, contradiction—seen variously as strife, self-evasion, and originary paradox—serves as a primary source of inventive or creative activity. Whether it be for the gods of Hesiod or Milton or the philosophers and rhetoricians of Plato, contradiction appears as a basic dilemma and insistent goad toward further thought, self-subsumption, and creative self-reinvention. Such continuous recreation occurs on the level of both character and cosmos, human and divine. Moreover, Altieri and Clark show ways in which characters (Socrates, God) and authors (Plato, Milton) pursue avenues toward managing potentially threatening contradictions. Such management occurs through the installation of a ternary model of contradiction. Some needed third term answers to the potentially paralyzing hazards of pitched oppositions or polarized contradictions. In the case of Altieri's reading of Plato, the self-subsuming activity of the philosopher-critic provides a way to dramatize and overcome the self-evasions and incapacitating contradictions of the sophistic rhetor and unwise lover. And in the case of Clark's reading of *Paradise Lost*, the institution of the principle of non-contradiction aids both Milton and Milton's God in handling the divisive contradictions that threaten to fracture God's being and the rationality of his creation at their seams. Marc Shell's essay, "Money of the Mind: Dialectic and Monetary Form in Kant and Hegel," exhibits the persistence of a three-termed model for handling the nature of contradicion. However, Shell also calls attention to the high ethical and philosophical cost of the third terms that Kant and Hegel seek out in the development of their own philosophical systems.

Shell's essay, much like Johnstone's, engages in a thorough and highly informative use of etymological and philological tracings. He carefully discriminates the notion of logical contradiction from the more supple and provocative notion of "real opposition," and he traces the philosophical itinerary of the latter notion through Plato and Aquinas and into the philosophical thought of Kant, Hegel, and (though briefly) Marx. The key issue for Shell is at root a historical one: the rise and varying fortunes of philosophical thought are cognate with economic form. For instance, Platonic dialectical generation and division finds a prime analogue in the collection and division of monetary denominations. Centuries later, "the moderns"—namely, Kant and Hegel—still preserve "the historical fact of the internalization of economic form in philosophy." Shell tracks an overriding concern throughout Kant's philosophy to balance self-cancelling oppositions. Credits and debits in Kant's systematic thought balance one another and tend toward the ground of zero. The problem with Kant and many post-Kantians, however, is that such a view of the calculus of thought presents time and again a formalist system of set oppositions, "as though thinking were merely double-entry bookkeeping." Needless to say this model of thinking still has powerful contemporary adherents—for instance, the rage for binary and digital analogues for thought in computer science and artificial intelligence.

Cyborgs, indeed, seem 'high-tech,' fully 'digitalized' accountants who channel all discrete bits of information in terms of factorable inputs and outputs.

Shell himself contends that Hegelian dialectic strives to overcome the formalism of the Kantian system. In place of the third term or the zero ground toward which Kantian thought attempts to resolve various real oppositions, Hegel institutes a different ternary model by redefining the nature of the third term. Hegelian thought hinges upon "the mutual cancellation of two partial *Hypotheses* in polar opposition to each other, and their incorporation and transcendence by a third." The nature of this "incorporation and transcendence" is central to Hegel's thought. Hegel does not suppress or cancel oppositions to zero or to a zero ground. His sense of cancellation (*Aufhebung*) involves the sublation of opposites—that is, self-conserving mediation between opposites.

Hegel's sense of sublation or mediation between opposites, as Shell demonstrates, draws upon three "traditions in which *Aufhebung* is associated with counting, exchange, and interest." With regard to monetary exchange, a canceled note or bond was not merely a null and void—a zero—but "still had positive value as a receipt or discharge from debt." Correspondingly, within Hegel's thought, "the nought of cancellation (*Aufhebung*) is, like this bond, both null and positive." Additionally, there's a logical connection between sublation and difference in the Hegelian dialectic; for Hegel, one must "look the negative in the face and abid[e] with it." Thus the sublation of real opposites does not cancel all to zero but leaves one with the reality of difference, with the idea of both positive and negative value.

Shell's illuminating discussion of the historical contexts informing "the internalization of economic form" in idealist dialectic and speculative philosophy does "put dialectic down to material conditions" and opens up a vista onto the connections among money, language, and philosophy that Karl Marx has characteristically been known to explore. Shell calls attention to the materiality of the trope for thought—"the money of the mind"—in such a way as to reveal it as a third term striving to cancel the bonds of filiation and fealty that it owes to the inescapably real and ineffaceably different material oppositions that give rise to it. Philosophical thought, just like economic thought, needs to remain perpetually cognizant of the real oppositions that cannot be canceled, transcended, or idealized to zero or to the ideal All. Shell's essay, then, mounts a critique of the high cost of speculative thought unwittingly indebted to the tropes of monetary practices and to ternary models for dealing with the real oppositions that constitute and engender philosophical practice. His essay demands the articulation of a binary model of dialectical thinking, a model of thought that fully sublates or mediates between real oppositions rather than constructs a calculus for reductions to zero or abstracts a pathway to an absolute idea of all.

In the words of Jacques Derrida that I place as the epigraph to my own contribution to this collection, "Metaphor as Contradiction," I attempt to "admire the generosity" of the conflation of signified and signifier in the articulation of sense and try to "interpret its hidden sublation speculatively and dialectically." That is to say, I pursue a study of a binary model of the dialectical co-presence of opposites—what I call "contradiction"—opposites that do not cancel themselves out or seek a third term in order to overcome or transcend the opposition. My particular subject involves the grammar and epistemology of poetic metaphor, and I generate what could very loosely be called an 'Anglo-Hegelian' reading of this pivotal rhetorical trope.

My essay examines the implications of two interrelated problems that arise in a grammar of poetic metaphor: (1) the insufficiency of grammatical types alone to account for the process of metaphor; and (2) the need to assume an extra-syntactic context as the way toward achieving explanatory adequacy. I carry out this examination by reconsidering the work of Christine Brooke-Rose and I. A. Richards and through reading a poem by the Japanese haiku poet Bashō. I argue that a grammar of poetic metaphor is bound up with the idea-content of metaphors and that meaningful analysis must take the whole process of metaphor, ideational as well as syntactic, into account. The course of the argument broaches questions bearing on the epistemology of metaphor. Poetic metaphor seems best described as the interaction of two opposed or contradictory thoughts or mental events. As I portray it in my essay, poetic metaphor involves "a contradictory display": Wordsworth's Cumberland Beggar, for instance, is seen as utterly nonhuman and a mere feature of the natural landscape yet this metaphorical seeing contains just that measure of his and the narrator's humanity. Indeed, the epistemological structure of poetic metaphor exhibits the co-active exchange of two elements—one a feature of the natural world or physical environment and the other a feature of the human community or cultural environment. Both elements are bound together in mutual co-presence in the experience of metaphor and in the analytic unpacking of a metaphor's cognitive force and ideational content. In addition to this binary bond that structures the cognitive experience of poetic metaphor, the mutually bound elements can be typed and categorized as opposites, incongruous polarities, contradictions. Poetic metaphors—and metaphorical perception in general—dialectically mediate and sublate polarized or contrary features: a human (or communal, cultural) feature is seen or spoken in terms of a natural (or elemental, non-cultural) feature, or vice-versa.

I also anticipate possible deconstruction of my concept of metaphor, especially my conception of the epistemology of poetic metaphor. My defense pivots upon discriminating two modes or functions of irony. I contend that deconstructive irony, "a fundamental tool of thought," operates according to the law of contradiction—or what is elsewhere called the principle of non-contradiction. Deconstructive irony faults discursive constructions that weave illusions of continuity and coherence that transgress the law of contradiction. Aesthetic irony, however, functions differently. It exhibits the error, the transgression, the contradiction, that structures metaphorical perception. Aesthetic irony discloses the synthetic fusion of categorically opposed elements within aesthetic experience. This constitutive principle discloses the virtually inexhaustible chiasmus of counterposed elements that articulate the metaphors of poetic discourse, metaphors that all too often become the literalized counters in discursive constructions that aspire toward philosophical or narrative continuity and coherence.

The final essay offers a sustained discussion of three seminal modern authors—Herman Melville, Sigmund Freud, and Bertrand Russell. Moreover, it underscores the persistence of a binary model for handling the nature and occurrence of contradiction. In many important respects, the essay by Richard Kuhns significantly broadens and deepens my contention concerning the inescapable primacy of contradiction for metaphorical perception. Kuhns mounts an eloquent exposition and articulation of the conflictual and inventive power of paradoxical language; the texts of our culture as well as the texts of our selves tellingly imbed contradictions and compound paradoxes and then dare us, demand of us, to determine what they might mean, what truth-claims they might utter.

In his essay, "Contradiction and Repression: Paradox in Fictional Narration," Richard Kuhns yokes together two unlikely concepts—contradiction, "a property of sentences," and repression, "a property of psychic conflict." Kuhns argues that both concepts "interinanimate one another when they work in the shaping of sentences the truth or falsity of which we are challenged to determine." Essentially, Kuhns finds new and intriguing application for the age-old paradox of the liar, the traditional *topos* of the problem of the undecidability of truth and falsehood. He reads Bertrand Russell on paradox and negation in ways that open onto psychological and psychoanalytic theories of meaning. In doing so, Kuhns reveals a connection, perhaps a homology, between Russell's laying bare the underlying structure of primary language and its hierarchy of secondary languages and

Freud's therapeutic desire to lay bare the primary language of the psyche by undoing or decoding the layers of repression and interpretations that the psyche has generated. Moreover, Kuhns links the developmental emergence of the notion of truth within the world of storytelling in childhood to the psychoanalytic model of "slow growth towards the lifting of repression." Kuhns contends that both processes exhibit homologous developmental models for learning how to use the notions of truth and falsity.

Perhaps even more intriguingly, Kuhns examines the function of negation in repression. He argues that logical contradictions, when viewed in a psychological context, afford a way to say what is "*both true and false.*" Contradictions generate psychic conflict and the force of repression, but they also provide a paradoxical way of speaking what is, at least in part, true. Furthermore, storytelling can be a significant avenue for speaking what is both true and false. Indeed, fiction "allows the introduction of sentences that are properly speaking both true and false"—that is, that violate the law of contradiction. In examining his major example, Melville's *The Confidence Man*, Kuhns notes the author's multilevel play on the intimate connection between storytelling and the liar's paradox:

> We are in a narrational world that resists, almost to the point of total indeterminacy, the application of the logical techniques employed to discover truth in paradoxical sentence structures.

The compounded paradoxes that commence and accumulate from the first page of the narrative throw "doubt on every sentence we have endlessly rehearsed" in such major texts of the culture as the New Testament. Such compounding of paradox eventually discloses the "deeper paradox" of *The Confidence Man*:

> Persons are like texts, texts are like persons. Both embed within themselves paradoxical assertions that deny the possibility of a determination of value; neither truth nor falsity attaches to sentences and actions. For within every text is another text; within every person is another person, and the embedded natures exist in contradiction to the encasing nature.

The inescapable and imbedded nature of paradox precludes any facile, comfortable or unquestionably authoritative determination of value, truth or identity. Texts and persons speak in paradoxes and exist in contradiction.

Two conclusions follow for Kuhns. For one, human beings "can affirm the inescapability of paradox"—"texts, like persons, are indeterminate in their claims to be true, to be false." However, on the other hand, "texts, like persons, secret within them a hidden inner that can, under the appropriate conditions, be revealed." For Kuhns, "we remove each covering of the hidden inner as we encounter negation. Where truth is denied, truth may be found." The activity of negation in the process of lifting repression discloses a way to read those possible truths that persons and texts must negate as false because they are true. These two conclusions appear contradictory and seemingly incommensurable, yet they are bound together. Where determinacy is negated or indeterminacy affirmed, there truth may be slowly and carefully uncovered. The liar's paradox so projected is a binary structure that cuts across logical, psychological, and fictional discourse and discloses the pattern of truth's slow development or discovery. The liar's paradox is the harsh, threshing-machine-like paradox of the "indeterminacy of the truth of beliefs." It is the fictional or narrative equivalent of the elusive aesthetic irony that I contend constitutes the play of poetic metaphor. Fictional projection of the liar's paradox in such a work as Melville's *The Confidence Man*, furthermore, yields the most cunning and most telling example of contradiction as intimate conflict: storytelling harbors truth-claims among its weltering profusion of falsehoods. Within the logical and psychological paradoxes of tales, speakers and listeners must depend upon the generative possibilities of verbal and psychic conflict to render the truth of persons, texts, and things.

Without further delay, I would like to release the readers of this text to the energies and shaping desires of the following essays. No single introductory narrative can constrain the intellectual possibilities and subtle divergences of the collection. Instead, the very nature of the topic—contradiction in literary and philosophical discourse—demands the generation of differences and multiply arrayed voices in order to render it.

## Notes

1. Some primary references for the principle of non-contradiction, the law of identity, the law of contradiction, and the law of excluded middle—the axiomatic laws or fundamental presuppositions of formal and symbolic logic—are the classic statements by Aristotle and their modern rearticulations by F. H. Bradley and Bertrand Russell. See Aristotle, "Book Gamma," *Metaphysics*, trans. Richard Hope (N.Y.: Columbia University Press, 1952), pp. 61–86; and Chapter 10, "Categories" and Chapters 6–24, "Interpretation" in *"Categories" and "Interpretation" from "The Organon"*, trans. Le Roy F. Smith (Fresno: Academy Guild Press, 1959), pp. 29–35, 48–72. See also F. H. Bradley, "A Defense of the Principle of Contradiction," *The*

*Principles of Logic* (Oxford: Clarendon Press, 1928), pp. 141–56, and Bertrand Russell, "The Law of Excluded Middle," *An Inquiry into Meaning and Truth* (London: Allen & Unwin, 1940), pp. 274–88.
2. Ludwig Wittgenstein, *Tractatus Logico-Philosophicus*, trans. D. F. Pears and B. F. McGuinness (London: Routledge & Kegan Paul, 1963), p. 69. Additional citations, including Wittgenstein's propositional numbers, will be made parenthetically with the abbreviation *TLP*.
3. Jacques Derrida, *Positions*, trans. Alan Bass (Chicago: University of Chicago Press, 1981), p. 75.
4. Ibid., pp. 74–5.
5. Martin Heidegger, "The Origin of the Work of Art," *Poetry, Language, Thought*, trans. Albert Hofstadter (New York: Harper & Row, 1971), pp. 15–87. All quotations from this essay will be from this translation and will be cited with the abbreviation OWA and the relevant page numbers in parentheses. The translation presents Heidegger's final revised version of "Der Ursprung des Kunstwerkes," as published in 1960.

In his essay "Heidegger and the Work of Art," *Aesthetics Today*, ed. Morris Philipson (New York: New American Library, 1961), pp. 413–31, Hans Jaeger outlines and evaluates at some length Heidegger's concept of truth with regard to the work of art, and I refer the reader to this elucidation rather than to try to summarize it here. See especially Jaeger, pp. 421–3.
6. For extensive background and commentary on these issues, see John D. Caputo's two excellent studies: *The Mystical Element in Heidegger's Thought*, rev. ed. (New York: Fordham University Press, 1986) and *Heidegger and Aquinas: An Essay on Overcoming Metaphysics* (New York: Fordham University Press, 1982).

Of course, especially since 1987, Heidegger's philosophical and artistic preoccupations have been examined within a sharply socio-political context. For three excellent studies with regard to this important problem, see Jean-François Lyotard's *Heidegger and "the jews"*, trans. Andreas Michel and Mark Roberts (Minneapolis: University of Minnesota Press, 1990); Nicholas Rand, "The Political Truth of Heidegger's 'Logos': Hiding in Translation," *PMLA* 105 (1990): 436–47; and "Heidegger: Art and Politics," a special issue, *Diacritics* 19, 3–4 (1989), ed. Rodolphe Gasché and Anthony Appiah.
7. Jacques Derrida, *The Truth in Painting*, trans. Geoff Bennington and Ian McLeod (Chicago: University of Chicago Press, 1987). All citations of this text will be noted by the abbreviation *TP* and the relevant page numbers in parentheses.
8. I take the liberty of briefly summarizing—actually thematizing—the drift of a complex " 'polylogue' (for n + 1—female—voices)" that is the articulated form of Derrida's work (*TP*, p. 256). This "polylogue" has definite affinities with the polyphonic discourse and linguistic playfulness of Virginia Woolf's *The Waves* and James Joyce's *Finnegan's Wake*. I merely note these intertextual possibilities here but do not rehearse them in the body of my text.
9. I am not deceptively rephrasing the concept of the hermeneutical circle

here. Instead, recognition of the fact that we project our presuppositions upon what we take to be the truth of things in themselves can be a way toward seeing and adjusting those presuppositions by which we see. In certain respects, this view resembles that espoused by André Maurois in *Illusions* (New York: Columbia University Press, 1968). Moreover, I explore this problem at length with regard to theories of reading and Joyce studies in my book *The Joyce of Reading: The Problematics of Reading "Ulysses"* (forthcoming).

10. Douglas R. Hofstadter, *Gödel, Escher, Bach: An Eternal Golden Braid* (New York: Basic Books, 1979). All citations of this text will be designated by the abbreviation *GEB* and the relevant page numbers in parentheses. It is noteworthy that Hofstadter deliberately links the notion of strange loops to its ancient form, the liar's paradox of Epimenides. In his essay for this collection, Richard Kuhns discusses Bertrand Russell and the fictive implications of the liar's paradox—Epimenides, himself a Cretan, asserts that "All Cretans are liars."

11. Two writers, working within different schools of thought, have assessed the cognitive and philosophical patterns at play in the absurdity or undecidability of self-referring paradoxes. Both writers cover the same lexicon of paradoxes with which Hofstadter preoccupies himself. See W. V. O. Quine, "The Ways of Paradox," *The Ways of Paradox and Other Essays* (New York: Random House, 1966), pp. 3–20; and Susan Stewart, "Paradox Regained," *Nonsense: Aspects of Intertextuality in Folklore and Literature* (Baltimore: Johns Hopkins University Press, 1979), pp. 206–9.

12. Denys Chevalier, *Paul Klee*, trans. Eileen B. Hennessey (Naefels, Switzerland: Bonfini Press, 1979), pp. 50, 57. The original name of the miniature is "W-geweihtes Kind"; it measures 5 1/8 x 9 inches and is painted in oil and watercolor.

13. See Will Grohmann, *Paul Klee* (New York: Harry N. Abrams, n.d.), pp. 90–93; and Karl Nierendorf, ed., *Paul Klee: Paintings and Watercolors, 1913 to 1939* (New York: Oxford University Press, 1941), pp. 30–31.

14. See *The Book of the Dead*, trans. E. A. Wallis Budge (New York: Dover Publications, 1967; orig. pub. 1895), especially pp. lv–c, cxi, cxv, 1, and 252.

15. Jacques Derrida thinks through the notion of "rendering reason" (*reddere rationem*) in an analogous way to what I do with the notion of contradiction. See his "The Principle of Reason: The University in the Eyes of its Pupils," *Diacritics* 13, 3 (Fall 1983): 3–20. Pages 7–11 and 14–16 are particularly interesting in this regard.

16. For Anaximander and Empedocles, see John Mansley Robinson, *An Introduction to Early Greek Philosophy* (Boston: Houghton Mifflin, 1968), pp. 23–40, 151–73. For Aristotle, see note 1 and John Peter Anton's excellent study *Aristotle's Theory of Contrariety* (London: Routledge and Kegan Paul, 1957), especially pp. 31–102.

17. For Immanuel Kant, see *Critique of Pure Reason*, trans. F. Max Müller (Garden City, New York: Anchor Books, 1966), especially pp. 19–384. For Bradley and Russell, see note 1. For Ogden, see especially his brilliant little study *Opposition: A Linguistic and Psychological Analysis* (Bloom-

ington: Indiana University Press, 1967; orig. pub. 1932). For Piaget, see particularly the late work as represented by *Experiments in Contradiction*, trans. Derek Coltman (Chicago: University of Chicago Press, 1980).
18. Peter Mark Roget, *Thesaurus of English Words and Phrases*, rev. ed. John Lewis Roget (Boston: DeWolfe, Fiske, and Co., 1879; orig. ed. 1852). See especially pp. v–xlv.
19. Maire Jaanus Kurrik, *Literature and Negation* (New York: Columbia University Press, 1979). See also the oppositional qualities of the grotesque in Geoffrey Galt Harpham, *On the Grotesque: Strategies of Contradiction in Art and Literature* (Princeton: Princeton University Press, 1982).
20. See Robinson, pp. 87–105, 127–39. Also see G. S. Kirk and J. E. Raven, *The Pre-Socratic Philosophers* (London: Cambridge University Press, 1957), pp. 182–215, 286–97.
21. For Hofstadter, see note 10, and see also his *Metamagical Themas: Questing for the Essence of Mind and Pattern* (New York: Bantam Books, 1985).
22. For two philosophical analyses of this situation, see Galen K. Pletcher, "Mysticism, Contradiction, and Ineffability," *American Philosophical Quarterly* 10, 3 (1973): 201–11; and Morris Lazerowitz, "Mystical and Logical Contradictions," *The Language of Philosophy* (Dordrecht, Netherlands: D. Reidel Publishing, 1977), pp. 76–92.
23. T. S. Eliot, *The Complete Poems and Plays, 1909–1950* (New York: Harcourt, Brace and Co., 1952), p. 129.
24. On this point Mircea Eliade's *The Two and the One*, trans. J. M. Cohen (New York: Harper & Row, 1965) is the classic study.
25. Hegel, *The Phenomenology of Mind*, trans. J. B. Baillie (New York: Harper & Row, 1967), pp. 161–78; *Science of Logic*, trans. A. V. Miller (N.Y.: Humanities Press, 1969), pp. 429–43.
26. Cleanth Brooks, "The Language of Paradox," *The Well Wrought Urn: Studies in the Structure of Poetry* (New York: Reynal & Hitchcock, 1947), pp. 3–21.
27. For Marx, see his *Economic and Philosophic Manuscripts of 1844*, trans. Martin Milligan, ed. Dirk J. Struik (New York: International Publishers, 1964), especially pp. 31–47, 170–93. For Engels, see his *Anti-Duhring*, trans. Emile Burns, ed. C. P. Dutt (New York: International Publishers, 1969).
28. Sigmund Freud, *The Interpretation of Dreams* in *The Basic Writings of Sigmund Freud*, trans. & ed. A. A. Brill (N.Y.: Modern Library, 1938), pp. 530–32 and 319–549 in passing.
29. See Norman Knox, *The Word Irony and Its Contexts, 1500–1755* (Durham, N.C.: Duke University Press, 1961), pp. 3–7, 38–41.
30. See notes 7 and 15. Also see the essays collected in Jacques Derrida, *Margins of Philosophy*, trans. Alan Bass (Chicago: University of Chicago Press, 1982).
31. See René Descartes, *Discourse on Method and Other Writings*, trans. F. E. Sutcliffe (Harmondsworth, England: Penguin, 1968), pp. 29, 95–169; Blaise Pascal, *Pascal's Pensees*, trans. W. F. Trotter (New York: E. P. Dutton, 1958), pp. 96–112; Søren Kierkegaard, *Philosophical Fragments*, trans.

David Swenson and Howard Hong (Princeton: Princeton University Press, 1962), pp. 46–67, and *Concluding Unscientific Postscript*, trans. David Swenson and Walter Lowrie (Princeton: Princeton University Press, 1941), pp. 345–519; and Paul Ricoeur, *Fallible Man*, trans. Charles Kelbley (Chicago: Henry Regnery, 1965), especially pp. 122–224.
32. Henry W. Johnstone, Jr., *The Problem of the Self* (University Park: Pennsylvania State University Press, 1970).
33. Charles Altieri, "Plato's Performative Sublime and the Ends of Reading," *New Literary History* 16 (1985): 251–73; see especially pp. 255–60. The essay is reprinted with a brief postscript in Charles Altieri, *Canons and Consequences* (Evanston: Northwestern University Press, 1990), pp. 163–88.

# 2

# *Strife and Contradiction in Hesiod*

## Henry W. Johnstone, Jr.

Logically, a contradiction is the conjunction of a sentence with its negation (for example: "Callias sits and Callias does not sit"). Not both conjuncts can be true, and not both can be false. In a more extended sense, a contradiction is the conjunction of a sentence with one of its contraries (for example: "Callias sits and Callias stands"). In this case, one conjunct must be false, but both may be. (Callias may be lying down.)

The fact that a certain conjunction is a contradiction does not tell us which conjunct is false, or whether both are. The existence of a contradiction is merely evidence that at least one conjunct is false. As we shall see, on at least one occasion Hesiod used the word *strife* to refer to a contradiction and saw strife of this kind as evidence that someone was lying, although at the outset neither we (the hearers of the poem) nor Zeus himself can tell who. Zeus and we, as well as perhaps some of the parties to the strife, are thus faced with a contradiction.

An important aspect of Western civilization is its concern with contradictions. The experience of being faced with a contradiction is typically Western. This experience is a kind of anxiety. When we are faced with a contradiction, we feel that we must deal with it as quickly as possible, for we regard it as a threat to the integrity of life or thought, and we doubt that it will spontaneously disappear. There are various characteristic ways of dealing with a contradiction. One is to make a saving distinction. For example, "It is raining and not raining" will pass muster if rain is understood to be falling in one place but not in another. Another device is dialectical synthesis: "All is Being" and "All is Nothing" turn out to be moments in "All is Becoming."[1] Again, we might resolutely embrace both poles of the contradiction, affirming the perspective from which they are seen as contradicting one another rather than as mere schizophrenic alternatives.[2] Or we might simply try to find out whether any or all of the inconsistent propositions are false. For perhaps the contradiction we are faced with arises from a mistake on someone's part or from a lie. If so, we can clear it up if we can detect the statement not in keeping with the facts. Zeus, as we shall see, does not deal with the contradiction he is faced with in quite any of these ways.

Hesiod's reference to the experience of being faced with a contradiction and to the assumption that this contradiction arises from a lie occurs in his *Theogony*:

ὁππότ' ἔρις καὶ νεῖκος ἐν ἀθανάτοισιν ὄρηται,
καί ῥ' ὅστις ψεύδηται Ὀλύμπια δώματ' ἐχόντων,
Ζεὺς δέ τε Ἶριν ἔπεμψε θεῶν μέγαν ὅρκον ἐνεῖκαι.
Theogony 782-4)

("Whenever strife breaks out among the immortals
Because someone having an Olympian home is lying
Then Zeus sends Iris to fetch the great oath of the gods.")

The καί heading line 783, which I have translated "because," must be clearly understood. Let S stand for "Strife breaks out," L for "Somebody is lying," and Z for "Zeus sends Iris." Now καί normally means "and." But Hesiod is not saying (S ⊃ Z) & (L ⊃ Z); for that is equivalent with (S v L) ⊃ Z, but S and L are not seen as alternative conditions under either of which Zeus sends Iris. What Hesiod means is more like (S & L) ⊃ Z.[3] But this formulation might suggest that independently of the strife we know that someone is lying. If we know that, then we must know who the liar is, and the errand of Iris becomes pointless.[4] Clearly Hesiod wants to treat the strife as *evidence* that a lie has been told in a situation in which we do not yet know who the liar is. Thus we must translate καί ῥ' ὅστις ψεύδηται as "because someone is lying."[5]

Hesiod's treatment of strife of a certain kind as evidence that a lie has been told may well be the earliest among the Greeks.[6] It seems to have no precedent in Homer or other poets who are thought to have flourished before Hesiod. Characters in Homer lie, and their lying sometimes gives rise to strife, but the existence of the strife is never our sole evidence that a lie has been told. In *Iliad* 4.364ff., for example, we see Agamemnon falsely reproaching Diomedes and Sthenelus. Sthenelus reacts; here is strife, albeit mild—but Diomedes remains silent; there is nothing in his stance that could be called strife at all. Yet we are aware of the falsehood and would have been aware of it even if Sthenelus had not reacted. We do not need strife as evidence.[7]

Of course, there are many kinds of strife described by Homer and Hesiod which are not contradictions. If a battle is called an *eris* (as at *Iliad* 3.7) or a *neikos* (as at *Iliad* 11.721), the strife may simply be a physical clash. Sometimes it is an athletic contest (as at *Odyssey* 8.209-211). Often, however, an *eris* or a *neikos* is a clash of competing *claims*. This is the case in the quarrel between Achilles and Agamemnon in *Iliad* 1. The latter claims to deserve a prize to replace Chryseis, while the former denies this claim. But the claims of Achilles and Agamemnon are not specifically *truth*-claims. Achilles can relevantly insult Agamemnon in many ways (e.g., as *demaboros* and *oinobares*), but it would not be relevant for him to accuse his antagonist of being a liar.

Let me try to put my point in another way. A strife arising from competing truth-claims is a contradiction. If the strife arises because someone is lying, it is clearly one arising from competing truth-claims, and hence a contradiction. A strife arising because someone is *mistaken* would also be of this kind, but I know of no example of such a strife in early Greek epic. A contradiction does not in itself tell us who is lying or mistaken, only that someone is. If we can already identify the culprit, nothing is gained by treating the strife as a contradiction. Since we readers, hearers, and critics can identify the culprits in Homer, we make no point worth making when we say that whatever strife may be occasioned is a contradiction. When Odysseus lies, for example, we are not 'faced with a contradiction.' But neither we nor Zeus can identify the culprit or culprits in Hesiod's example, and we know we must look for them only because we are faced with a contradiction.

It might be objected that Homer *implicitly* appeals to the principle of non-contradiction whenever he identifies any utterance as a lie: Odysseus' lying tales and the truth cannot both be true. But that is not the issue. My contention is only that Hesiod *explicitly* describes one form of contradiction—namely, a strife arising from competing truth-claims—and that Homer offers us no such description. An implicit appeal to the principle of non-contradiction is not a description of a strife arising from competing truth-claims.[8]

## Notes

1. See, for example, *The Logic of Hegel*, trans. William Wallace, 2nd Ed. (Oxford, 1892), §§86–88.
2. Among writings recommending this approach is my book *The Problem of the Self* (University Park: The Pennsylvania State University Press, 1970).
3. I am symbolizing logical connectives in the following way. By "X ⊃ Y" I mean "If X, then Y." "X & Y" means "X and Y," the conjunction of the sentences "X" and "Y." "X v Y" is the disjunction of these sentences; it means "X or Y or both."

4. I assume that the primary function of the Styx water, which Iris was to fetch, was ordeal, not punishment. To be sure, having served as ordeal, it did then serve as punishment for those it convicted. How the water works as ordeal, convicting the liar who quaffs it, is delineated by Walter Leaf in *The Iliad* (London, 1900–1902), Vol. I, *ad* 2.755.
5. The use of καί here is something like that noted in L. S. J. "to add a limiting word or defining expression" (see H. G. Liddell and Robert Scott, *A Greek-English Lexicon*, rev. Sir Henry Stuart Jones [London: Oxford University Press, 1968]) or that noted by Bonitz, "ut καί explicandi magis quam copulandi vim habere videatur" (*Index Aristotelicus* [Berlin, 1870], p. 357). Thus that someone is lying *explains* the strife.
6. Of course there are even earlier examples from Hebraic literature. See, for example, 1 Kings 3.16–28, which is structurally very similar to the Hesiod passage.
7. Two passages that might be adduced as counterexamples to my thesis are *Iliad* 20.250–255, the brief simile of the women who χολωσάμεναι ἔριδος πέρι θυμοβόροιο go forth quarreling πόλλ ἐτεά τε καὶ ουκί, and *Iliad* 18.497–501, describing the representation on Achilles' shield of an assembly where a *neikos* had arisen, one disputant avowing that he had paid the bloodprice of a man, while the other ἀναίνενο μηδὲν ἐλέοθαι. But in the first case Homer does not treat the lies as the cause of the strife, or the strife as evidence that lies were told, and in the second it seems clear that the phrase I have quoted must be translated as "refused to accept anything" rather than as "denied that he had received anything" which would require οὐδέν rather than μηδέν (See L.S.J. under ἀναίνομαι and Leaf, *The Iliad*, Vol. II, Appendix I, pp. 610–611.)
8. I am very much indebted to Professor Richard Hamilton of Bryn Mawr College for his criticisms of an earlier version of this paper.

3

# Plato's Masterplot: Idealization, Contradiction, and the Transformation of Rhetorical Ethos

## Charles Altieri

I know of nothing more characteristic of living in a postphilosophical age than the strange feeling one finds oneself experiencing as one reads a text like Freud's *Dora*. On the one hand one cannot avoid a sense of awe at Freud's analytic intelligence and at our nakedness and smallness before such an intelligence. Yet, uneasy in the self-consciousness that one needs such stances for self-defense, one is also likely to think there is something terribly comic and pathetic about the whole enterprise of Freudian analysis as *Dora* exemplifies it. The sense of power is easy to explain: Freud in effect creates a new discourse by providing a different map of the psyche, the forces it depends on and the ways coherence is possible in our descriptions of experience. What seemed coherent is shown to be contradictory so that Freud can dramatize and explain a different model of mastery. But that same process leads our attention to other contradictions which Freud apparently cannot master, indeed which ironically place Freud within classic tragic patterns of blindness and insight. Without Freud we might not recognize how much of his behavior in the Dora case is motivated by his own sexual desire. Freud's analytic acumen becomes a form of sexual possession as he tries to convince Dora that she was really thrilled by Herr K.'s advances and that her resistance derived from sympathetic identifications with Frau K. and the serving girl. Even Freud's doggedness (with his marvelous use of footnotes as obsessive instruments to possess Dora long after the encounter) comes to appear a perverse pursuit of power enjoyed both as intellectual mastery and sexual possession. It is no wonder that it is here Freud discovers transference, for this allows him to have his Dora and explain her too. The imaginary's might-have-beens are the ultimate theatre for Freud's erotic play:

> Might I perhaps have kept the girl under my treatment if I myself had acted a part, if I had exaggerated the importance to me of her staying on, and had shown a warm personal interest in her—a course which, even allowing for my position as her physician, would have been tantamount to providing her with a substitute for the affection she longed for? . . .
>
> "Now," I ought to have said to her, "it is from Herr K. that you have made a transference on to me. Have you noticed anything that leads you to suspect me of evil intentions similar (whether openly or in some sublimated form) to Herr K.'s? Or have you been struck by anything about me or got to know anything about me which has caught your fancy, as happened previously with Herr K.?"[1]

There is no talk of counter-transference in this tale. Freud will eventually develop that concept but without ever applying it to Dora, so this particular work fails to account for its own energies, and then the claims Freud makes begin to appear more symptomatic than heuristic. Arguments seeking authority to shape how we think in fact tend to reinforce contemporary suspicion of all self-projection, especially in relation to therapeutic ideals. Nonetheless, it is difficult simply to dismiss the work without explaining how it engages our energies and produces in fascination the authority it lacks as analysis. There seem two other options available, significant largely because they become our only ways to praise or idealize texts within the hermeneutics of suspicion Freud fostered. We can simply accept Nabokovian qualities of the work and give the work what I call the authority of pathos. *Dora* becomes a profound example of self-betrayal and delusion, heroic because of its ambitions and the strange power of the work to at least indicate its own errances. If this seems too indulgent, we can reinvent another modern author, this time a critic's model, called Monsieur Textualité. We can give *Dora* authority because as a text it displays the problematic nature of the discourse it inaugurates.

I find both models relevant to Freud but neither adequate as a general critical stance. The two options I propose simply suspend contradictions by preserving their functions within the text. There is no author to suffer contradictions and no larger interpretive framework—in history or in the sphere of conceptual arguments—by which we can treat the contradictions as illustrating a general problem and requiring a dialectical resolution. For example, it seems to me crucial that Freud's self-evasions occur within the difficult act of balancing two quite different forms of authority. He wants to master the psyche in terms of *logos*—that is, by the authority of a descriptive science with general rules—and in terms of *ethos*—that is, by the authority of an exemplary reader of particular cases. Ideally, the two will reinforce one another, but in *Dora* the impersonal nature of scientific generalizations provides a form of coherence which masks the text's fundamental contradictions on the personal dramatic level, while the personal coups of interpretation seem to justify the scientific pretenses. Freud need not take personal or intellectual responsibility for his emotional involvement with Dora because the passion can appear as a general one, a passion for the lofty heights of truth from which one thinks wistfully of personal interests as part of the possible stage play of analysis. However, so long as the responsibility lies beyond Freud, the person, Freud remains the somewhat pathetic slave of his passions. Then the model of interpretation he exemplifies comes to occupy what might be called the pivot of deconstructibility, where our passions war with our interpretive languages and our general truths seem our most vulnerable modes of self-exposure.

My subject is Plato, not Freud. Yet Freud makes an appropriate introduction because he epitomizes therapeutic ideals at odds with mainstream social values. For Plato and for Freud, curing a person involves redefining what a person is. And to redefine what a person is, one must inaugurate new models of analysis which change the nature of what we can take as contradictory, what coherent. The process of change must take place under some values and interpretive principles the thinker shares with his audience. Otherwise there is no point in discourse, as Freud probably recognized when he decided to keep his work under the general rubric of a scientific practice. But once one enters a common discourse, one becomes subject to the reversal, which I think applies to Freud in the case of Dora, if not elsewhere. Now the basic contrast emerges. Freud does not succeed in having his own interpretation shape our understanding. In fact, the more we believe his doctrine, the harder it is to believe his concrete analysis; the more we concentrate on the analysis, the harder it is to trust the man who created the doctrine. Plato does not become the same kind of victim, guilty before his own ideas on the one hand and before those he has not managed to transform on the other. The contrast with Freud thus affords a useful measure of the force and exemplary value of the Platonic way of treating contradiction. First of all, Plato foregrounds the question of who has the power to show that beliefs are in contradiction by revaluing virtually everything that might be used to criticize him. This occurs most obviously in his continual self-scrutiny: with an ideal of science somewhat less deceptive than Freud's, he is free to base his own authority primarily on his capacity to provide a coherent account of the nature of his revolutionary motives and the character his form of scrutiny can produce. Plato thus makes his struggle with sophistic rhetorical notions of ethos the basis for a new philosophical version of ethos. And as he seeks this, he eventually elaborates what I take to be a very powerful version of the process of identification made basic to our understanding of rhetoric by Kenneth Burke. I shall argue, in fact, that the idea of justice worked out in the *Republic* gets strong support simply from its power to resolve central rhetorical questions about how it makes sense to see philosophers sharing the discourse of the community they want to reform.

These rhetorical issues depend on a second contrast to Freud if we are to appreciate their full significance. Part of the problem in *Dora* is that Freud cannot fully defend the idealized self-image he projects as therapist and employs as a seducer to hide his fantasies. Freud is typically modern in his having a flexible and strong form of suspicious hermeneutics but no decent model, except the problematic one of science, in order to defend the idealizations of ways of thinking and powers of the psyche inherent in his work. Plato, on the other hand, makes the capacity to offer idealizations and defend them in ways they might be defended the core of his work. Since we are at a point where irony is almost a reflex habit capable of anything except taking responsibility for itself as the ideal it is, we have a lot to learn from the thinker who offers the *Phaedrus* to cover many of the same issues that emerge in *Dora*.

# I

I can give a somewhat more precise description of the issues at stake in this essay if I pause for a moment on the nature of contradictions. This should indicate what a thinker faces who tries to base his authority on his handling of them in discussion of human values. Contradictions are not natural facts—that may be why they are so important for the theory of value. Nature contains all sorts of incompatibilities. These only become contradictions when claims about phenomena compete for the same discursive space. Thus one cannot be and not be at the same time. In terms of predicates we apply to human beings, this simple fact can get quite complex. In one sense there should be no problem in thinking I was courageous today and a coward yesterday. But imagine saying I will be courageous tomorrow and a coward the day after. In the second case we introduce an implicit will, and that seems to require both some notion of coherence of self over time and some set of terms or community which gives meaning to the ideas of will and coherence. Natural facts and deeds seen from a naturalistic perspective only present differences; cultural frameworks establish contradictions. Conversely, once we can locate contradictions, we can begin to recognize the complex levels inherent in a culture, or even in an argument, by which some contradictions can be posed and resolved within the system's different standards of coherence. One could, for example, simply find new ways to define the cowardly act so that some community one wants to be heard by will grant it is consistent with courage. One could also redefine the self, a more difficult task, or one could become a dialectician claiming that the reinvention of the self is required by the contradiction and sustained from within it because one can interpret what led to the claim of contradiction.

Suppose that one makes the last claim, as I think great dramatistic thinkers like Plato do. What then might serve as proof that one has succeeded? The thinker claims to alter the model which created the contradiction and in so doing to demonstrate a new form of power. Then he has the dual task of proposing and evaluating an ideal without simply relying on charisma. Charisma might gain converts, but it will not rationalize the power or give it a form of intelligibility which can survive the master. How we produce power with intelligibility is the subject of several dialogues, especially the *Phaedrus*. But in order to have appropriate terms for reading them, we need one gloss from Robert Nozick—the principle of self-subsumption:

> Self-subsumption is the way a principle turns back on itself, yields itself, applies to itself, refers to itself. If the principle necessarily had the features it speaks of, then it necessarily will apply to itself. . . . a reflexive fundamental principle will hold merely in virtue of holding, it holds true "from the inside." . . . Perhaps it cannot be shown that specific principles are fundamental, but a sign that they are . . . is that they fall under themselves, as instances, and they subsume other things standing in the relevant relation (evidential or justificatory), including to themselves. Note that this self-subsumption is a mark not of truth (quite false principles can exhibit it) but of fundamentality.[2]

Plato himself spends considerable efforts exploring just what can produce self-subsumption—principles, persons, or dialectical ladders, and he hopes in doing so to combine the fundamental and the true. Despite this difference, Nozick's principle captures the central power Plato seeks in his treatment of contradictions, and it helps us clarify just what Plato must encounter if he is to achieve his goal. For example, a self-subsuming presentation takes on itself the burden of elaborating a situation and a responding mind worth subsuming. It must create a space of discourse where contradictions are teased out and competing levels of analysis exposed so that an audience can see the need for and power of the subsuming principle or person. Second, the process of self-subsumption encourages taking full responsibility for one's arguments as forms of idealization, not simply as forms of description. One calls attention to method because one wants to show that even if the facts do not change, the approach to facts must because new powers can be inferred from the methods. Self-subsumption succeeds as rhetoric when it persuades us of the limits in purely descriptive claims. For the trap of description is its incapacity either to interpret the motives and needs of the describer or to account for any original constitutive act the motives might produce. Psychoanalysis describes Dora, not Freud; physics describes laws, not responses to nature; and both disciplines depend on laws they must appear not to create. Yet neither discipline can discuss why their enterprise is valuable, or even why the agent chooses the discipline unless they turn to methods which can handle idealization. Finally, idealization requires a thinker to create within his self-subsuming strategies principles which enable others to identify with the values proposed and means used to resolve contradictions. Otherwise the one claiming self-subsumption is merely a solipsist or dreamer and the idealization nothing but a fantasy. A self-subsuming argument about values becomes significant to the degree that it exemplifies a way of being in the world which unites the spheres of *ethos* and *logos*, self and principles which tie the self to other persons.

I think we still have a good deal to learn from Plato, so long as we can concentrate on the principles developed in his dialogues rather than the specific claims. In this essay I shall concentrate on his ways of projecting contradictions which then create a theater revealing the values in and power of a process of self-subsumption which I consider necessary for contemporary practices of idealization. In the process I shall combine two basic forms of inquiry. The first involves tracing Plato's understanding of the dramatic method as a model for gaining authority by subsuming contradictions and, eventually, as something philosophy must subsume. Plato's initial strategy is to preserve from the rhetoric he attacks its reliance on *ethos*, but to transform *ethos* so that philosophy proves the more potent source of cultural strength. The philosopher shares the struggle for power which rhetoricians describe, but only philosophy can take responsibility for the idealizations it produces when it engages in that struggle. For philosophy creates a new form of *ethos*, a hero who is concerned for *ethos* as an image of conceptual, dispositional, and affective coherence over time (not simply for rhetorical occasions). Coherence, in other words, can be articulate self-subsumption based on reasons which define the self rather than flatter the audience. These reasons, in turn, can compete with rhetoric in the practical world because they align reflection with deep sources of action and of satisfaction so that one can carry oneself in public without the danger of self-contradictions which bring shame and mockery.

A second form of inquiry is needed if we are to project a coherent development for the dialogues and understand that development as a conceptually significant unfolding of tensions inherent in the process of idealization and self-subsumption. So I shall derive from Plato's *Apology* a three-term model for the way self-subsumption sustains the idealization process. Then I shall use the model as a grammar for locating changes in Plato's career. The three terms are the projection of ideal qualities exemplified by the work, the division enabled by that ideal of the self into contaminated and potentially noble parts, and the creation of transitional qualities inviting an audience to identify with the idealization as a way they can achieve the potentially noble identity. In the *Apology* Plato defines Socrates' heroism by having him exemplify traits which warrant his judging and exposing the contradictions in those who would put him on trial. He knows what his opponents conceal from themselves about their motives for the prosecution. So as readers come to understand what most of Socrates' original audience could not, they are in effect led to take responsibility for their own contradictions. To read this work well is to divide ourselves into features we share with those corrupted by society and features we can align with the example of Socrates. Finally the *Apology* in effect offers the philosophical life as our way of identifying with the Socratic powers and thus of aligning ourselves with what is best in our nature.

Since everything turns on what I want to call idealization, we should be clear on its components.[3] First of all, idealization is self-consciously constitutive. It is not content with description, nor with the simple givenness of states of affairs. It entails projecting and testing ways of engaging in states of affairs and of getting beyond established social practices. This refusal of the familiar, however, makes idealization very dangerous. Modernism, from Bacon to Carnap, has as perhaps its strongest shared trait a distrust of all edification as both an evasion of things as they are and an invitation to make identifications only with fantasized versions of the self. Yet even this critical position involves an idealization. Thinkers choose this stance as better, and they try to illustrate why it is better in their work, usually by presenting the contradictions it avoids or resolves. So our choice is probably not between idealizing and not idealizing, but between idealizing well and idealizing badly. For Plato, one does it well when one supplants or supplements dogma by a dramatic process of projecting an attitude and testing it against the typical attitudes prepared by other modes of being in the world. Drama is the easiest form of self-subsumption because one can expose and explore one's own motives in the discourse (at least to some degree of self-reflection), and one can articulate specific psychological and affective powers which underlie claims to resolve contradictions. Finally, the dramatic model can be concrete enough to lead beyond the specific parameters of philosophical argument and allow philosophical claims to authority to be tested by the practical powers they give those who might learn to identify with what a dialogue exemplifies.

Despite all these generalities, the dramatic model will not suffice for Plato. He cannot reject it but must incorporate it by elaborating a new philosophical rather than dramatic form of dialectic. The abstract nature of my three terms should allow us to specify the important features of this transformation. In doing so I run the risk of returning to an old, largely discredited form of Platonic scholarship, the study of his 'progress' as we trace a theme through a series of works. The reasons for distrust are obvious, given the fact scholars often construct the order of texts they use from the issue they trace.[4] Nonetheless, if we are to speak of self-subsumption, the best way to define that process as a dynamic imperative within Plato's thinking is to see how he uses his own career as a basic source of significant contradictions. Moreover, if we follow Plato the self-critic, we find him grappling with precisely the problems the best suspicious minds in contemporary society level against philosophy. For both features—the celebration of Plato's 'progress' and the resistance to contemporary analytic fashions of philosophy—Hegel's *History* proves our best guide—for his sense of how contradictions foster and test idealizations, for his criticism of the concrete personal stance Socrates presents and, above all, for his dialectical sense of how idealization must finally rely on a complex interrelationship between abstracted personal powers and some immanent transpersonal potential which in the *Republic* provides the basis of possible identifications.

Contemporary criticism of Plato makes excruciatingly clear the need to return to the principles of Hegel's commentary. We might describe the state of affairs as a perverse form of self-subsumption. A cultural inability to appreciate the necessity for determinate procedures of idealization is paralleled by a critical incapacity to appreciate some basic features of the dramatic method as well as the turn to a philosophical dialectic. Most commentators pay lip service to the dramatic method, but there remain very few who attribute sufficiently rich motives for the effort Plato expended or who capture its contemporary relevance. The Plato scholarship I have read seems to be divided into those philosophers who keep Plato current by emphasizing the value of his arguments and those who stress the importance of taking the drama seriously by putting it into historical contexts. But once the context is established, those under the influence of Leo Strauss deny the power of dramatic idealization by emphasizing irony or esoteric doctrine; others, such as John Sallis, so stress the play of mind that they miss the overall organizing purposes.[5] The most interesting and revealing example of social attitudes limiting our response to Plato takes place in the work of Stanley Fish, an extremely subtle and careful critic. Because he relies heavily on the best modern way we have of interpreting Plato's dramatic method, Robert Cushman's therapeutic analogies, Fish combines the orientation of a philosophical analysis with the typical interests of one of our best literary critics. The results cry out for a Platonic treatment of the limitations of the interlocutors.

Fish bases his *Self-Consuming Artifacts* on a central contrast in the Platonic dialogue between 'rhetoric' and 'dialectic.' Where the rhetoric of Gorgias and Lysias panders to self-flattering public categories of thought, dialectic in dialogue

> ... requires of its readers a searching and rigorous scrutiny of everything they believe and live by ... It does not preach the truth, but asks that the readers discover the truth for themselves ... often at the expense not only of a reader's opinions and values, but of his self-esteem. If the experience of a dialectical form is humiliating ... [Ultimately] a dialectical presentation succeeds at its own expense, for by conveying those who experience it to a point where they are beyond the aid that discursive or rational forms can offer, it becomes the vehicle of its own abandonment.[6]

Such negative freedom is perfectly suited to the Christian works Fish goes on to study, because where the human mind fails in its effort to make determinations, there God can be. In our negations is his presence. But Plato does not share this faith, nor the humility that accompanies it. To him these would be strange idealizations indeed: love is lack, yes, but not lack one wants to stay lack. Rather, lack begins a quest for dialectical determinations which can fix and reinterpret what is initially negated. Fish reduces Plato to Socrates, and he treats Socrates as himself having no mode to create except one that erases itself. Fish's form of self-scrutiny has no qualities of other selves to use as a measure and no concern to lead the audience to make identifications. It is true that dialectic depends on exploring margins and exposing contradictions, but—as Hegel says—Plato goes beyond the discursive features of language in order to show not only what lies beyond thought but what lies immanent within its unfolding contradictions. We need not stay on this level of abstraction. The proof is in the *ethos* Fish's method allows him. He treats the *Gorgias* and *Phaedrus* as if all the action could be summarized in terms of a simple process of therapy, and therapy could be accomplished by freeing the spirit from its illusory means of knowing. This misses all the self-irony of Socrates' desires, all the efforts on Plato's part to draw specific determinate contrasts between the philosophical and the rhetorical lover, and all the complexity of trying to authorize the right to make philosophy a deeper form of producing and eliciting desire than is rhetoric. Fish is correct in seeing that authority cannot be justified by arguments, but he fails to see how a process of arguments may function to show, not to state, powers which allow us to integrate and possibly to make sublime the contradictions in our erotic lives:

> The dialectician selects a soul of the right type, and in it he plants and sows his words founded on knowledge, words which can defend both themselves and him who planted them, words which instead of remaining barren contain a seed where new words grow-up in new characters, whereby the seed is vouch-safed immortality, and its possessor the fullest measure of blessedness that man can attain unto. (*Phaedrus*, 276e)

If Fish's reading is representative, it signifies a good deal more than myopia in the scholarly interpretation of Plato. The myopia stems from deep intellectual suspicions of all explicit, positive claims about values, ironically most prevalent at a time when we increasingly need to be able to offer and defend idealizations. Although modernist thinking officially separated value from fact, it proceeded on the assumption that scientific or 'rational' inquiry into facts and fundamental laws would suffice to establish the basic values society needed. However, in recent years this dream has turned problematic. Myriad critiques of objectivity in the physical and natural sciences as well as the work of philosophers such as Habermas and Richard Rorty have made it increasingly difficult to defend practices or ideals solely on the basis of facts. Only the most foolish relativist denies that we can make judgments about objects or laws which others can verify. But there are strong doubts whether these judgments will suffice for determining values, even the values which should predominate within a scientific community.

The relevance of Plato to this condition should become clear if we spend a moment on Richard Rorty's formulation. Emphasizing only philosophy, Rorty insists that recent intellectual shifts create in outline an imperative for rejecting the foundationalism at the center of post-Cartesian thought. Foundationalism has two basic components— claims that philosophers can describe how the mind best mirrors reality and thus the discipline possessing such knowledge (which, I add, is probably not philosophy) has authority to evaluate and direct in general terms the work done by other disciplines. Scientists make discoveries; philosophers establish what is to matter in these discoveries for the larger community. If we then generalize from Rorty, we can see why all the analytic disciplines seem so little concerned with values. Values will flow from empirical discoveries, which will also set priorities for further research. But as foundationalism wanes, as we attend to cases like Freud's where personal, social and scientific motives conceal one another and absolve responsibility, we see that we need ways to reason about choices in terms of different criteria. Unable to rely on foundations, we must reinvent teleology, if only as a secular discipline for proposing and assessing goals in terms of the qualities of personal and social life that actions might produce. Rorty sees the need for different kinds of philosophy if we are to address this condition. But his contrast between analytic and edifying philosophy in my view only deepens the case for giving Plato an attentive hearing. Here is a typical passage carving out the space where the discussion of values as values will be necessary:

> . . . I interpret Sellar's attack on "givenness" and Quine's attack on necessity as the crucial steps in undermining the possibility of a "theory of knowledge." The holism and pragmatism common to both philosophers, and which they share with the later Wittgenstein, are the lines of thought within analytic philosophy which I wish to extend. I argue that when extended in a certain way they let us see truth as, in James's phrase, "what it is better for us to believe," rather than as "the accurate representation of reality." Or, to put the point less provocatively, they show us that the notion of "accurate representation" is simply an automatic and empty compliment which we pay to those beliefs which are successful in helping us do what we want to do.[7]

There is, however, very little in the book which gives any content or context to expressions like "better" or "what we want." Rorty defines edifying philosophies as those which promise to make the agent a new person, but he seems to share the optimistic sense of his pragmatist masters that one need not provide any mechanism for adjudicating or guiding our value decisions. If we are left free, our nature will govern us by seeking optimum living conditions. Plato is less optimistic because he sees all decisions as involving the demands of two competing natures. There must then be a technique for dividing values. To handle this, Plato poses what seems an unverifiable foundation, the idea of the good and the methods of philosophical definition. This foundationalism cannot be defended. Nonetheless, there remains in Plato much that I think proves useful in establishing rough criteria for grounding and judging proposed idealizations in loosely dramatistic terms, even when he rejects the dramatic example of Socrates. As Ilham Dilman points out, we must distinguish between arguments which serve as verifiable warrants for a descriptive claim and the presenting of reasons which elucidate a character's way of life by connecting various features of his behavior and plausibly linking means to possible ends.[8] I want to illustrate the complex grasp Plato has of this latter procedure—both for its own sake and for ours. The intricacy of moral consciousness taken in itself makes available a moving portrait of the complexity of self-reflexive moral life. If we can also establish a general grammar from such an example and show how in engaging his own contradictions Plato defines possible ways to present and justify claims about values, we may begin showing that edification too depends on fidelity to specific practices of reasoning within a cultural rather than a natural framework.

## II

The best way to illustrate the elements that go into a convincing idealization is to trace Plato's struggle with contradictions inherent in public life and in the roles one can play as a critic of that life. I will confine myself here to four texts, The *Gorgias*, *Phaedrus*, *Symposium*, and *Republic* because they most fully illustrate the possibilities and pressures which shape Plato's attempts to synthesize the process of idealization, the projection of contradictions, and the elaboration of possible principles for identifying with the idealized state.

The *Gorgias* brilliantly dramatizes the problem of gaining authority for the ideals carried in philosophical discourse without in the process making Socrates appear to be just another rhetorician. The text in effect defines philosophy by its power to reveal contradicitons in rhetoric which the philosopher can handle by creating new—and not simply philosophically based—conditions of identification between the speaker and his audience. It will not suffice simply to show that someone contradicts himself. He could say, with Whitman, "Very well I contradict myself, I contain multitudes." Perhaps it is only philosophy, not life, which punishes contradictions. Perhaps philosophy's fear of contradiction is precisely the sign and cause of its impotence. One might be speaking for Derrida here, but in fact I summarize the position of Callicles, Socrates' last antagonist in the *Gorgias* and his best spokesperson for those who complain that Socrates is "always set upon victory":

> If you are serious [Socrates] and what you say is true, we shall have human life turned completely upside down; we are doing, apparently, the complete opposite of what we ought. . . .
>
> The reason for your present outbreak of claptrap is that the very thing has happened to Polus that he blamed Gorgias for allowing to happen to him . . . Gorgias said in answer to a question from you that if a would-be oratorical pupil came to him ignorant of the right he would teach it to him, and Polus declared that this answer was dictated by a false shame, because a refusal would outrage the conventional notions of society, and that it was this admission that involved Gorgias in self-contradiction. . . . But now Polus has suffered the same fate . . . as a result of this admission [that "doing wrong is baser than suffering wrong"] has been entangled by you in his term and put to silence, because he was ashamed to say what he thought. The fact is Socrates, that under pretence of pursuing the truth you are passing off upon your audience a low, popular notion of what is fine, a notion which has its foundation merely in convention and not in nature. . . .
>
> That is the truth of the matter, and you will realize it if you abandon philosophy and turn to more important pursuits. Philosophy, Socrates, is a pretty toy, if one indulges in it with moderation at the right time of life; but if one pursues it farther than one should it is absolute ruin. . . . Such a person . . . will never be a real man; shunning the busy life of the heart of the city and the meetings in which, as the poet says, men win renown, he will spend the rest of life in obscurity, whispering with three or four lads in a corner and never uttering any sentiment which is large or liberal or adequate to the occasion. (*Gorgias*—481c, 482c-e, 484c, 485d)

Plato's task is to refute this statement without relying on the authority of philosophy. Instead of justifying descriptions by their truth value, he must give power to a nonsophistic notion of truth by demonstrating its dramatic functions in practical life. The means are hermeneutic: Plato asks us to read Callicles and to recognize how much he suffers from not being able to read his own contradictions. Callicles' problem is not that he contradicts himself but that in not recognizing his contradictions he loses two kinds of social power—a power to make the most forceful defense of his own case, and a power to retain a cultural identity not reduced to statements and acts which would shame him before almost any audience as well as reducing him to a self-divided dupe within the Socratic theater. Still we must grant him his strengths.[9] (Without them there would be no pathos to his condition.) He is not a skeptic. He simply subscribes to a hierarchy of values in which 'truth' is not a very significant factor so long as one knows what one wants to do. From this position he can play an interesting dialectical role. He recognizes the central contradiction in philosophy—that it posits a hierarchy of values inconsistent with appearances—and he even catches the Socratic trick of manipulating the rhetorical category of shame. However, the more he sees the negative truth about philosophy, the more he needs something like philosophy to help him state the truth in determinate form. Lacking that, not only his words but also his public identity itself begin to unravel. He simply has no principle which will allow a coherent relation between parts of the self or between words and deeds. And while this lack is exposed by philosophy, it has real consequences, as most readers of the tale can attest. Callicles sees that Socrates manipulates shame, but because he cannot distinguish kinds of shame, his awareness only intensifies our sense of his lack of self-knowledge. Plato uses two kinds of contradiction to make clear the consequences of such images. First Callicles gets confused on nature and convention. He sees shame as created by convention shackling nature, yet his own account of "the truth of the matter" with regard to real manhood depends even more on social conventions than any ploy of Socrates because his only criterion is effect on an audience. Similarly this realist is entirely absorbed by his role and the fantasy identity it creates. There is no way outside fantasy because he plays to an audience, yet has as his basic value only the desire to be reflected in a mirror. He cannot even imagine the shame that might occur if a more critical audience were to make him confront his own contradictions.

Several structural features of the dialogue reinforce this sense that Callicles' refusing the discipline of self-reflection makes him a pathetic figure. Notice how the opening stresses the relationship between the dialogue form and questions like "What sort of man" is Callicles and what sort of answers will different modes of inquiry produce. Then while all the rhetoricians insist on the criterion of satisfying the immediate audience, Plato insists on revealing the price they pay. They cannot produce consistent identities and cannot withstand challenges. Callicles is right that Gorgias and Polus are too easily shamed, but the cause is less Socrates' manipulation than the sensitivity to judgments which rhetors develop. Callicles can escape this form of shame, but the alternatives available to him are considerably worse. Once he denies social constraints, Callicles has only the stubborn persistence of impulse uncontrolled by principle. Then this stubbornness itself will create conditions where Callicles can only postpone recognizing shame. That he *should* feel shame, even by the rhetorician's criteria, is all too evident when he completely reverses his political principles. This lover of democracy becomes a raving aristocrat who sets natural strength against the weak masses bound to conventions. Callicles reveals himself as using, rather than holding, beliefs because he epitomizes those not born with privilege who make democratic ideals their ticket to the aristocratic life. Eventually he does in fact feel shame, but he cannot acknowledge it. Plato makes the moment one of his greatest dramatic touches (repeated with Thrasymachus). Defeated and forced to admit that there must be a hierarchy of pleasures, this person who dreams of performing the self nobly before an assembly wants in defeat only to escape entirely from this philosophical theater and simply play his part by rote (501c). But Socrates will not allow that. He compels Callicles to writhe in agreements wrenched from him even as he tries to assume some purely functional identity. But if one refuses philosophy one risks having no identity at all. This seems Plato's point, especially since he soon produces the text's most horrifying contradiction, as Socrates taunts his victim: "It seems that we have here a man who cannot bear being improved and submitting in his own person to the correction that we are talking about" (505c). The self-defined hero, now reduced to a desperate effort not to be himself, becomes only a nameless exhibit for Socratic analysis, a metonymy of the bold realist whose first words interrupted proceedings in his desire to take the stage.

This is not humility on Socrates' part. It cannot be, because he must establish a sharp practical difference between the way of life he exemplifies and that exemplified by Callicles. The 'realist' has no identity; the dreamer who speaks with boys can reduce the realist to the most childish of roles. Without the theater of cruelty, each could accuse the other of contradictions, and Socrates ironically would become only the double of the rhetorician, a realist with a different scam. But Socrates conquers—not because his arguments are true, but because he has found a way to use arguments to exemplify and interpret personal power, while the power in effect subsumes the arguments.[10] Perhaps the most important feature of Callicles' defeat is the starkness of the contrast. Whether or not philosophy is only a new rhetoric or carries a technique for seeing the good, the dialogue tries to make manifest the fact that there are for almost any audience manifest differences in the quality of lives led by two people not very different in raw intelligence.[11] There are, as Robert Nozick has argued, different levels of integrating or failing to integrate features of one's experience.

And there are, Socrates makes clear, radical differences between forms of thinking that by concealing their motivating energies condemn an agent to misuse his powers and those which help one understand and manipulate one's interests. As Plato shall elaborate later in much richer terms, philosophy produces a continual dialectic between the power to control ourselves in discourse and the power to use discourse to define ourselves as worth controlling and as worthy of eliciting identifications from others. Socrates' composure allows him to keep addressing Callicles as friend, and not only for ironic reasons. The appeal splits Callicles into contaminated and politically noble features, and it sets a context for Socrates' final offer of guidance to Gorgias. Moreover, the appeal leads us back to Socrates' function as an idealized example. Philosophy not only gives him a power to act, it also gives him the power to interpret and test his own powers. Because his arguments are not simply descriptions, they articulate an *ethos* which at the same time they dramatize. Arguments become the philosophical alternative to epic narrative. They allow the philosopher to act as his own bard while becoming a representative for all who learn to question their narcissistic needs.

If we redefine the role of the bard, we must also redefine our sense of audience. Once we make character central to philosophy, or to any discourse, we can hope to judge it by questions of what it allows us to do. And we can hope to judge claims about what we can do by questions of what the actions would allow us to become. It should be no surprise, then, that Plato closes this dialogue with an elaborate myth of the need to have souls judged in their nakedness after death by divine judges who are similarly naked. Conquering rhetoric means providing a model of self-definition which appeals to the best in ourselves by appealing to the best features in our idea of judgment.[12] Developing adequate concrete tests for these imaginary acts of judgment may never be an easy or even clearly specifiable task. But once we are convinced that there are people whose acts require such audiences, and once we see how argument allows us a form of self-presentation before these idealized tribunals, we may have to be content with nothing less.

## III

It is by no means certain that the Socrates of the *Gorgias* would make out very well before this ideal tribunal. In the give and take of argument the Socratic virtues win, but the concluding fiction about judges is not a very secure way to make general the possibility of there being common criteria rhetoric and philosophy must satisfy. More dangerously, Socrates here is almost as contentious and unsympathetic to others as Callicles accuses him of being. In addition, Socrates is terribly moralistic and hortatory, perhaps in compensation for the gulf Callicles insists upon between ideals and a 'realistic' awareness of social practices. By the end one is tempted to treat Socrates as the object of considerable irony. But this readerly stance is incompatible with the general economy of the dialogue's structural contrasts, and is very difficult to motivate. Resorting to the idea of progress in Plato's career seems to me a more plausible alternative. While it is difficult to imagine the author of the *Gorgias* treating Socrates ironically, it is easy to see the author reading the work as inviting ironic critical distance and hence recognizing the need to alter Socrates' role. It is certainly appropriate that the creator of the myth of naked judgment be the first writer we know who constantly reflects upon and changes his stances. In the obviously later dialogues on rhetoric Plato carefully endows Socrates with a good deal more self-irony and free play of mind while tamping down the self-righteousness. Idealization always raises two dangers—of turning models of processes of mind into dogmatic assertions and of making the dogma a narcissistic mirror in which to assert one's superiority. Only the myth of self-scrutiny keeps such indulgences under control. Plato's problem is how to idealize this self-scrutiny without having it become only negative dialectics. His solution is to elaborate and deepen the sense of personal qualities which can reflect clearly on the motives informing speech. These qualities allow him to dwell in a space of discourse capable of integrating and subordinating to his own purposes what leaves others in paralyzing contradictions. Eventually, this process of self-reflection will lead beyond the personal to the more complex model of idealization worked out in the *Republic*, but in order to appreciate the terms of the conflicts and the possible values of that resolution we must imitate Socrates and work through the contradictions that result as the *Phaedrus* and the *Symposium* return to the related questions of authorizing philosophy and creating a new hero.

The central myth of the *Phaedrus*, the story of the two steeds and the charioteer, captures the same process of idealization, contradiction, and realigned identifications which I described in the *Apology* and demonstrated at work in the *Gorgias*. But now Plato makes the central process of contradiction and self-division much more complex. Socrates too is victimized by all the divisions *eros* produces, and this in turn creates identifications that threaten to deny the Socratic program. Only Callicles and his ilk would insist that the Socrates of the *Gorgias* shared the identity of a rhetorician, but now Socrates must recognize how desire leads him to identify with Lysias and thus to turn philosophy into a rhetorical tool. This recognition, however, will instead prove a philosophical tool because the temptation in effect both grounds and tests Socrates' powers to reflect on and reconcile the contradictory features of erotic motives which most of us share. By becoming more complex he becomes a richer figure of philosophy's power to transform the human and to create in sublimation different bases for the identifications we take as basic to identifying our own humanity. Instead of requiring the gods to serve as judges, Socrates projects constant self-reflection as serving the same task. It is then not inappropriate to dream of philosophy producing for men forms of self-coherence which rival that possessed by the gods. These seeds laid down in the *Phaedrus* blossom fully in the *Symposium*'s celebration of the Socratic character. Yet at this climax, comic celebration becomes inseparable from a new awareness of the tragedy inherent in all acts of idealizing single human exemplars, so the quest for a philosophical *ethos* must take the different turn represented by the *Republic*.

I expect my readers to be familiar with the plot and ideas of the *Phaedrus* and the *Symposium*, so I shall try to deal only with the relevant dramatic features. The *agon* of the *Phaedrus* is not a simple therapeutic confrontation of the *ephebe* or *eiron* and the wisdom figure. There is no self-delusion about disinterested analysis or the possession of truth separate from the play of desire and need for power. The philosopher must acknowledge his having the same role as the rhetor: he wants to possess Phaedrus. Within this sameness, however, the philosopher can both produce differences and reconcile what he makes contradictory. So by identifying with the rhetor, and especially by subsuming all the rhetor's needs and tricks under his self-consciousness, Socrates creates a stage where he can produce an identity with strong claims to be able to include and transcend rhetoric. Dialectic, we might say, begins in the sublating of rhetoric. For instead of simply trying to satisfy a desire, Socrates distances himself from it, reflects on the complex of energies producing his state, and finds in those energies a way of freeing desire from its immediate object so that the thinker can create a state of desire capacious enough to allow his identity to be expressed and his beloved to know what he would identify with.

The structure of the dialogue focuses attention on the kinds of desire emphasized by different modes of expression. The opening and closing discussions emphasize the limitations of writing, while the middle discussion demonstrates those personal qualities writing blocks or distorts. Writing is not dialectical because it fixes thought into fixed patterns. More important, in that fixing writing also captures the subject in a variety of specular stages. Writing creates enough stability to seduce us into turning reflection into a static act of mirroring the self. Instead of scrutinizing motives, we treat the self as if it were as substantial and fixed as a finished artifice, valuable for the performance it monumentalizes. Phaedrus admires Lysias because of the elegance of his language and his Barthesian capacity to cover all the relevant topics so as to leave no room for rival suitors (235b). By expressing these desires, Phaedrus seduces and manipulates Socrates. In posing a rival he makes the challenge clear. But the danger of any challenge is that competition entails likeness. To win as a rhetorician may entail confining the self to the identity of a rhetorician. Socrates' first speech, in fact, is deeply perverse (from a Platonic point of view) because it treats the philosophical tool of definition and the philosophical ideal of self-control as mere instruments in the pursuit of pleasure. But Socrates speaks; he does not write. So he can recognize the terrible contradiction involved in ignoring all those contradictions of the lover's life which make it, and Phaedrus, worth pursuing. Here the philosopher's love of contradictions gives him access to both the reality of love and the complexity of his own psychic states in the dramatic moment. Philosophy may not provide truths, but it articulates a dramatically appropriate world of contradictions, suppressed by other orientations, as its means for testing and projecting new identities.

Socrates had uttered his first speech as if he were the defeated Callicles. He offered the speech as only poured into his mind; he spoke with his head covered, and, in imitating Lysias, he put himself into a double contradiction. He ceased to express his own nature, and he belied his own immediate and long-term desires by idealizing the role of the one "possessed of reason and not in love" (241c) as his means of seducing the boy he is in fact mad for. Soon, however, we see that the only truth of this speech was its being spoken in another identity. Love has such power over us all. But the philosophical mind can reflect in and use these multiple identities. That, indeed, is what makes true education possible. Socrates cannot finish his first speech, because to do so would entail actually praising the nonlover—that is, not only becoming other but collapsing critical consciousness into the role. What he has done is all too clear as Phaedrus begs him to go on. For to the narcissist there is no point in being cast as the beloved unless he hears praise of the one pursuing him. Even when Socrates tries to change themes, Phaedrus still imagines only his status as beloved. Now he says he will be able to tempt Lysias to a competition, a remark Socrates answers with a rueful self-knowledge; "I am sure of that so long as you continue to be the man you are" (243e). Socrates' problem is double. He must try to recoup his identity as philosopher and as lover, and he must try to turn Phaedrus from his narcissism. The way is to take on another identity, this time Stesichorus, which enables

Socrates to open a new space of discourse about love that addresses the complexity of motive and idealizes the possibility of conversion from Phaedrus's blindness. This speech will allow Socrates to reconcile *eros*, philosophy, and education, so he can—even to the beloved—eventually speak *in propria persona* and offer an example of the power to distinguish between destructive and constructive forms of *eros*.[13] When the lover tries to speak the language of practical, commonsense analysis which prefers empirical clarity to passion, he in fact acts out a madness and hides from himself the grounds of his own speech. Only when he begins in purely abstract, self-reflective meditation on the nature of the soul can he get far enough from mimesis to discover mythic terms capable of simultaneously expressing and analyzing the states love makes possible. And only by the dramatic presentation of contrasting states of soul can we see what madness philosophy must be able to speak in order to free us to see who we can become as lovers. Only in idealization does philosophy begin to articulate the nature of what moves it and what it must serve as 'truth.'[14]

Now, however, a more disturbing contradiction emerges, one which Socrates will never be able to resolve, although the *Symposium* will at least articulate its ramifications and prepare for the new dialectic elaborated by the *Republic*. Plato can use Socrates' awareness of division as the basis for celebrating the dialectical powers of the lover. But these very powers seem to make the process of identification impossible. By healing his divisions within, Socrates creates an irreconcilable difference between his example and the powers of his audience. Plato can show why and how the audience should be educated, but Plato cannot muster much hope that they have the power of self-consciousness to need or win coherence among their desires. The gods may be able to judge the hero who devotes himself to speaking what is pleasing to them (273l), but, as even Phaedrus recognizes, men may never interpret the example correctly or try to imitate it (274a). Phaedrus, though, does not see why he cannot see. That we do may suggest some hope for the Socratic strategy. We see Phaedrus completely won over by the rhetoric of Socrates' speech, but oblivious to the content. In Phaedrus's eyes, Socrates can do nothing nobler than compete on Lysias' level and be a performer for the delectation of one whom he would educate. It is this inability of Phaedrus, and not some metaphysical desire for presence, which is primarily responsible for the subsequent attack on writing. Writing reinforces Phaedrus's world of spectators and performances because it distances all discourse and prevents any challenge from emerging. Or, to put the same point another way, writing always has coherence because it has form as an object. There is no pressure to face contradictions, to experience lack, or to win coherence, and thus there is no way Phaedrus can understand a discourse on love. The dialogue leaves Socrates recognizing that his teaching is a sublimated form of insemination (278a) and hoping that his beloved, the poet Isocrates, is not a Phaedrus but is capable of philosophical reflection. Yet all we see as his audience is someone who makes all discourse the flamboyant dissemination of a writing which can always be manipulated to flatter the critic.

Socrates' plight is concisely summarized in the last argument of the *Symposium*—that the same man can write comedy and tragedy. The same man has become both comic in his powers of consciousness and tragic in his distance from those he would educate. The *Symposium* is Socrates' greatest triumph as a dramatic dialectician because he completely integrates the positive elements in the other discourses while identifying and overcoming the source of their self-contradictions.[15] As Socrates' speech points out, none of the other speakers can know what love is because each lacks a sense of lack. Their praise of love consists primarily in idealizing their own dominant traits, so each figures himself only as a beloved, someone to be reflected, rather than a lover who seeks completion in something beyond the self. In the process, they pervert the terms of idealization I have been developing. Idealization becomes self-flattery, and identification fosters contradiction because those who should be exemplars instead identify with those who should be led to imitate them. The only positive feature of such self-luxuriating is its making emphatically clear by contrast how lack can function as the emotional correlate of Socratic wisdom and must be allowed the same dialectical role of thrusting the self outside its standard assumptions in pursuit of a new coherence. Imagining this openness is no easy job. It takes contrasts with the other characters, especially with Aristophanes, who sees the motivating force of lack but absorbs it into a self-congratulatory version of his own sexuality. More important, it takes a brilliant reversal of the obvious charge of contradiction against Socrates. Is not Socrates guilty of simply creating love also in his own image? Plato, I think, anticipates this, so that in thwarting the charge he once again indicates that although there may be infinite regress in language, there are clearly levels of mastery over the self and the world which are describable in terms of self-subsumption. Socrates insists that his view of love is not self-generated. Indeed, he learned it precisely through the dialectic that the story presents. His account in the present is a circular demonstration of what one gains by identifying with Diotima's lessons. Socrates did not learn a doctrine about love, but experienced a process which the doctrine at once illuminates and partially constitutes. Learning here is purely a matter of exemplification. Plato makes Socrates an exemplary student in a story about imitating examples told in order to teach a lesson. By imitating and identifying with a model, Socrates prepares for later self-reflective moments which exemplify on a deeper, enduring level the model's powers to comprehend the lives that need change and to endure as value for the one who changes:

> Like him [Agathon] I shall begin by stating who and what Love is, and go on to describe his function, and I think the easiest way will be to adopt Diotima's own method of inquiry by question and answer. I'd been telling her pretty much what Agathon has just been telling me—how Love was a great god . . . , and she used the same arguments on me that I've just brought to bear on Agathon to prove that, on my own showing, "Love was neither beautiful nor good." (*Symposium*, 201d–e)

Finally he shows how well he has learned his lessons by virtually embodying in speech a form of the dialectical ladder. He abstracts from the contradictions in others and builds from that process a capacity to respond to and absorb what is good within them, to beget and be begotten.

So noble a view of education, however, returns us once more to the tragedy of Socrates. The framing structure captures what Hegel would later describe as the limitations of defining the universal entirely through the powers of a single consciousness. The opening materials on transmission parallel in their embodiment of time the dialogue's closing image of Socrates isolated in space. The multiple narrators indicate how difficult it is to preserve personal examples as models of value.[16] Even if one has the fidelity of Apollodorus or Aristodemus, one then binds oneself to bitterness about the rest of the world (173d, e) or, worse, becomes only a recording machine entirely ignored by Socrates as he pursues the challenge of seducing more recalcitrant youth. Then the plot captures the full complexity of the dilemma. Its initiating condition is once again Phaedrus's desire to hear love praised. But in the *Symposium* Lysias is divided into several competing discourses and, most important, Phaedrus is soon absorbed into the roles of Agathon and Alcibiades. Agathon has no awareness of lack. He combines all the allure and all the pathos of poetry and of power. Alcibiades, one can guess, was once Agathon until he encountered Socrates as Socrates did Diotima. However, he emerges from that encounter primarily as an emblem of the pathos of his society. As its best representative, he can understand the value of Socrates. He has been made to feel deeply all that he lacks. Yet, as a public man, he cannot turn lack into any form of dialectic. He becomes a figure of unruly violence, able to express his wisdom only in destructive acts which make the external world mirror his inner emptiness. Lack breeds contradictions for which his form of life has no resolution, indeed which his power only exacerbates because he can command everything but himself. As politician *par excellence*, Alcibiades recognizes the values in others. Yet he needs to be praised in return for his praise, and he needs to love and be loved by individuals. He cannot abstract from Socrates; his paean to love is idolatry of a man and hence he has no freedom except in superficial irresponsibility intended to mask his pain and, above all, his shame. Alcibiades is Plato's greatest audience figure, less because his subsequent actions had such enormous consequences than because he is the only one who fully knows that he is in contradiction and has only contradictory ways to express that fact. His contradictions reveal by contrast the necessity and power of the Socratic personal dialectic. However, they all embody a lack which cannot find identity in that dialectic, but instead becomes a destructive force precisely because Alcibiades knows, loves, and must resist what he cannot be. By idealizing Socrates, Plato creates a provocative which threatens everything he tries to create. Alcibiades becomes what he is because he absorbs Socrates' lessons as fully as one can while remaining in control of the public power doomed to repeat a tragic history.

## IV

The *Republic* makes explicitly thematic these dramatic oppositions between the ideal and the real. In doing this, it sets the stage for a different, more distinctly conceptual dialectic with the power to turn the real/ideal contradiction into the basis for a profound synthesis between what I shall call immanent and idealized features of philosophical construction. Instead of dramatic forms of coherence based on an individual's power to reconcile contradictions, the *Republic* tries to show how the contradictions are inherent in the life of thought itself as it deals with fundamental questions about human values: the task of the philosopher is to integrate the mind's desire to produce ideal constructions with a cogent picture of immanent capacities to satisfy those desires as one adapts the proper discipline. The *Republic* keeps in the foreground the powers of mind dramatized in Socrates, but it does so in such a way as to suggest a ground for them which is inherent in the psyche and in our constitutional need for constitutions. Where the *Phaedrus* could locate in madness and desire the possibility of Socratic philosophy, the *Republic* makes justice a plausible ideal by rooting it in the fundamental needs of citizens not satisfied by empirical descriptions of the state. But now it is the concept itself rather than the personal stance of the thinker which inherently resolves the contradictions once we learn to understand its complexities. Justice is simply an impersonally grounded relationship with two basic components—the capacity of some agent to grasp the overall good and the capacity of all agents to define their identity as based on serving that ideal.

My view of the *Republic* is by no means original. Commentators such as Julius Stenzel recognize the *Republic* as "the critical turning-point in Plato's philosophy, as regards the interrelation of form and content."[17] And Hegel treated the argument about justice as a paradigm for Plato's shift from the Socratic location of universal principles in the individual as giver of reasons to the idea of the universal as immanent in the unfolding of thought. After Alcibiades, Hegel says, Plato had to overcome the essentially negative dialectic of Socratic freedom and anchor particulars in a purely ideal, and hence real, set of relations:

> This determination [of the universal] is the relation which the dialectic movement in thought bears to the universal, for through this movement the idea comes to these thoughts which contain the opposites of the finite within themselves. For the idea as self-determining is the unity of these differences and thus the determinate idea. The universal is hence determined as that which resolves and has resolved the contradictions in itself, and hence is the concrete in itself; thus this sublation of contradiction is the affirmative. Dialectic in this higher sense is the really Platonic; as speculative it does not conclude with a negative result, for it demonstrates the union of opposites which have annulled themselves.[18]

Nonetheless, as perhaps Hegel always lets us claim, there is considerable room for clarifying how the process of exploring contradictions in the *Republic* can become a form of dialectical resolution. Moreover, I think there is a compelling social need to get straight on these Platonic strategies because, as I have tried to indicate, we simply do not know how to create, discuss, or evaluate forms of idealization which are basic to the imaginative force and potential social power in many of the texts our culture has most consistently honored. The need often seems great enough to require moves like Hegel's or Plato's establishing a metaphysical foundation for the ideals. However, if we pay careful enough attention to Plato's strategies of argument, I think we can preserve a sense of how to make and assess idealizations compatible with our distrust of foundations. I once thought the dramatic dialectic of the Socratic dialogues would suffice for this because it so powerfully addressed the issues of rhetorical *ethos* central to discussions of authority and idealization in even the most skeptical of cultures. And indeed their example can suffice if we are willing to be judged by some ideal community in our capacity as performers. But if we are to have public and socially responsible models for idealization, we probably must heed Plato's tragic sense and see what we can recover from the intricate ways he establishes social correlates for the idea of the good. In other words, the dialectic of the *Republic* seeks at once to reach an original foundation and to show how that foundation anchors what is in fact immanent in social life. In a moment I will try to describe the dialectic. Now I want only to suggest that we can read the efforts to locate in social life the need for ideals and potential of achieving them as simply an example of how we might proceed in our discussions without posing any foundation beyond what any given rhetorical case makes plausible. I want to treat Platonic dialectic as a rhetorical model indicating how we might organize discussions about values. There need not be certainty or single answers, so long as there are principles for our talking about the creation and application of ideals. In this respect, the *Republic* exemplifies the richest way I know of denying the hegemony of empiricism and using self-subsumption as the test for successfully reconciling contradictions and posing plausible identifications in the development of ideals. Not only does the *Republic* itself subsume the basic contradictions of the social order and of Plato's previous career, it also defines a logic I think we can find informing the arguments of superb contemporary thinkers like Nozick and John Rawls.

The opening books of the *Republic* follow the dramatic model. Against a background of civil crisis,[19] Socrates exposes the personal and intellectual disorder inherent in the naturalistic and historical ways of interpreting values represented by Thrasymachus. But then Socrates becomes so absorbed in the contrast he constructs that he becomes a devotee of his own utopian ideals. There is almost no concern for either the grounds of his own knowing or the entrenched emotional assumptions of his audience which as a rhetor he must deal with. In Book 5, however, the tables are turned, and a new adventure in thought begins. It is Socrates' audience that insists on his contradictions, and it is Socrates who begins to squirm. He eventually dominates, but only by recognizing the limitations of his reasons and specifying the dialectical process needed for his inquiry (508d–513e). As I trace the major contradictions, I want to concentrate on two basic features of that dialectic to which I have already alluded—its way of reconciling immanence and idealization and its creating a space of thinking, analogous to that of the *Symposium*, where one can see the remarkable complexity of identifications required for the concept of justice to prove a plausible principle on which to base the social order. Plato claims there are two paths to the dialectic—one which advances from assumptions and hypotheses "to a beginning or principle that transcends assumptions" (510b) and the other "taking hold of the first dependencies from it [the first process] so to proceed downward to the conclusion" (511b). I want to emphasize this downward progression in order to show how the drama of thinking anchors the idea within our dependencies, so that the ideal is immanent as potential and as need and so that the structure of needs makes justice a clear transpersonal principle warranting identifications.[20] Justice is inherently a relational principle not a specific power like courage (425d; 443d) so that all can partake of its distributive function in their different ways. Thus it can ground analogies between the psyche and the state, and it can as a principle reconcile contradictions that required the Socratic example. Finally, if we turn to the process of reading, our deepening awareness of what justice is is inseparable from our deepening awareness of the common properties in what we need, what we desire, and thus who we are. One might even say that contradictions are finally resolved only in the projected reader's will as she understands and chooses the Platonic idea of social and personal order. Hegel complained, perhaps correctly, that Plato lacks any sense of modern autonomy. But, conversely, he saw that Plato offers perhaps the deepest model we have of what may anchor and extend that autonomy within the social order.

I must be concrete. Book 5 opens with strange, much too empirical objections by the group. Instead of allowing Socrates to continue his plan (which must wait till Book 8), they want to discuss in detail the communist arrangement of women and children he has proposed. Socrates' response seems odd: "You don't realize what a swarm of arguments you are stirring up by this demand, which I foresaw and evaded to save us no end of trouble" (450b). Their mistaken projection of pure self-interest onto the proposed polis is exactly what Socrates should want to purify. But here the purification involves painful admissions and a crucial problem of philosophical authority which only the dialectic can resolve by aligning Socrates with those he must now claim he should be able to rule. Plato sets the stage for this confrontation nicely by modulating from concrete arguments on procreation to the general claim about the greatest good for the constitution of a state and the proper aim of the lawgiver: "Do we know of any greater evil for a state than the thing that distracts it and makes it many instead of one, or a greater good than that which binds it together and makes it one" (562a, b). The empirical case sustains and is sustained by a general principle. But again Socrates simply claims a principle of identification without either clarifying the link between the ideal and actual possibilities or fully characterizing the unity he proposes so that he can demonstrate it is clearly different from tyranny. He is repeatedly not practical enough in resisting the narrow empiricism of his auditors. So again pressure is brought to bear, and again Socrates gets uneasy and defensive in his insistence that he must deal with paradises and prejudices (471c–472b). The question raised now perfectly duplicates the issues created by the methodological drama, so that what one says about the ideal and how one can be in a position to say it become completely interwoven, while our attention to the how is deflected from the person who stumbles to the argument which makes sense of the stumbling. The specific question put Socrates is simple: in what way is "the realization of this polity . . . possible" (472b)? However, a simple answer would be disastrous because it would reinforce the empirical attitude Socrates can't seem to get his auditors to shake. So he carefully asks his audience to remember "that it was the inquiry into the nature of justice and injustice that brought us to this pass" (472b). For this strategy is basic to dialectics. It emphasizes necessary links between hypotheses and questions asked within an internally consistent process. One does not learn about justice by asking a range of discreet practical questions, but only by tracing the needs within the whole discourse and the various twists and turns they create. If the discourse seeks to satisfy needs which description cannot, and if the internal development is coherent in response to those needs, the question of realization is not quite appropriate. Because the philosophy has a viable theory of how ideals might be imitated, social ideals need not become actual facts in order to have effects in the real world:

> If we do discover what justice is, are we to demand that the just man shall differ from it in no respect, but shall conform in every way to the ideal? Or will it suffice if he approximate to it as nearly as possible and partake of it more than others. . . . A pattern, then, said I, was what we wanted when we were inquiring into the nature of ideal justice and asking what would be the character of the perfectly just man, supposing him to exist . . . We wished to fix our eyes upon them as types and models, so that whatever we discerned in them of happiness or the reverse would necessarily apply to ourselves in the sense that whoever is likest them will have the allotment most like to theirs. Our purpose was not to demonstrate the possibility of the realization of those ideals. . . .
> Do you think, then, that he would be any less a good

painter, who, after portraying a pattern of the ideally beautiful man and omitting no touch required for the perfection of the picture, should not be able to prove that it is actually possible for such a man to exist. (472b–d)

The seeds for this affirmation of pattern as shaping behavior were sown much earlier in the work. There Plato has Glaucon ask the question which clearly distinguishes Socratic heroism from both epic and Sophist ideals:

> Socrates . . . of all you self-styled advocates of justice, from the heroes of old whose discourse survive to the men of the present day, not one has ever censured in justice or commended justice otherwise than in respect of the repute, the honors, and the gifts that accrue from each. But what each one of them is in itself, by its own inherent force, when it is within the soul of the possessor and escapes the eyes of both gods and men, no one has ever set forth adequately in poetry or prose—the proof that the one is the greatest of all evils that the soul contains within itself, while justice is the greatest good. (366d–367a)

Notions of inherent force and qualities which escape even the gods depend on abstract philosophical constructs. But it is only the contradictions we encounter at this point in the text which specify the two competing moments such an ideal depends on—one a condition of inwardness by which one defines one's identity and the other a condition of pure abstract knowing by which one knows what to identify with. Distance from empirical life is precisely what makes the ideal patterns worth pursuing as the foundations of a new heroism. However, simply speaking of patterns to be imitated will not suffice. At least three further problems arise for one who wants to defend Plato's case and thus must enter the paradoxes of dialectics: one must say how ideals differ from opinions, since both in a sense deal with what is not (478d); one must say who can know the ideals; and one must link the knowing to practice because the knower will dwell in a different mental world from those governed by descriptions and opinions. As the text faces these contradictions, all the answers point toward the same unifying principle—that of the philosopher-king who knows the good, is motivated by it, and thus finds himself in the same conflict with society as Plato does when he expresses the ideals. But to the extent that the philosopher in this text can reach the dialectical ideal of showing "things in their connections" (537) and still mollify his audience, "harmonizing and adapting the citizens to one another"

(519e; cf. 501), one can hope the king will be able to govern. This harmony, after all, is simply justice, and the mutual desire for it expresses the motive power of the good on which the philosopher can rely in his governing.

Each step in Book 5 up to the discussion of dialectic plays on contradiction between the ideal and the empirical as Socrates tries to engage the problems I have just mentioned. If ideals are not empirical descriptions, there still must be a "possibility of realization" (473) if they are to be distinguished from fantasies. But the possibility rests on what may be the greatest fantasy, the philosopher's image of his own power. This is why Plato offers the solution of the philosopher-king only with the greatest trepidation. Yet this trepidation also functions as a sign of strength—that Socrates can know and govern himself and, structurally, that such a risk can produce significant dialectical results. The strength is superbly manifest. The philosopher-king is the perfect governor because his way of knowing, the pursuit of the good, entails a bond between the cognitive pursuit of the ideal (484e) and the practical pursuit of justice. Justice only makes sense as an ideal. There is no partial justice, and there are no empirical tests for it. So one might say that we understand what a philosopher is when we recognize that he must resolve the contradiction between the conceptual and the practical quests which we needed earlier in order to pose the relevant issues. This is the effect of dialectic if we have eyes to see.

The eyes necessary for this, however, need a good deal of schooling. Of course the philosopher as Plato conceives him unites the realm of knowledge and social order. But the very definition of the philosopher is an ideal one, convincing perhaps only to the philosopher or the fool. Plato comes close to mocking Socrates as his passions build to the following double-edged coda: "Then in addition to our other requirements, we look for a mind endowed with measure and grace, whose native disposition will make it easily guided to the aspect of the ideal reality in all things" (486d). It seems then that if we ask how the ideal can be realizable, our only answer is to trust the one who alone knows ideals. Socrates now anxiously repeats three times a request that his audience concede the argument has no faults. Adeimantus seizes the opening to offer a long Callicles-like speech to the effect that because we can find no faults in the argument, we find philosophy itself at fault (489b–e). In response, Socrates shifts the mode of discourse to parable and shifts his theme away from the glories of the ideal to the pathos of those who lack it. Form and content both reverse what had been the philosophical method—I think, in order to show how philosophy can adapt itself to the practical order. Plato has philosophy and the philosopher turn on themselves the more to become themselves, thus realizing in the concrete what this inverse idealization asserts. Philosophers suffer in the real but are thus revealed as necessary to it. Philosophers cannot be honored precisely because the state needs philosophers to educate it to honor philosophers. Otherwise there is only the perversion of ideals, as we see in the audience, until the environment makes even the philosopher's seed idealized in the *Phaedrus* produce misshapen fruit (492a).

This reversal may seem simply a clever rhetorical ploy. However, the more we reflect on it, I think the more we are likely to be struck by its power, especially its capacity to subsume all that has gone before. Plato is brilliant in this regard. On the conceptual level, the spheres of nature, society, and psyche all participate in the same relational function of justice. The concept of relations then explains both why we need a class of thinkers who are not trapped in natural appearances and how others participate in orders they cannot perceive. On the dramatic level, Book 6 has developed from the problem of how to show that ideals can effect the actual, through an exercise in idealization on the nature of the philosopher, to a picture of how desperately a state without someone to see and impose ideals destroys any possibility of education or good government, thus returning us to the world Thrasymachus proposes. Each time we are tempted to deny the need for ideals, we are drawn back to the picture of life without them, especially to the desperate blindness regarding philosophy which seems an infallible sign of bad government. The nonphilosopher with power is finally the best justification for philosophy, a common state of affairs that only philosophy is strange enough and idealistic enough to be able to explain.

As Book 6 draws to a close, it becomes increasingly insistent on this circular defense of the philosopher's power, for which the statement on dialectic will prove a climax. The parable of the ugly philosopher, for example, emphasizes a gulf between the philosopher and the multitude. But the difference only reinforces the need to understand relational concepts. Justice can acknowledge differences, *must* acknowledge differences if it is not to grow monstrous, yet the concept can justify for all the privilege of the few. Identity in a community does not entail each substituting for each, as one of Plato's progeny, Rawls's difference principle, makes clear. At the same time, philosophy is a powerful force for producing harmonious identity, both in principle and in the process of coming to the agreement Plato dramatizes (e.g., 500–502). The relational nature of justice creates an ideal which all can share even within their differences: "We all so far as possible may be akin and friendly because our governance and guidance are the same" (590d). Similarly, the rulers need not be in conflict, to the extent that they understand a good which does not depend on but guides personal will. The good offers principles of imitation not necessarily mediated by personal example (550c), so they are available in a variety of ways to those in different social categories. The dialectic of sameness and difference to be teased out in the *Sophist* begins here.

Finally, Plato so describes the good as to make it at once the climax and the source of both the arguments and the strategies presented by the text:

> For you have often heard that the greatest thing to learn is the idea of good by reference to which just things and all the rest become useful and beneficient. . . .
>
> That, then, which every soul pursues and for its sake does all that it does, with an intuition of its reality but yet baffled and unable to apprehend its nature adequately, or to attain any stable belief about it as about other things, and for that reason failing of any possible benefit from other things . . . (505a, e)

I speak of both arguments and strategies because the good is as elusive as it is potent. The philosopher can try by dialectics to reach it directly, but this vision is incommunicable. In fact, the enthusiasm Socrates relives in the effort to describe only the offspring of the good (i.e., good things, not the idea of good) rapidly approaches the unintelligible, demands his description of dialectics, and (again) elicits a shift out of philosophy to a parable, here of the cave. But these problems seem to me to affect only the upward way. That failure I take as a provocative to explore other, self-reflective dimensions of these discussions which I think embody and complete the downward way. Here, in this final contradiction between the empirical and the philosophic vision, we most fully see how ideals can be correlated with immanence so that ideas speak to society's needs without a dramatic example. In looking for the meaning of justice, the text has in effect been asking what it is that people seek. If we know what they seek, we can see how the good enters their lives. Then we can see how philosophy is necessary as a therapeutic tool, even if one cannot describe its grounds, for the philosopher elaborates relationships between assumptions and possible grounds, both by correcting those errors which produce contradictions making the ground inaccessible and by dramatizing the presence of powers which in seeking the good reveal it as an idea because we know what it must satisfy. Because the empirical fails, we begin to see the true shape of desire.

As he turns to discuss the good, then dialectic, we see why Socrates does not simply describe justice. He elicits its nature by asking two basic questions of his audience and by showing how their initial answers contradict the force of the good motivating them. After the negative example of civic disorder, Socrates begins his reconstruction by inquiring into hypothetical origins. Not unlike Rawls, he wants his audience to imagine what they can see as a plausible set of human needs giving rise to the state, and he wants them to see how their innate tendencies to idealization get most clearly and fully expressed when they think about how they would educate anyone, especially those who would govern (376c). Education is inherently constructive, inherently connected to our ideas of the good because it is a projection of what we think we can make of ourselves and of our society. (Its demise as an ideal and locus of ideals is perhaps the saddest feature of contemporary American society—which, in justice, gets a ruler whom almost no one would educate for.) Socrates does not expect his audience to see the good, but he can ask questions which demand abstraction and self-projection. These questions allow desire to express itself in ways somewhat free of acculturated empirical interests while preserving the concrete constraints afforded by education in social practice.

The *Republic* clarifies an idea of good that everyone possesses, and in that it demonstrates the social use of philosophical ideals and the precondition of all definitions of justice. The argument finally subsumes itself by becoming a form of articulate speech for desires the whole society possesses. In recognizing this, Plato confirms the power of philosophy to elicit identifications with the nondramatic, with what he actually deepens by speaking abstractly. In abstraction the text unites strands that confirm community and direct common needs to a goal that can be stated in a transpersonal language resolving the conceptual and personal contradictions between philosophers and practical citizens. Socrates himself becomes most human (that is, most anxious and confused) precisely when he is forced to digressions which in their practical demands bring him closer to a good he cannot reach nor even appreciate simply by argument. Socrates' needs and fears are the beginning and end of the dialectic when seen from the practical world. They derive first from a desire for justice he shares with all citizens, and then from his awareness of all the problems one must face who cares to return with the truth. In these moments of vulnerability, the philosopher's role as idealist and suffering citizen stands out most clearly. And this role in turn explains the nature of the arguments he must make. In one sense all he can do is provide a circular argument, based on what he shares with the *polis*. The self-subsuming expansiveness of that circle separates the philosopher from others such as the sophists by demonstrating that it is he who articulates what all need. Plato does that so well that his may be the model we still need for grounding idealizations and appreciating how dialectic must, above all, manifest the internal connectedness of thoughts that taken in isolation often seem arbitrary, trivial, or contradictory. Self-subsumption allows ideas to stand as ideals grounded by integrative powers one no longer needs to place in a personal exemplar. So psychology and politics are free to enter the circle where immanence and idealization sustain one another.

I am painfully aware of how abstract I have been in my attempts to defend a Platonic model of thinking, if not his specific formulations, as in fact concretely valuable, even necessary, for contemporary culture. I see no alternative way to make the case while reveling in Plato's inventiveness as a dramatic thinker in pursuit of his own contradictions. I cannot claim that the effort is well handled, but I can conclude by expanding my claim that it is certainly worth making. Few contemporary thinkers face the challenge of justifying the making of cases which proclaim specific idealizations for society or practices within it. Among those who do, the distance from Plato is almost as depressing as the conditions we must idealize from. Robert Nozick cannot get past a Socratic sense of individual integrations, while John Rawls constructs a powerful model of social interpersonality, but at best by a hypothesis that has no dialectical thrust. Yet these thinkers seem to me to be far and away our best on questions of social value. Consider the alternative grounds of idealization in concepts like the political unconscious, or the force of the carnival spirit, or the dialectical shape of history, or critical rationality, or emancipatory interests. Forms of idealization such as these obviously have very little determinate content as concepts. How do we identify attributes of the political unconscious or critical rationality in any systematic way? Those that do have content are very hard to place within the state, since they either lack clear form within society (e.g., the carnival spirit or negative dialectics) or they ignore competing interests (as in the case with Habermas's rationally derived emancipatory interests). The minimal lesson Plato offers is a sense of the contradictions we must explicitly face in our efforts to produce self-subsuming states—as arguments and as forms of self-scrutiny. Any adequate case on values must account for its own interests, handle contradictions between the ideal and the empirical, connect example or charisma to some transpersonal or rational links among concepts, and—above all— connect the activity of the thinker to the needs of the populace he speaks for and thus threatens. Plato makes it a good deal easier to define the problems and above all to account for the thinker's own interest. In doing so, he exemplifies an *ethos* of self-construction so powerful in its capacity to efface the personal that one wants to identify oneself as seeking to play a part in his *Republic*.

## Notes

1. Sigmund Freud, *Dora: An Analysis of a Case of Hysteria* (New York: Collier Books, 1963), pp. 131, 140.
2. Robert Nozick, *Philosophical Explanations* (Cambridge, Mass: Belknap Press, 1981), pp. 137–38, 278. Self-subsumption obviously goes back to the activity of Spirit in a Hegelian dialectic as it circles back on itself. But Nozick sees, as Hegel does not (crucially for his reading of Plato) that persons as well as ideas can demonstrate powers of self-subsumption. Nozick's introduction also taught me to ask why contradictions should be considered as disqualifying an argument.
3. I work out some of the issues connected to this topic in two essays, "An Idea and Ideal of a Literary Canon," *Critical Inquiry* 10 (1983): 37–60, and "Going On and Going Nowhere: Wittgenstein and the Question of Criteria in Literary Criticism," in William Cain, ed., *Philosophical Approaches to Literature* (Lewisburg, PA: Bucknell University Press, 1984), pp. 202–26. Both essays appear in the first part of my *Canons and Consequences: Reflections on the Ethical Force of Imaginative Ideals* (Chicago: Northwestern University Press, 1990).
4. For a statement of the problem in the progress view, see John H. Randall, *Plato: Dramatist of the Life of Reason* (New York: Columbia University Press, 1970).
5. For the philosophical approach see Volume I of Gregory Vlastos, ed., *Plato: A Collection of Critical Essays* (Notre Dame: University of Notre Dame Press, 1978); for the historical critics influenced by Strauss (who are often the best commentators on drama as dialectic) see Jerome Eckstein, *The Platonic Method: An Interpretation of the Dramatic-Philosophic Aspects of the Meno* (New York: Greenwood Press, 1968), and especially Stanley Rosen, *Plato's Symposium* (New Haven: Yale University Press, 1968); for Sallis, see John Sallis, *Being and Logos: The Way of Platonic Dialogue* (Pittsburgh: Duquesne University Press, 1975); and for a full range of these stances on materials relevant to my argument but usually not taken up, see Keith V. Erickson, ed., *Plato: True and Sophistic Rhetoric* (Amsterdam: Rodopi, 1979).
6. Stanley Fish, *Self-Consuming Artifacts* (Berkeley: University of California Press, 1972), pp. 1, 2, 3. For Fish's most revealing statement on dialectic, see p. 13. He grants no levels of reflection, has no sense of preserving by sublating, and is not concerned with measuring acts of spirit by the determinations they make available. His dialectic ought to be humble and "a radical criticism of the ideal" (p. 13), because it has almost nothing in common with Hegelian dialectic or, more controversially, with the Plato who has Socrates say "I am the only man now living who puts it [the genuine art of statesmanship] into practice." I quote from 521d of the Walter Hamilton translation of *Gorgias* (Baltimore: Penguin Books, 1971). All references to other dialogues will be to the translations in Edith Hamilton and Huntington Cairns, eds., *The Collected Dialogues of Plato* (Princeton: Princeton University Press, 1961).
7. Richard Rorty, *Philosophy and the Mirror of Nature* (Princeton: Princeton University Press, 1979), p. 10.

8. Ilham Dilman, *Morality and the Inner Life: A Study in Plato's Gorgias* (London: Macmillan, 1979), pp. 170–74.
9. Dilman, pp. 86–104, is good on Callicles as preferring idealizations which must rely on philosophy if they are to be treated in discourse at all.
10. Adele Spitzer, "The Self-Reliance of the *Gorgias*," in Erickson, ed., pp. 143–53, is very useful on the way the dialogue idealizes the powers exemplified in Socrates' arguments.
11. In order to avoid putting even more pomposity in my text, I reserve for this note the reminder that the more deconstruction succeeds in undermining rational processes of justification the more it requires that all philosophical stances submit to some form of this dramatic test.
12. It is this doubling or interrelation of a property of ideas and a property of our practical psychological lives which I shall claim blossoms in the *Republic* into a full dialectic of ideality and immanence. Similarly, the *Republic* 366d–367a will spell out the reversal of epic notions of the hero I allude to in the following sentences.
13. The deconstructionist point holds here: What is destructive and what constructive depends on circular arguments which are likely to contain numerous contradictions. Nonetheless, some circles are a good deal larger than others and have more articulate internal relations. As a rhetorician, Plato tries to make the circle that sustains his reading of "constructive" appeal to a better and to a larger community (or, more precisely, to a community desirable for most of those who reflect critically on their second-order desires). The burden, then, is on others to present, and maintain, competing idealizations.
14. It will be important to my discussion of the *Republic* that we see Plato here deriving the idea of the good from the nature of the human practice of philosophy. If we are to philosophize, as opposed to describe, we must have an idea of the good. He need not say further that the idea exists beyond our discussions, but he does. In another essay on Plato that repeats some of the claims I make here about the *Phaedrus* and *Symposium*, "Plato's Performative Sublime and the Ends of Reading," *New Literary History* 16 (1985): 251–73, I try to develop further the role of personal example in carrying this idea of the good, but always with a measure of irony. This essay is reprinted, but with a postscript, as the sixth chapter of my *Canons and Consequences*.
15. For example, he treats the need for hypothesizing origins one finds in Agathon and Aristophanes; he shows that immortality provides the enduring state Pausanias seeks in society; he shows the dialectical place of Eryximachus' concern for natural procreation; he shows Love's relation to Agathon's perverse theology; and, above all, he redefines the model of lack and longing Aristophanes creates. Socrates even has in his provoking Alcibiades a sublimated form of the cough which as natural force gently mocks Aristophanes' lyrical stance. It is, of course, only because one values lack that one attends to others sufficiently to include their concerns. I must add that all my remarks on the *Symposium* are very heavily indebted to David Tarbet's class lectures on the subject.
16. Stanley Rosen is so affected by this opening to irony that he speculates on

what Aristodemus might have missed when he began to get sleepy (p. 9). One sees why Christ invented a church as the rock to secure his example.
17. Julius Stenzel, *Plato's Method of Dialectic*, trans. D. J. Allan (New York: Arno Press, 1973), p. 15.
18. G. W. F. Hegel, *Lectures on the History of Philosophy*, trans. E. S. Haldane and Frances Simpson (New York: Humanities Press, 1955), p. 52. Hegel's specific account of dialectics in the *Republic* is on pp. 90–95. For Plato on dialectic in the *Republic*, see 508d–513e and 532d–541b. I find support for my reading in a fine, non-Hegelian essay, Richard Robinson, "Hypothesis in the Republic," in Vlastos, ed., pp. 97–131, especially 125–131.
19. Eric Voegelin, *Order in History*, Vol. 3: *Plato and Aristotle* (Baton Rouge, La.: Lousiana State University Press, 1967), is superb on how Plato's first book renders this crisis.
20. I quote selectively in order to avoid dealing with the difficult phrase "making no use whatever of any object of sense but only of pure ideas moving on through ideas to ideas and ending with ideas" (511c). I proceed on the assumption that one is proceeding by ideas when one attends to how ideas are formulated and contextualized, but I wish I had more confidence that I understood Plato's full meaning.

4

# The Mechanics of Creation: Non-Contradiction and Natural *Necessity in* Paradise Lost

## Mili N. Clark

*To the Memory of C. A. Patrides*

The myth of *Paradise Lost* is stated by God, who asserts that he made man (and all rational beings) "Sufficient to have stood, though free to fall" (III.99).[1] God's statement juxtaposes sufficiency and falling as the opposite terms of the myth's synchronic structure, and sufficiency includes actual freedom, for the freedom to fall is the potential loss of freedom. A bare paradigm to be conjugated throughout time until the renovation of the just, the statement does not supply a principle or cause to explain the change from sufficiency to falling, even though the whole story of *Paradise Lost* clothes the paradigm in enough practical information to account for the falls of these rational beings who have the wherewithal to stand. Satan's pride and envy, Adam's passion for Eve, Eve's vanity and sense of inferiority, mankind's appetite for power, glory, and pleasure are reasons why particular individuals fail in their obedience to God. But such reasons are the embodiment in individuals of a causality that the reasons tend to obscure and deny. Specifically, they cannot transcend their particularity to become the third term that is needed in the myth's paradigm to mediate between sufficiency and falling. Without the third term, sufficiency and falling would remain synchronically inert contradictions lacking the energy the myth obviously possesses to keep on repeating itself diachronically in the falls of successive generations of God's creatures.[2] On the metaphysical level, not the practical, there ought to be a causal principle that provides both the attractive identity between

75

sufficiency and falling which yokes together these two terms and the repulsive dissimilarity which drives them apart.

Much of the poetic believability of *Paradise Lost* flows from Milton's vivid portrayal of the psychological states, social circumstances, and physical surroundings of his characters. Poetically the epic succeeds in convincing us that characters who really are sufficient to stand nevertheless choose to fall. Adam's ability to reason his way to general truths on the basis of what he sees around him is little short of miraculous. Even the less intellectually endowed Eve reasons as well as the Milton of the *Areopagitica*, whose arguments for an uncensored press are remarkably similar to her arguments for working apart from Adam in the face of Satan's threatening presence in Paradise (see esp. IX.322–41). The poetic credibility of *Paradise Lost* may be called the poem's 'physics,' in which the causes of the Fall are immediately intuitive and demonstrable to the postlapsarian reader's own experience. However, since the myth's paradigm originally signifies the pre-fallen state, the reader requires the causality, or at least the logic, of a metaphysical explanation of why sufficiency is defined by the freedom to fall. In particular, this reader shares the Platonic concept of the sufficient being as one who would have stood despite the poem's physics. Sufficient to have stood, though free to fall is a contradiction in concept and is the contradiction which the mythic structure of *Paradise Lost* repeatedly strives to overcome.

# I

So many reasons offered in the poem's physics for failure to stand, while believable as reasons, argue so much deficiency in the characters that we are driven to look for the source of a deficiency that God and Raphael deny exists (V.524–28; VIII.561, 640–43).[3] There is a general structure of deficiency in *Paradise Lost* which is easier to point to than to account for. Fully one-third of the angels and more than one half of mankind fall (XII.334–36, 533–35). "Freely they stood who stood, and fell who fell," says God (III.102), and we must believe him because God is Truth. God did not plot the downfall of his creatures because God is good. Conversely, God did not prevent their downfall because God is just; he could not rescind the free choice he gave each one of them.

There is more than enough proof of the freedom to fall, and were it not for the sheer magnitude of the numbers involved, we would search no further for the cause of failure than the reasons that Milton's physics provide. But these numbers are vital statistics that add up to a failure rate of only slightly less than one-half of God's total production of rational beings, angelic and human. The impersonality of great numbers resists the personal explanations for failure and demands an equally impersonal accounting. Viewed historically, sin is a monstrous repetition compulsion, devoted merely to self-perpetuation and devoid of progress or purpose. Mindless as a machine, history relentlessly grinds out its record of unrighteous deeds: "So shall the World go on, / To good malignant, to bad men benign" (XII.537–38). Milton's vital statistics do not admit of the easy and dogmatic solution taken by Reformation theology. There, the only numbers that matter are those of the elect:

> We say, then, that Scripture clearly proves this much, that God by his eternal and immutable counsel determined once for all those whom it was his pleasure one day to admit to salvation, and those whom, on the other hand, it was his pleasure to doom to destruction. We maintain that this counsel, as regards the elect, is founded on his free mercy, without any respect to human worth, while those whom he dooms to destruction are excluded from access to life by a just and blameless, but at the same time incomprehensible judgment.[4]

Theology, the church, sacraments, exist to benefit the elect, since no benefit could accrue to the reprobate by definition. Without God's election of some from the uniformly reprobate condition of all humanity, human life would be pointless. As it is, even with election, God's restraining grace is necessary to preserve 'all that is' by preventing man's corrupt nature from following its own inclinations into total chaos.[5] In the Reformed context, it makes no sense to speak of a 'rate of failure' because all persons are failed after Adam; the success of the elect is due entirely to God's will and power.

The physics of Milton's poem, however, do invite the reader to speculate about the causes of a rate of failure because Milton presents God as far from being the arbitrary predestinator posited by Reformation dogmatics[6]. To all persons God gives sufficient grace to "clear thir senses dark" (II. 188) and conscience as their guide. Sufficient grace becomes man's power to *use* his own free will in order to strive for salvation.[7] Only those who refuse God's offers of grace will be lost. Although the renewed powers of man fall short of Adam's original sufficiency, the paradigm of "Sufficient to have stood, though free to fall" is reinstituted and its contradiction repeated in the continuing myth of man's historical adventure. Once more, it becomes necessary to ask why any person who is upheld by God would choose to fall. Conversely, given that the majority of mankind does fall, it becomes problematic why those who stand are the exception. Milton could have chosen the Reformation solution to the problem of numbers, and its theology offers enough contradictions around which to construct a myth; indeed the founder of the Protestant revolution Martin Luther defines the heart of religious experience as contradiction:

> [Paul] says: I do not do the good I want (v. 19). Because the same person is both spirit and flesh, therefore what he does in the flesh the whole man is said to do. And yet because he resists, it is rightly said that the whole man is not doing it, but only a part of him. Therefore both expressions are true, that he himself does it and he himself does not do it.
> . . . Note that one and the same man at the same time serves the law of God and the law of sin, at the same time is righteous and sins!
> In the light of these points it is obvious that the idea of the metaphysical theologians is silly and ridiculous, when they argue whether opposing appetites can exist in the same subject, and when they invent the fiction that the spirit, namely, our reason, is something all by itself and absolute and in its own kind and integral and perfectly whole, and similarly that our sensuality, or our flesh, on the opposite end likewise constitutes a complete and absolute whole.[8]

Luther's exposition of St. Paul is an intimate and psychological account of how one person can be simultaneously righteous and sinful, and such is the experience of the elect after the Fall. Milton's contradiction between sufficiency and falling, which exists both before and after the Fall, subsumes Luther's. Had Milton accepted the doctrine of predestination, the continuity of his myth would have been broken. Conversely, since he did not accept predestination, Milton needs the myth in order to justify God.[9]

As it is, God keeps reinstating the original terms of the myth throughout human history in his attempts to save his latest image from becoming a failed experiment in creation. As man exercises his freedom to fall, God finds new ways of re-establishing his sufficiency to stand—which in a moment sin changes into the preterit sufficiency *to have stood*. Apparently opposed to the compulsion of sin to repeat itself are God's attempts to mitigate its vicious circularity and redirect history toward blessedness by cultivating a morally healthy stock of human beings—"the divine gardener's constant efforts to replace withered roots by fresh ones."[10] He experiments many times with recreating the human race through Noah, Abraham, Moses, David, Jesus, (and perhaps even the Puritans), but the virtue of these men is not communicated naturally to their descendants. Individuals such as Abdiel among the angels and Noah among the mortals stand out as spiritual exceptions unable to propagate their virtue to others. Goodness is an individual not a racial virtue, explainable on neither genetic nor cultural grounds. The Son's payment of the "rigid satisfaction, death for death" (III.212), gives the human race a second chance, but neither his teaching nor his self-sacrifice alters the genetic or cultural propensity to sin. "Indebted and undone" man is bankrupted by original sin, and the Son, so to speak, gives him a loan of fresh capital. But beyond the loan, which man is free to use as he will, the Son's redemption of the original bond between man and God does not account for why some persons choose to be saved, much less for why others choose to be damned. Under close scrutiny, Milton's physics loses any outward appearance of the Reformation doctrine of election, according to which Christ's merit is an effect but not the cause of God's saving grace.[11] Both Christ's merit and man's sincere intent are operative causes in man's salvation (III.290, 192).

The mechanics of creation are such that sin is naturally propagated, "traducted" biologically from Adam and Eve to their children and down through the generations, but virtue is not: "This depravity was engendered in us by our first parents. . . . those even who are born of regenerate parents; for faith, though it takes away the personal imputation of guilt, does not altogether remove indwelling sin. It is not therefore man as a regenerate being, but man in his animal capacity, that propagates his kind; as seed, though cleared from the chaff and stubble, produces not only the ear or grain, but also the stalk and husk" (*CD* XV, pp. 196–97). Milton's grain analogy, consonant with traditional Christian metaphors of fruit, seed, tree, stock, conveys that sin is a distinguishing characteristic of the human species. In terms of modern genetics, God's attempt to repropagate the human race from the seed of Noah fails in adapting man to salvation because Noah's righteousness is a non-inheritable acquired characteristic.

The interference of Milton's God in the natural development of mankind does slow down the rate of failure in the species. Milton has a clear idea of the genetic transmission and conservation of sin from generation to generation, and there is this implication to be drawn from Milton's presentation of history in Books XI and XII: that the rate of failure in the species is a function of the natural evolutionary development of sin. Left unmodified by God's experiments, the dominant strain of sin would evolve man's capacity to respond to God's grace out of the species. God reconstitutes man's sufficiency to stand and the freedom of his will to respond to grace at just those moments in history when sin has brought mankind to the point where righteousness is on the brink of extinction. God's experiments redirect the natural tendency of sin to evolve linearly into the repetitively cyclic movement of a plant that grows, flowers, and then is cut back to its roots only to grow again (as Herbert portrays his own spiritual cycles in "The Flower"). After the Fall, human nature and grace are in conflict.[12] History is the perpetuation of the central contradiction in the myth of *Paradise Lost*.

Just as God has not predestined individuals to salvation or damnation, he has left history free of any internal teleology, which is not to say that history does not serve his purpose. His original purpose in creating mankind was to make a race which would "open to themselves at length the way / Up hither [Heaven], under long obedience tri'd, / And Earth be chang'd to Heav'n, and Heav'n to Earth, / One Kingdom, Joy and Union without end" (VII.158–61). After the Fall, his purpose remains, albeit much modified from a race of humans to a collection of virtuous human individuals who will be gathered up to form the "multitude" of redeemed (III.26) united under the Son. The race will fail to realize God's plan, while a multitude of individuals will succeed. Human history begins with the precipitating event of the Fall; but how long will it, or must it, continue so that God will realize his purpose in creating humans? History is indeterminate insofar as God does not predestinate individuals. His infusions of sufficiency into mankind at certain historical moments serve to keep history indeterminate, that is, the events of history do not come about in such a way that it is impossible for them to be otherwise. Nor do God's interferences in history subject it to divine compulsion, unless it is the compulsion that humans be free, for they hold at bay the destruction of the entire race through sin. God knows the termination date of the world, but that date is indeterminate insofar as it is contingent upon the free choices of individuals who will or will not realize his purpose. The world's termination date is externally arrived at in a peculiar way by God. It is statistical: a time shall come "When this world's dissolution shall be ripe" (XII.459), and that time is when Hell—"her numbers full" (III.332)—has no more room for sinners. Milton's solution to history's termination date may be unorthodox, but it does reconcile the indeterminacy of man's free will with God's determined plan for a final creation free from defect. Before he creates mankind, God makes a place for sinners which is Hell, and Hell has room for a fixed number of sinners, angelic and human. We may suppose that God fixes only the numbers of the damned, not those of the saved. When Hell is full, time ends, and the number of saved is the sum of all those individuals throughout history who have themselves chosen obedience to God's will. The contradiction in the poem's basic myth is finally never *overcome* because the contradiction is *real* (see note 2). God puts a stop to it by separating sufficiency from its negation and thus eliminating the indeterminate from the cosmos.

Although the number saved was known in advance by the omniscient God, it was not predetermined, nor were the individuals predetermined who comprise either group. The indeterminacy of free will is displayed by the fact that God will create the new heavens and new earth after history terminates. Milton's solution to the numbers problem is Baroque: it allows for the containment of the indeterminate within the determinate, for the possibility that history might have been otherwise within the necessity for it to be what it was when it was. That history is indeterminate is shown by the startling contrast of the final four lines of *Paradise Lost* with the terrible vision of history in Books XI-XII. Into those lands where Adam has seen history unfold, as if from a script in the divine archives for which in time there will be human actors, Adam and Eve wander to find a world utterly open to choice, utterly contingent upon free will.[13]

For Milton, man's free will is a mysteriously spontaneous power independent of genetics, evolution, and predestination. There can be no science of free will, including theology, in Milton's cosmos. Free will is similar to chance: its effects happen neither always nor for the most part.[14] Given that there is no science of free will, the statistical probability of free will's issuing in either damnation or salvation is that of chance, what Aristotle calls the luck of "persons who play at even and odd."[15] The proportion of either damned or saved to the total number of mortals is calculable by statistical probability. Were it not that the dice are loaded by the conservation of sin, the proportion would be one-to-one. On the other hand, it may be pure coincidence that the predetermined number of damned is greater than that of the saved.[16] But, for reasons which I shall explore presently, coincidence is an unlikely explanation. The cosmos itself is an order imposed upon the randomness of chaos.

That both God will realize his purpose and man will be free to choose to join him in it or not makes for a more complicated physical and moral cosmos than allowed for in the Protestant doctrines that preceded Milton's. To bring it all off, God must be intimately involved with helping the individuals who want to be saved and at the same time he must provide impersonal means of guaranteeing everyone's freedom. Stopping history when Hell's numbers are full is one such impersonal means. Another has to do with the natural law by which all are created equal. Because they are created equal, a virtuous parent cannot pass his or her virtue onto offspring. The justice of God's predestining some individuals to salvation bothered Milton enough to dispense with the doctrine of predestination. He does not, however, dispense with Original Sin; it is the bottom line of equality, the great leveler at birth. Never content with purely doctrinal explanations of anything, detesting intellectual slavery and superstition (*CD*, Preface, p. 3), Milton wanted a scientific explanation of sin as well. How did sin come to be one of the laws of nature, encoded in human genetics?

The term *genetics* and the biological knowledge it implies for us today had not yet been broached by the seventeenth century, but the general subject and curiosity about it existed. From his study of the chicken egg, William Harvey drew some conclusions which would direct later scientists to investigate possibilities they might have taken longer to treat seriously. For instance, he refuted Aristotle's assertion, which still dominated medical thought in the seventeenth century, that only the male supplies the vital principle (*anima*) of generation, while the female supplies only the matter from which the male vital principle generates the offspring. Since a partridge and a common fowl will produce a hybrid "as like the female as it is like the male in vital endowment," Harvey concluded that the female is equally efficient in the work of generation as the male.[17] The same is true of human generation: "And, therefore, it is that the male and female by themselves, and separately, are not genetic, but become so united *in coitu*, and made one animal, as it were; whence, from the two as one, is produced and educed that which is the true efficient proximate cause of conception" (*Animal Generation*, p. 395). But the 'influence' of the male semen on the female ovum cannot alone account for the development of the foetus into an individual of its species: "Lastly, not only is there a soul or vital principle present in the vegetative part, but even before this there is inherent mind, foresight, and understanding, which from the very commencement to the being and perfect formation of the chick, dispose and order and take up all things requisite, moulding them in the new being, with consummate art, into the form and likeness of its parents" (p. 455). What Harvey is searching for is the genetic code, but he must make do with a mysterious, intelligent vital principle.

Whether or not Milton read Harvey is less relevant to the physics of his cosmos than that he lived when he did, at a time when scientists, the 'virtuosi,' were searching for the causes, by which they meant the laws, of nature. Those laws, according to the guidelines Bacon set forth in *The New Organon* and *The Advancement of Learning*, must be mathematical, uniform, and unvarying.[18] Having been set in motion by God they probably could not be broken by God. There was debate over whether or not God could or did interfere with nature's laws, as in the production of miracles, which might have scientific explanations. Nature's mechanical laws, which are God's general providence, seemed to contradict the traditional Christian belief in God's particular providence. The discovery of a contradiction, such as that between God's general and his particular providence, in many cases led the seventeenth-century philosophers to discard the half of the contradiction that was inconsistent with natural law. By the end of the century, writes Richard Westfall, "the virtuosi were finding it more and more difficult to admit any providential interruptions of nature, until finally some of them even denied the reality of miracles themselves." Boyle's diffident yet decided preference is characteristic: "And that having, when all these things were in His prospect, settled among His corporeal works general and standing laws of motion suited to His most wise ends, it seems very congruous to His wisdom to prefer unless in the newly accepted [sic] cases catholic laws and higher ends before subordinate ones, and uniformity in His conduct before making changes in it according to every sort of particular emergencies."[19]

By now it is a truism in the history of ideas that Protestantism aided the spirit of the scientific revolution because both rejected the mediating tactics by which the medievals had reconciled contradictions:

> As an example of the indirections by which, in the history of ideas, directions are so often found out, the anti-metaphysical bias of Calvinism is at this point relevant. For Calvin, like Luther, held reason to be futile when applied to the search for righteousness, and taught that we deserve only God's hatred. . . . his distinctiveness lies in the very clarity of his insistence on unmediated grace imputed to individual souls in an otherwise profane and secular world. His argument thus has the effect of separating in a novel way the inscrutable economy of the first cause, the divine will, from whatever concern reason may otherwise have with the world of secondary causes.
>
> I stop short, here, of explaining the rise of science unilaterally in terms of Puritan thinking along the lines of the 'Merton thesis,' but wish rather to indicate merely the similarity between Calvin's anti-metaphysical stress on divine transcendence and certain equally anti-metaphysical tendencies of the new method. Calvinists, that is, could insist on a transcendent God in the name of Christian piety with the same kind of confidence as scientists who asserted (for fear of offending piety) that God was really none of their business.[20]

When Milton tried to avoid science's despiritualization of nature, he could not turn to Protestantism for support, because it had thrown out many of the fruits of Catholic philosophy's cultivation of nature. Boyle's conviction that God's wisdom manifested itself in the uniformity of his conduct is scientific, Protestant—and mechanical. The other side of this zeal for uniform laws is that not all the contradictions of medieval thought were able by their very nature to yield to *new* rationalizations. While that side of Milton which believes in particular providence and which portrays so convincingly his characters' personal reasons for failure denies the impersonal, mechanistic, and mathematical interpretation of natural law, he is a man of his time and cannot evade mechanism altogether, although in *Paradise Lost* he hides it under the gorgeous vitality which flows through the cosmos. It surfaces when Milton alludes to the numbers of angels and humans who will not realize God's plan for his final All-in-All. One major effect of the contradiction between sufficiency and falling is the waste of created things. One-third of the angels and the majority of mankind is an enormous waste of God's resources even if his resources are infinite. From the point of view of the finite universe, the waste is a measurement of the loss of energy from a closed system. In the science of theology the waste is the by-product of the entropy of sin, and sin is the angels' and man's willful misuse of their own resources. The dogmatic answer to waste is simple and requires no thought beyond the tautology that because man is sinful he sins. In *Paradise Lost*, Milton searches beyond the tautology for an answer which not only begins with the Fall and its disjunction of nature and grace, but also, in a scientific fashion, reveals itself as a law unifying God's conduct from before the foundations of the world were laid. This is why an analysis of the physical processes of Milton's cosmos in terms of a rough concept of evolution is not so anomalous as it may seem at first blush.

Milton's materialism (the creation *ex deo* rather than *ex nihilo*) is a scientific notion, one that the seventeenth-century search for unifying laws suggested to him as much as did Aristotle's *nihil ex nihilo fit*. Milton's materialism underlies the genetic transmission of sin:

> Again, if sin be communicated by generation, and transmitted from father to son, it follows that what is the πρῶτου δεκτικὸυ, or original subject of sin, namely, the rational soul, must be propagated in the same manner; for that it is from the soul that all sin in the first instance proceeds, will not be denied. . . . If the soul be equally diffused throughout any given whole, and throughout every part of that whole, how can the human seed, the noblest and most intimate part of all the body, be imagined destitute and devoid of the soul of the parents, or at least of the father, when communicated to the son by the laws of generation (*cum gignendo*[21])? It is acknowledged by the common consent of almost all philosophers, that every *form* to which class the human soul must be considered as belonging, is produced by the power of matter [*omnem certe formam, cuius generis et anima humana est, ex potentia materiæ produci omnes fere consentiunt*]. . . . There seems therefore no reason, why the soul of man should be made an exception [to the general law of creation[22]]. For, as

has been shown before, God breathed the breath of life into other living beings, and blended it so intimately with matter, that the propagation and production of the human form were analogous to those of other forms, and were the proper effect of that power which had been communicated to matter by the Deity [*humana quoque forma ex potentia materiæ a Deo indicta*[23] *propagaretur et produceretur*]. (*CD* I, pp. 47–53)

The power matter possesses to propagate and produce all living species is given to it by God.[24] Matter follows whatever instructions God has given it for producing creatures. While matter may seem to act autonomously in generating the mineral, vegetable, and animal kingdoms, it does so as God's faithful agent and steward. Milton, along with the Cambridge Platonists, stressed the compatibility of religion and science at a time when the theories of Hobbes and Descartes were positing nature as an autonomous system of laws regulating the motions of matter.

In *A Discourse on Method* Descartes summarizes the plan he followed in his treatise *Le Monde* (a work whose publication he suppressed after Galileo's trial and which was published posthumously in 1664):

> Without being obliged either to follow or to refute the opinions accepted among the learned, I here resolved to leave all this world to their disputes and to speak only of what would happen in a new world, were God now to create enough matter to make it up, somewhere in imaginary space, and if he were to put in motion variously and without order the different parts of this matter, so that he concocted as confused a chaos as the poets could ever imagine and that later he did no more than apply his ordinary conserving activity to nature letting nature act in accordance with the laws he has established. . . . one can believe—without belittling the miracle of creation—that by such activity alone all the things that are purely material could have been able, as time went on, to make themselves just as we now see them. And their nature is much easier to conceive, when one sees them coming to be in this manner, than when one considers them only in their completed state.[25]

The great difference between Milton's and Descartes' theories lies not so much in whether or not the species developed gradually out of nature or sprang full grown from it but in Milton's insisting that God first made matter able to be an efficient cause of species, whereas in Descartes' hypothesis God just introduces natural laws into a chaos of matter and they go to work in chaos until material things are able to produce themselves. By breathing his breath of life into matter, Milton's God first changes chaos utterly before matter can become productive of species. Milton illustrates in *Paradise Lost* the danger of Cartesian materialist theory, while at the same time acknowledging that to an atheistic eye such as Satan's his materialism might appear similar to Descartes'. Aware of the vitality of nature and of the power of matter, Satan argues that not God's hand but their own "quick'ning power" created the angels:

>     self-begot, self-rais'd
> By our own quick'ning power, when fatal course
> Had circl'd his full Orb, the birth mature
> Of this our native Heav'n, Ethereal Sons.
>
>                                         (V.860–63)[26]

A theory of the power of matter as an efficient cause of species, of which evolution is the latest and most sophisticated, is compatible with belief in a god as creator of all things. It differs from a literal reading of Genesis in that it aims to be a scientific interpretation of *how* God created the world, a distinction Descartes feared the ecclesiastical authorities would not appreciate, and indeed, his one-time friends the Cambridge Platonists, who for a time believed Descartes was one of them in spirit, later decided he was a thoroughgoing mechanist. They, however, saw no incompatibility between their religious piety and their own theory of the power of matter which they termed *plastic nature*. Plastic nature is a creative but unconscious spirit working in matter, according to the ideas and purposes in the divine intellect, to produce the mineral, vegetative, and animal species. (Because for them the soul was not material, the Cambridge Platonists stopped short of including man in plastic nature's productions.[27])

> It is a certain *Lower Life* than the *Animal*, which acts *Regularly* and *Artificially*, according to the Direction of *Mind* and *Understanding*, *Reason* and *Wisdom*, for *Ends*, or in Order to do *Good*, though it self do not know the Reason of what it does, nor is *Master* of that Wisdom according to which it acts only a *Servant* to it, and *Drudging Executioner* of the same; it operating *Fatally* and *Sympathetically*, according to *Laws* and *Commands*, prescribed to it by a *Perfect Intellect*, and imprest upon it; and which is either a *Lower* Faculty of some *Conscious Soul*, or else an Inferiour kind of Life or *Soul* by it self; but essentially depending upon an *Higher Intellect*.[28]

Not only does Plastic Nature save God the drudgery of attending to the generation of every single leaf, insect, chicken egg, etc., but it also accounts for the imperfections in nature which, without the theory of Plastic Nature, would be attributable to a perfect God:

> This Opinion [that everything is done immediately by God himself] is further Confuted . . . by those *Errors* and *Bungles* which are committed, when the Matter is Inept and Contumacious; which argue the Agent not to be Irresistible, and that *Nature* is such a thing, as is not altogether uncapable (as well as *Humane Art*) of being sometimes frustrated and disappointed, by the Indisposition of Matter. (Cudworth, pp. 292–93)
>
> For *Physis* (as I said) is not the divine Understanding it self, but is as if you should conceive, an Artificers imagination separate from the Artificer, and left alone to work by it self without animadversion. Hence *Physis* or Nature is sometimes puzzeled and bungells in ill disposed matter, because its power is not absolute and omnipotent.[29]

Milton's metaphysics in *Paradise Lost* is a poetic concoction of God's immediate acts of creation in Genesis, Lucretian atomism, the Stoic doctrine of the seeds of things, and the Cambridge Platonists' plastic nature. Plastic nature in her youth in the newly created world is sister to More's Divine Artificer's imagination, separate from the Artificer, producing prolifically and wildly:

> Nature here
> Wanton'd as in her prime, and play'd at will
> Her Virgin Fancies, pouring forth more sweet,
> Wild above Rule or Art, enormous bliss.
>
> (V.294–97)

This nature, or power of matter, as an efficient cause of species, was made capable by God of changing the natures of the species as he originally created them, as nature must do after the fall of man when man, and all the species, become mortal and vitiated in their moral constitutions. As outlined to the angels, God's original plan for mankind included a gradual adaptive change to fit humans to the environment of Heaven, an ascent of man "by degrees of merit rais'd / They open to themselves at length the way \ Up hither" (VII.157–58). The power (*potentia*) of matter is, strictly, the potential for all forms in the scale of nature, a theory implicit in Aristotle "of matter proceeding to formed substance, which in turn furnishes the matter for a higher substance, and so on" (Hunter, "The Power of Matter," pp. 143–44). Either the power of matter appealed to Milton because he disliked the idea of power exclusively descending from high to low, or the idea of power ascending from low to high was a consequence of his scientific predilection for a materialist biology. Either way,

> By postulating a world in which generative influence not only descends from active agents to their subjects, but responsively reascends from subjects to superiors, Milton converts the traditional hierarchy of causation into an interdependent system of interacting influences. He thereby creates a world susceptible to pollution on account of original sin, just as it is capable of progressive development as long as human integrity endures.[30]

Raphael speculates that since everything is made of one first matter, and since the angelic species, made of more refined matter than are humans, can eat human food, that humans will be able to work their way up the matter chain (or, eat their way up the vegetable food chain) to become angels:

> time may come when men
> With Angels may participate, and find
> No inconvenient Diet, nor too light Fare:
> And from these corporal nutriments perhaps
> Your bodies may at last turn all to spirit,
> Improv'd by tract of time, and wing'd ascend
> Ethereal, as wee. . . .
>
> (V.493–99)

The devils in Hell have a rather more modern concept of evolution and try to comfort themselves with the prospect that forced to adapt to their changed environment, they will. Both Belial and Mammon speak to the hope that the raging fires of Hell, now so painful, will seem mild when the essential nature of the devils has become a creature of Hell:

> Our purer essence then will overcome
> Thir noxious vapor, or enur'd not feel,
> Or chang'd at length, and to the place conform'd
> In temper and in nature, will receive
> Familiar the fierce heat, and void of pain.
>
> (II.215–19)

> Our torments also may in length of time
> Become our Elements, these piercing Fires
> As soft as now severe, our temper chang'd
> Into their temper.
>
> (II.274–77)

Milton's concept of the power of matter considerably exceeds the Cambridge Platonists' power of plastic nature or that of Descartes's. There is a strong implication that the power of matter itself, given a certain tract of time in which to work, will effect some change. Since the souls of rational beings are made of this same matter, however refined a degree of it, their rational faculties are impelled to change from the way they were originally created. Adam and Eve simply could not have remained in their original perfection even if they had not yielded to Satan's temptation. Not yielding, they would have advanced a step up on their ascent to becoming angels, but they would have advanced anyway, provided they did not commit impiety on their own. Unfortunately, eating the forbidden fruit sent them down from perfect to imperfect human. As his career as fallen angel goes on, Satan becomes aware of the long descent down which his chosen course of action will send him: "In the lowest deep a lower deep / Still threatning to devour me opens wide" (IV.76–77). The forbidden fruit was more than just a sign of Adam and Eve's obedience. The fruit was alien to the food chain which Raphael celebrated as sustaining the entire universe. It was not a "corporal nutriment" which would aid in man's evolution into angel, as are all the other foods on earth. The power of matter did not produce the Tree of the Knowledge of Good and Evil any more than it produced the Tree of Life: both were placed in the garden by God. Both trees signify the limitations of potent matter which cannot give the gift of immortality, because matter is not itself immortal, or give the gift of knowledge of good and evil, because matter is not itself rational.[31] Eating the alien fruit, Adam and Eve begin to change their essential natures, so that they are no longer adapted to live in Paradise. They would not be fit to live anywhere, except Hell, did not God change the conditions under which the power of matter operates (having the angels tilt the earth's axis, calling Sin and Death to infest the earth). The power of matter will now produce species adapted to the changed environment of earth while itself remaining essentially good because it is executing the plan of the divine intellect.

Before the fall of man, then, Milton's power of matter could evolve or devolve humans up or down the scale of nature, depending on whether human actions were ecologically conservative or destructive. The alien fruit that Adam and Eve ate severely damaged matter's power and limited it to generating the damaged seeds of all the (fallen) species. Sin is transmitted from parents to children regardless of the virtue of the parents. This is so because Milton's thinking is limited to the precepts of Aristotelian metaphysics and Christian theology, as were the ideas of his contemporaries in the sciences. Among the "paradoxes and problems" of animal generation to which Harvey hasn't an answer, he lists "a remarkable fact, that virtues and vices, marks and moles, and even particular dispositions to disease are transmitted by parents to their offspring; and that while some inherit in this way, all do not" (*Animal Generation*, p. 455).[32] Centuries of thinking only in terms of how a species (the formal cause) is present in the individual habituated philosophers to conceiving of inheritance as passed downward from the general to the specific to the individual. In addition, Adam and Eve were not individual humans; they were the human species; its whole potential was in their seed. That an individual could pass onto the species a 'new' trait, say a virtuous trait, is barely conceivable because the terminology and the metaphysics did not exist to explain how that could happen.[33] Such a notion is also completely at odds with Christian theology, because it obviates the need for Christ's sacrifice and for grace, and, though Milton was a radical thinker, his purpose was not to do away with Christianity but to reconcile it with seventeenth-century science. Because there was always some metaphysical principle none of the philosophers was willing to sacrifice, none of their theories of matter actually did open up a theory of evolution. (Descartes' materialism was limited by his dissociation of matter and spirit.) Despite their implied or overt concept that matter itself is capable of producing gradations of species, from lower to higher, species in themselves did not derive from lower species. In the absence of a belief that a virtuous individual could contribute his genetic complement to the species as a whole, Milton developed (or borrowed) other explanations for why the human race continues to survive despite the fact that it is stuck with this extraordinarily maladaptive trait, sin.[34]

If Milton had accepted the tautology 'because man is sinful he sins' as adequately justifying God's ways, he would not have needed to write *Paradise Lost*. He may not have foreseen before he began writing that his epic would raise questions better left unasked if one is defending God against charges of injustice toward humans. One of those questions concerns the wasteful economy of the universe, specifically the great numbers of damned angels and humans. Those numbers are a necessary by-product of God's determination to realize his All-in-All, the multitude of redeemed who will be united with him at the end of history. It just so happens that in order to insure the multitude of redeemed, the generative process must produce a staggering total of human beings of which the number of bad will exceed many times over the multitude of good. God infuses new supplies of sufficiency into the human race in order that history continue long enough to produce the multitude of redeemed. History as Milton summarizes it in Books XI-XII is a record of the misery man inflicts on man; the more God's infusions of sufficiency prolong history, the more misery ever new generations of humans must suffer that God obtain his All-in-All. Milton does not evince any sympathy for the damned. His problem is that the sheer number of them implies something is wrong with God that he can't generate his multitude of redeemed in a less wasteful manner—that their sufficiency to stand was at no time sufficient enough.

Here, too, evolution is an instructive analogy because the multitude of redeemed is God's Idea of the human species, which he preserves at the cost of the individuals who are the subjects of his, rather than nature's, experiments in survival. The seventeenth-century scientists understood the implication that mechanical natural law places individual and particular creatures below the welfare of the whole system, and particular creatures may have to suffer to preserve the whole (Westfall, p. 86; also pp. 79–80). Before early modern science had entwined itself into the problems of theology, Thomas Bradwardine made a fascinating observation on the problem of numbers during the course of refuting the argument that: "If Adam had not sinned no one would have been reprobated. Therefore, predestination or reprobation corresponds to individual merit."

> One answer would be that if Adam had not sinned, only those who are now elect would have been born, that is to say, only that number of those now elect would have been born. If Adam had not sinned, God would have created only those souls as are now given to the elect, although some he might perhaps have joined to other bodies than they have now. Or, if we wish to keep body and soul together as an elect unit, only those would have been born who are now elect. In that case an elect who has actually been born of a reprobate parent would have instead been born of another father who belongs to the elect.

Aware that even entertaining the possibility of only elect persons being born was giving ammunition to "the argument which accuses God of injustice and cruelty," Bradwardine quickly advances the deterrent defense of the death penalty:

> If a man may undergo temporal punishment for the temporal benefit of others, why should he not be punished temporally and eternally for the temporal and eternal benefit of the elect, in order that they might all the more flee from evil and choose the good in the present, that in the future they might have greater joy, deeper love, and higher praise for God?
>
> Thus great profit, both in the present and in the future, accrues to the elect from the reprobate, indeed the whole

purpose of being for the reprobate is that they have been created for the sake of the elect. ("The Cause of God Against the Pelagian," *Forerunners*, pp. 152, 160–61.)

Bradwardine's explanation for the existence of the damned, when it was possible for God to have created only elect souls, will not serve Milton's justification of God's ways. His seventeenth-century scientific impulse led him to look for a law which would account for the way things are without indicting God for premeditated murder. Because he believed in a theocentric universe, this law had to proceed from God, and since it was a law, it had to be unitive, operative throughout creation before as well as after the Fall.

The law through which God accomplishes his generation of numbers—as mechanical as any seventeenth-century scientist's conception of natural law—is the law of non-contradiction. The law of non-contradiction has been around a long time, arbitrating the propositions of philosophers and the jurisprudence of judges and juries. But it was Milton who saw the frightful implications of one traditional use of it and nonetheless resolutely set out to display and defend it in his epic.

## II

There is an argument, derivable from *Paradise Lost* and *The Christian Doctrine*, one which centers on God rather than on man's willful disobedience, that explains the structure of deficiency: why defect but not virtue is propagated; what the third term is between sufficiency and falling in the myth's paradigm; why *Paradise Lost* is formally a tragedy. The argument justifies God by revealing that both he and the creatures are victims of his own matchless perfections. The argument also reveals why God's ways have to be justified, because it leaves him formally responsible for evil on the metaphysical plane. Although the sources of Milton's argument are in medieval theology, in his use of them they undergo a seventeenth-century transformation consonant with the search for natural law. The argument begins with the contradiction in God that corresponds to the contradiction between sufficiency and falling in the myth of *Paradise Lost*.

The contradiction in God is that he is two Gods—the God who is self-sufficient and without need of other beings and the God who creates other beings because he needs them to realize his perfection:[35]

> (a) God would not be perfect if he did not will and create things other than himself; *and*

(b) God would be perfect if he did not will or create any things other than himself.

As a historical conclusion, this is of fundamental importance for the understanding, not only of St. Thomas, but of most medieval philosophy, since the conjunction of the two contradictory theorems is by no means peculiar to him. What it signifies is that medieval thinkers for the most part believed in two Gods. The two were called one; but they were *thought* as having different and wholly inconsistent characters or essential attributes. . . . Consequently, for the intelligent reading of medieval theological and religious writings, the first thing needful is to note, in any given passage, *which kind of God* the author appears to be thinking of. . . . For the affective response to the conception of a God who by his intrinsic nature communicates his own good to creatures, who is a God of love and therefore needs other beings as objects of his love, and who desires their love and takes pleasure in their service—and the affective response to the thought of a God who is eternally impassible, whose good is completely realized without them, who is therefore indifferent to them, and to whom they can render no service which has any value for him: these two are polar opposites among the many varieties of religious experience. (Lovejoy, p. 85)

In their dispute with each other over the nature of St. Thomas' God, both Lovejoy and Pegis cite the doctrine of natural necessity, Lovejoy to prove that "there is in the Thomistic theology 'a strain of logical determinism' with respect to the creation of things other than God" (p. 72), and Pegis to prove that "the necessity of the divine willing comes from the perfection and goodness of the divine being; and this means to St. Thomas Aquinas that the divine will finds no necessary motives outside the divine being."[36]

Following is Pegis' translation of St. Thomas on natural necessity, a doctrine to which I shall refer again when I examine what Milton evidently intended it to mean applied to beings other than God:

God wills not only Himself, but also things other than Himself.

This is clear from the comparison made above. For natural things have a natural inclination not only towards their own proper good, to acquire it if not possessed, and, if possessed, to rest therein; but also to diffuse their own good among others so far as possible. Hence we see that every agent, in so far as it is perfect and in act, produces its like. It pertains, therefore to the nature of the will to communicate as far as possible to others the good possessed; and especially does this pertain to the divine will, from which all perfection is derived in some kind of likeness.

Hence, if natural things, in so far as they are perfect, communicate their good to others, much more does it pertain to the divine will to communicate by likeness its own good to others as much as is possible. Thus, then, He wills both Himself to be, and other things to be; but Himself as the end, and other things as ordained to that end, inasmuch as it befits the divine goodness that other things should be partakers therein. (*Summa Theologica*, I, 19, 2; Pegis, p. 60)

That God is 'pure act' is a correlative of natural necessity and also implicates God in logical determinism. Milton denies that God is pure act: "There seems, therefore, an impropriety in the term of *actus purus*, or the active principle, which Aristotle applies to God, for thus the Deity would have no choice of act, but what he did he would do of necessity, and could do in no other way, which would be inconsistent with his omnipotence and free agency" (*CD* XIV, p. 49). If God is pure act, then for God *velle alia a se* = *creare* (Lovejoy, pp. 72–75). Milton assumes that God's thinking about beings other than himself does not compel him to create them at some time. When Adam says that "Evil into the mind of God or Man / May come and go" (V.117–19), he is particularizing the more general postulate of the freedom of the intellect to think any idea whatever without the will acting upon it.[37] This separation of intellect and will does not accord with other statements in *Paradise Lost* about the dependence of will upon reason (III.108, IX.351–56).

Critics have been quick to notice that Milton's denial that God is pure act opens up the possibility that God "must include an element of potentiality."[38] If there is a potentiality in God, then he must be mutable; but Milton expressly states the immutability of God (*CD* XIV, p. 47). Milton's derivation of matter *ex deo* is consistent with his denial of pure act but inconsistent with his attribution of immutability to God, since matter is the potentiality from which God makes the creature and to which he can return the creature. A theology which posits a God who is not pure act but is immutable and yet creates *ex deo* is self-contradictory. By asserting that matter is substantially inherent in God, Milton "empties his theory of any usable provision for pure potentiality and hence leaves himself powerless to explain change in corporeal creatures. . . . [H]is doctrine of materiality in God . . . is on the whole a position not so much theologically heretical as logically contradictory and philosophically inadequate."[39]

Milton's sight is set so intently on God's free will that his peripheral vision misses the implication of potentiality. In another instance, Milton's sight is set so intently on the goodness of matter proceeding from the goodness and generosity of God that he misses the implication of natural necessity: "it is an argument of supreme power and goodness, that such diversified, multiform, and inexhaustible virtue should exist and be *substantially* inherent in God . . . and that this diversified and substantial virtue should not remain dormant within the Deity, but should be diffused and propagated and extended as far and in such manner as he himself may will" (*CD* XV, pp. 21–23). As does St. Thomas in his application of natural necessity to God, Milton argues the necessity of creation from God's goodness. God determines what sorts of things he will create, but since God is good, it follows that he cannot not will to create. The two Gods which Lovejoy finds in St. Thomas' God also appear in Milton's God; indeed, the contradiction is fundamental to Christianity.[40]

The contradiction between freedom and necessity reduces to two of God's perfections—his goodness and vitality—compelling another perfection—his will—to create. Pegis argues that, on the contrary, there is no contradiction in God between natural necessity and freedom because God's active power is always greater than the effects it produces; he could always have produced effects other than the ones he did produce. The end of the divine action, therefore, finds no necessity in any of its effects (St. Thomas Aquinas, *De Potentia*, III, 16; Pegis, p. 66). This statement of St. Thomas does not prove that there is no necessity in the origin of the divine effects. Milton is as aware as Lovejoy that the contradiction originates in the mutually incompatible perfections of God, but throughout *The Christian Doctrine* he prudently avoids direct confrontation with the issue wherever he discusses God's attributes of immutability, vitality, and will.

The issue surfaces, however, in Milton's discussion of omnipotence, for the contradiction constrains that attribute more than the others. We have seen already that under omnipotence Milton denies *actus purus* in order to affirm God's free agency. He adds a seemingly unobjectionable statement that actually has far reaching effects upon God's free agency and omnipotence: "It must be remembered, however, that the power of God is not exerted in things which imply a contradiction" (*CD* XIV, p. 49). God's omnipotence and free agency are internally limited by his other attributes. He cannot will an unjust or an evil or an inane act. Most important is that he cannot uncreate: "Now nothing is neither good, nor in fact anything. Entity is good, nonentity consequently is not good; wherefore it is neither consistent with the goodness or wisdom of God to make out of entity, which is good, that which is not good, or nothing. Again, God is not able to annihilate anything altogether, because by creating nothing he would create and not create at the same time, which involves a contradiction" (*CD* XV, p. 27). Since God is the material cause of things, for him to annihilate anything would include annihilating a part of himself—a contradiction indeed. The principle of non-contradiction is a favorite with Milton, who liberally applies it in order to solve diverse problems throughout *The Christian Doctrine*.

The principle of non-contradiction is a law of metaphysics such that two contrary properties cannot exist in the same subject at the same time. Its correlate in logic is the law of excluded middle such that any proposition is either true or false. A proposition is not just any statement, but a statement that is reducible to the law of non-contradiction. Since this tautology is self-evident, so, too, are all propositions that are reducible to the law of non-contradiction. It is remarkable that this law should ever have been applied to God; however, it is the legacy of Greek rationalism to Christianity, both Catholic and Protestant. The ascendancy of the law in Christian theology begins in the eleventh century,[41] although it was not the sole principle that rationalized God's ways to men, for there was the whole medieval system of mediation as well. When the dialecticians succeeded in destroying the system of mediation, only the law of non-contradiction was left to save the appearances. Before the Reformation, Ockham cut away from metaphysics all third entities such as real relations, divine ideas, quiddities of genera and species. He did so, not only to simplify the metaphysics, but also to assert God's freedom and omnipotence, which he thought had been constrained by all these metaphysical entities. For instance, God does not create individual human beings from a pattern of the human species which is in his mind, because such a pattern would prevent his freedom and power from doing anything he wishes. "Ockham's tendency was always to break through supposedly necessary connections which might seem to limit in some way the divine omnipotence, provided that it could not be shown to his satisfaction that denial of the proposition affirming such a necessary connection involved the denial of the principle of contradiction" (Copleston, p. 79).

It is a paradox in the history of ideas that when natural logic had freed God from metaphysical restraints, a law of logic became the arbiter of what he could or could not do. "God can do anything or order anything which does not involve a logical contradiction" (Copleston, p. 116). As one can readily tell from Copleston's ninth chapter on "The Ockhamist Movement," what did or did not involve God in a contradiction varied from philosopher to philosopher.[42]

The removal of all metaphysical constraints on God's will and power opened up the frightening possibility of an arbitrary God who could, if he so desired, change the ground rules on which the physical and moral order behaved. Although I doubt any philosopher or theologian would have so conceived the matter, the principle of non-contradiction was man's last safeguard against God's irrationality. For example, the early dogmaticians say that "goodness is good because God wills it," while the later dogmaticians say that "God wills the good because it is good": "'God is a law to Himself. Whatever He wishes done, it is right by the very fact that He wills it. Whatever God does He knows and wills.'—Yet the later dogmaticians let this idea drop. Voetius discusses the question, whether there is in the divine nature an immanent, necessary and independent law, which, if God would not deny Himself, God must maintain, and he answers Yes" (Heppe, pp. 93–94).

When the law of non-contradiction is discussed in terms of God's attributes, the matter is very complex, for a distinction should be made between what is intrinsically contradictory to God's nature and what is intrinsically contradictory to the nature of the creature. The attributes are only the way that man's discursive reason understands God, dividing him up into will, intelligence, power, goodness, whereas God's essence is simple, indivisible: "Rather the attributes of God are the divine nature itself in its relation to the world. And since God is essentially nothing else but absolutely single actuosity, every separate attribute of God is the identity of the whole divine being, as the latter is displayed in relation to a definite object. The doctrine of the divine attributes . . . rests upon the proposition of the Reformed dogmaticians that God is 'actus purissimus et simplicissimus' (purest and most single activity)" (Heppe, p. 57). It follows that the principle of non-contradiction is applicable to God only when his relationship to the creature is in question. On the one hand, non-contradiction seems to be a logical law which keeps man's concepts of God and of created things in order:

> "[Things] are the objects of omnipotence, according as of themselves they do not involve a contradiction. Only then is God related to them as omnipotent." From which it follows that "The absolutely possible as distinguished from that which is called possible comparatively and in relation to this or that power is that which does not involve a contradiction. Implying a contradiction is nothing else than repugnance of terms in the connection of predicate with subject and of subject with predicate. But what is repugnant to happening thus cannot possibly happen. All implication of impossibility consists in our conceiving alone, vilely conjoining ideas which are mutually opposed to each other." (Heppe, p. 101;

quoting from Abraham Heidan's *Corpus Theologiæ Christianæ* [1686])

On the other hand, non-contradiction seems to be a metaphysical principle, inherent in God's relation to the creation, which limits the effects of God's omnipotence to acts which are consonant with his nature (i.e., his other attributes): "The object of the omnipotence of God is anything that is not contrary to his nature and does not involve a contradiction, and so it is 'non-impotence' rather than the 'possibility of everything.' Therefore, dying, making undone what has been done, making a human body infinite, and the like, are not to be attributed to God, for they would be acts of impotence rather than of power."[43]

The definition of metaphysical non-contradiction as 'non-impotence' is a classic tribute to man's capacity for double-think. Anselm admitted that there is a paradox in our "attributing negative or apparently privative terminology to God" so that we designate God's strength "by words signifying weakness."[44] The logical law of non-contradiction, which is supposed to guarantee the truth or falsity of terms as they are used in propositions, fails its function when terms predicate a God who is *actus purus*. Therefore, the logical law of man's language does not prevent us from "vilely conjoining ideas which are mutually opposed to each other." For that reason, John of Mirecourt did not invoke the law to prove that God could not "bring it about that the world should never have been, that is to say, that God could bring it about that the past should not have happened" (Copleston, p. 145). For that reason, Milton's God is not *actus purus*.

Milton's use of non-contradiction is both the metaphysical principle of God's relationship to the world and the logical law of man's language. From the metaphysical principle that God cannot contradict himself proceeds the surety that logic enables man to speak truthfully. Since Milton's God is not pure act, there is even some doubt that non-contradiction applies to God only in his role of Creator. Although Milton also says that he is pure and simple essence, God's not being pure act must account for the inference the reader draws from Milton's writings that the terms denoting God's attributes are not mere conveniences of man's time-bound intellect, but also signify *real* attributes *in* God. Justice, will, freedom, and wisdom are literally signified by human language,[45] and it is just possible (although I would not press the issue) that in a God who is not pure act, non-contradiction holds all his attributes in harmony inwardly as well as outwardly toward the creature.

In Milton's Creator-God, non-contradiction locks together in perfect harmony and order attributes which in a lesser being than God could conflict with one another to the point of mutual repulsion. When God retires and does not put forth his goodness (VII.170–71), he releases his control over the part of himself which becomes Chaos. Non-contradiction is absent from Chaos, which is consequently forever at war with itself: "Chaos is possessed of forms—a good; it is composed of matter—essentially good. But it can not function in other than disordered fashion when Chance rules, when Providence provides no law, when Deity is absent. Strictly speaking, chaos can act neither for good nor ill; it exists in what More called the condition of 'Impossibility, which would be the state of all things, were there not a God.'"[46] Satan, the furthest removed from God of all creatures, experiences his increasing loss of self-control as a "hateful siege of contraries" (IX.121–22).

To produce other beings, God introduces into a portion of Chaos an order radically different from the order that matter possessed before he withdrew his control over that portion of himself. The rational beings made out of Chaos have finite perfections—understanding, reason, imagination, will, passion—which are ordered so as to bring matter from the condition of impossibility to the condition of possibility. The sufficiency to stand is their condition of possibility, which they are free to accept or reject. The finite perfections which make up the creature's sufficiency are ordered into a hierarchy from understanding to passion. In this respect the finite creature differs from God, whose attributes are not hierarchically ordered. Finite creatures do not intrinsically possess the metaphysical principle of non-contradiction. Indeed, God cannot communicate the principle to them, for he cannot make another being like himself, infinite and eternal. Finite creatures can contradict themselves; this is what "free to fall" means. Happily for man, as a fallen being his freedom persists in his ability to contradict his sinful deeds and desires with good ones.

The metaphysical principle of non-contradiction, possessed exclusively by God, is the third term which mediates the oppositions of sufficiency and falling in the myth's paradigm. Non-contradiction assures that God can only purposely make creatures, who are good, and whom he will treat justly. It cannot guarantee the finite creature the freedom from self-contradiction that God enjoys. Our discussion has come full circle, back to the fact that there is no conservation of virtue in created things. Adam and Eve would have passed on their acquired virtue to their descendants as a gift for having resisted the temptation of Satan, because their resistance would have brought their condition of possibility into actuality. They would have been by merit more than birthright children of God, and in a finite but real sense authors of themselves. The Son arguably becomes author of himself when he freely volunteers to die for man. Since God knows that the

Son will do what he has promised to do, the Son has earned merit above and beyond his birthright. This merit makes him parent of the human race in a way not shared by God, and his merit is spiritually, not physically, passed on to his children in faith:

> thy merit
> Imputed shall absolve them who renounce
> Thir own both righteous and unrighteous deeds,
> And live in thee transplanted, and from thee
> Receive new life.
>
> (III.290–94)

Milton uses a metaphor from the vegetable creation ("transplanted") because the original sin transmitted in sexual (animal) generation is a natural law which the Son's merit absolves in the individual believer.

What might have been testifies to the goodness and generosity of God's intentions. What actually does happen testifies not only to the failure of his intentions but to the inevitability of failure. While it is true that God's attributes have no end other than himself, it is also true that had God not created *alia a se* the issue of non-contradiction would have been moot. Because God creates, non-contradiction operates to assure his freedom, justice, will, and goodness *at the expense of the creature*. Woodhouse has noted that Milton's theology fails to provide a "solution of the problem of evil on the cosmological level" because it denies both the dualism of God and matter and the creation *ex nihilo*: "He rejects the latter doctrine because . . . it is in reality a concealed form of dualism since in effect, and at the additional expense of a logical contradiction, it exalts nothing (or not-being) to the rank of a principle or cause" (pp. 321–33). However, Milton exalts non-contradiction to the rank of cause, becoming thereby one of the most original of philosopher-poets. As a metaphysical cause, non-contradiction is not a communicable power. However, rational creatures have a finite version of it: natural necessity, which creature communicates to creature. Metaphysical non-contradiction is the cause of the structure of deficiency in creation, for, although as God is its object it harmonizes his attributes, as created things are its object it paradoxically renders his attributes contradictory toward them.

The macrocosm is the most visible indicator of non-contradiction at work in the structure of deficiency. Although matter is good and an inexhaustible virtue, things made out of it are ordered hierarchically in a descent from God, as they necessarily are in degenerative cosmologies where matter is the end product of an energy-exhausted series of emanations.[47] Non-contradiction necessitates that the Son and all created things together be less than God, and Milton apparently believes that non-contradiction and natural necessity are antithetical concepts with respect to God:

> For questionless, it was in God's power consistently with the perfection of his own essence not to have begotten the Son, inasmuch as generation does not pertain to the nature of the Deity, who stands in no need of propagation; but whatever does not pertain to his own essence or nature, he does not effect like a natural agent from any physical necessity [*naturae necessitate*]. If the generation of the Son proceeded from a physical necessity [*natura necessario*], the Father impaired himself by physically [*natura*] begetting a co-equal; which God could no more do than he could deny himself. (*CD* XIV, pp. 187–89; see also Pegis, p. 62)

There is necessity in the subordination of the macrocosm to God, but there should be no necessity in the subordination of created things to one another within the macrocosm, especially since matter is essentially good and the first, not last, of created things (see Chambers, pp. 69–81). Also, since generation does not pertain to the nature of God, there should be no necessity for all created things to be likenesses of God.

But God behaves as if compelled by natural necessity to create likenesses of himself, and the creation behaves as if it were a degenerative cosmology. The hierarchy of creatures begins with the Son, the first and highest born of all creatures, and ends with man, "God's latest Image" (IV.567) and humblest born. The infinite descent of God's images begins with the Son, who virtually images his Father—"in him all his Father shone / Substantially express'd" (III.139–40)—and ends with Eve, who resembles "less / His image" than does Adam (VIII.540–46). The descent of man is a fall from the universal (God) to the general (the Son) to the specific (angels; mankind as represented by Adam), to the individual (Eve): "She has an identity as unique as Adam's, and in fact, a superior independence. . . . [A]s the beautiful narcissistic image of Eve contemplating her own reflection shows us, she can tolerate aloneness better than Adam can. . . . She is, in short, the supreme human particular emerging from creation's individuating process."[48] Although she is inwardly and outwardly the least exact image of God, her tolerance for aloneness has a curiously inverted resemblance to God's unapproachable solitariness that is found in no other being. God is best by himself accompanied, but nevertheless creates other beings who are in no sense companions to him. Eve is best accompanied by Adam and was created to propagate mankind, a creativity she at first rejects, preferring herself to other beings. After the Fall, she proposes suicide in order to prevent the birth of sin-infested children. Although procreation does pertain to her nature, she is scarcely necessitated by it. Only at the end of the poem, when she has been assured that her procreation has a glorious purpose, does she accept motherhood as really defining her being.

It is as if God created Eve in order to disburden himself of the procreativity that does not pertain to his nature, and instead communicated to her his awesome solitariness. Adam is able to speak unabashedly, if deferentially, to God, whereas, he tells Raphael, before Eve's absoluteness he feels all the creaturely unworthiness that he might be expected to feel before the self-sufficient God who has no need of him and to whom he can give nothing (VIII.546–59). God and Eve are involved at opposite ends of the contradiction between self-sufficiency and procreativity. They each manifest the other's essential nature, thereby involving their proper attributes in a schizophrenic distortion, such as Adam describes to Raphael.[49] As long as God does not create, there is no contradiction and the potentiality for self-contradiction is occulted within him. However, creation forces the contradiction into the open, toward the finite creature and within time. It is appropriate that the contradiction should be fully manifest in Eve, the last and least exact image of God. Her inexactness inheres in her inferior degree of control—self-control and control of other creatures—as Adam notes (VIII.544–46). She has difficulty maintaining her self-control because she has two natures that are in conflict with one another, and she does not have the principle of non-contradiction to mediate them. One is centered in herself, the other in Adam and her procreative role. Her initial spontaneous preference for her own company erupts in her fatal desire to work apart from Adam. As the individual, her tendency is to reject subordination to her species (Adam); yet the individual is the means of perpetuating the species. Among the angels, Satan is the representative individual who rejects subordination to his species—although creaturely propagation is not involved. As Milton defines the individual in relation to its species, the individual is subversive of it. That is another reason why he could not conceive *scientifically* (apart from theologically) of the virtuous individual passing on to his progeny his trait (adaptive to salvation). In fact, the virtuous individual must be subversive of his fallen species if he is to be virtuous, as Adam understands from Michael's vision of history:

> Henceforth I learn, that to obey is best,
>
> . . .
>
> . . . with good
> Still overcoming evil, and by small
> Accomplishing great things, by things deem'd weak

Subverting worldly strong, and worldly wise
By simply meek.

(XII.561–69)

The contradiction in Eve and the contradiction in God which it inversely mirrors come together in Adam's story of her creation, although Adam is unaware of the contradictions. Indeed, Adam's superb right reason in its pristine state is not equipped to deal with paradoxes. Full awareness of ambiguities comes with the fruit of the knowledge of good and evil, as his soliloquy in X.720–844 shows. In the creation of Eve, we are able to see what happens when a finite creature takes part in the creative process, and from that to understand why the creative process is coded to perpetuate deficiency.

Adam is Eve's formal and material cause; she is his idea, and she is made from one of his ribs. Her final cause is God-in-Adam and her efficient cause is the Son. When he asks God for a companion, Adam does not think of Eve in much detail. He does not request a woman, although he understands that he needs someone to help him "beget / Like of his like" (VIII.423–24). It is not until he sees Eve that he spontaneously understands what begetting involves. His idea of her is primarily focused on his need for companionship, a need awakened by his perception of the disparity between himself and the animals. In his first reply to Adam, God asks if he seems to Adam "sufficiently possest / Of happiness, or not? . . . for none I know / Second to mee or like, equal much less" (VIII.404–08). Although human thoughts cannot know what it feels like to be God, Adam is sure that God does not need "Social communication" (VIII.429), because he is without deficiency. Only a few moments after he has created Adam, God is declaring his unequaled solitariness and Adam is, apparently correctly, affirming that God does not need other beings. This unique opportunity for Adam to ask God why he creates beings he does not need passes unheeded. Instead, Adam uses God's self-sufficiency to illustrate how different he is from God. Man, deficient by himself, needs a companion to solace his solitary deficiency:

But Man by number is to manifest
His single imperfection, and beget
Like of his like, his Image multipli'd,
In unity defective.

(VIII.422–25)

God is pleased that his latest image knows himself and will freely express himself with the wish for a companion—"Expressing well the spirit within the free, / My Image" (VIII.440–41). He promises Adam "Thy likeness, thy fit help, thy other self, / Thy wish, exactly to thy heart's desire" (Il.450–51). Since neither God nor Adam tells us whether or not God is happy in his solitary state, we are free to speculate that God's creation of self-images is the expression of his desire for companionship, since he evidently rejoices that some day he will be All-in-All.[50]

The exchange between God and Adam explains man's natural necessity to propagate. If we compare the three points St. Thomas Aquinas makes about natural necessity with Adam's exposition of it, we see a startling difference in emphasis. According to St. Thomas, the will (1) is inclined toward its own proper good, (2) is desirous of communicating its good to others, and (3) is productive of its like by communicating its good. This is consistent with the various statements about God in *The Christian Doctrine*, except that Milton denies that generation pertains to the nature of God. Applied to man, only point (1) of St. Thomas' natural necessity receives emphasis: Adam wills his proper good, Eve. While it is true that Adam wants to share his happiness in Paradise with another, he is not primarily concerned with communicating his good to others. Rather, he feels that without another being like himself he is deficient, lacking in some essential goodness. It is not desire to communicate a good possessed but desire to acquire a good not possessed that compels man to will *alia a se*. Both Adam and God affirm that natural necessity compels man to will and communicate his likeness to others. Adam recognizes the newly created Eve as "my Self / Before me" (VIII.495–96); the angel tells Eve that she is Adam's image (IV.473); elsewhere Adam calls Eve "Best Image of myself and dearer half" (V.95). Where theoretically God can choose or not choose to create and therefore ought to be able to create beings who are not his images, man has to propagate and has to propagate images of himself. Furthermore, man's images are expressions or likenesses not of his good (self-possession) but of his deficiency: "Man by number is to manifest / His single imperfection." To sum up, natural necessity for Milton means that man's will (1) is inclined toward its own proper good, (2) is desirous of achieving a good not possessed, and (3) is productive of its like by communicating its deficiency. Henceforth, I shall use the term 'natural necessity' in this sense.

The third point is the crucial difference between Milton's natural necessity and St. Thomas'. It explains Eve's tolerance for aloneness and her dual nature. In possession of Eve, Adam is no longer alone, but he has constituted her out of his aloneness; she *is* his aloneness. Her first natural and spontaneous impulse is to be alone with herself, and she rejects the company of Adam until she submits to her teleology of companionship. She is also the means by which man is to manifest his solitary deficiency in the begetting of children. She will bear to Adam multitudes like herself (IV.473–74). The logic here is exact: her multitude of self-images will all be images of Adam's solitary deficiency.[51] She is the logical reduction to the finite level of the Christian God's contradictory two natures (as analyzed by Lovejoy), at once the image and inversion of the divine self-sufficient solitary and of the creator of other beings.

Only God creates out of self-sufficiency, the true communication of inward good (self-possession) to another being. God creates (generates) only once out of self-sufficiency. Hence, the Son completely fulfills God's intentions in creating him. Although he is necessarily inferior to God, the Son is constituted of whatever God possesses that he wills to give to him. The principle of non-contradiction underlies the subordination of the Son to God, who cannot beget a co-equal any more than he could deny himself. The subordination of the Son is the most convincing evidence for Milton's literal understanding of the principle as signifying a real necessity within God. It is also ample evidence that language directly signifies realities, which are not to be distinguished into natural and supernatural realities, any more than in Milton's physics there is a separation between body and soul. Thus, there are not two kinds of logic for Milton as there are for Robert Holkot, who in other ways is a spiritual kin of Milton: "Theology, however, is superior to philosophy; and in the sphere of dogmatic theology we can see the operation of a logic which is superior to the natural logic employed in philosophy. In particular, that the principle of contradiction is transcended in theology is clear, thought Holkot, from the doctrine of the Trinity" (Copleston, p. 136).

Non-contradiction continues to operate in the subordination of all created things to the Son, who becomes God's efficient cause of creation. Beyond the descent from God to the Son to created things, there does not seem to be a principle to account for the thoroughgoing hierarchical procession of creation from angels to mankind-in-Adam to the individual-in-Eve. God does not repeat any single act of creation—there are not two species of angels, for instance, nor two individuals alike. It does not seem self-evident that if God created a second Son exactly duplicating the first, he would contradict himself. Likewise, it ought to have been possible, after the fall of the angels, for God to have created a new species higher than the angels rather than lower. God does create within a spatio-temporal matrix of high to low and first to last, however. Because he does so, space and time are asymmetrical, and exact duplication of any single act of creation is impossible.

Samuel Alexander, who like Milton believed that logic and nature are correlative, and who also interpreted the law of non-contradiction as being both metaphysical and logical, says that "order is a category of things because of betweenness of position in Space-Time. . . . Such betweenness can only be generated by a relation which being transitive has direction and is therefore asymmetrical." If we apply Alexander's thought to Milton's cosmos, we can say that if God generated a second Son, the latter would be dissimilar to the former if only because the latter would have to occupy a different space-time. The law of non-contradiction guarantees the asymmetry of space-time:

> The so-called Laws of Thought, regarded as metaphysical laws, follow at once from these considerations. The most important of them is the law of contradiction. Ultimately that law means that occupation of one piece of Space-Time is not occupation of a different one. A thing cannot be both A and not-A at once, for if so it would occupy two different space-times. Or more shortly the meaning is that one space-time is not another. . . . Considered on the other hand as a law of our thinking, the law of contradiction means that the thinking of one object and the thinking of its contradictory occupy mutually exclusive places in the mental space-time.[52]

Following Alexander, I think it safe to say that there is a category of order in Milton's cosmos which necessitates that God cannot duplicate a single act of creation, but which does not necessitate the hierarchy of descent through which he does create. It is simply a 'law' of Milton's cosmos that differentiation is accomplished vertically through hierarchical subordination (separate and unequal) rather than laterally (separate and equal). Upheld by non-contradiction, the asymmetry of God's acts and decrees means that God cannot undo what he has done or revoke a decree. The fulfillment of his decrees must take place within the asymmetrical irreversibility of time. This is why God prolongs time by successively re-establishing man in his sufficiency to stand in order to achieve fulfillment of the final All-in-All.

Non-contradiction remains contained within God and does not proceed from him into other beings. Instead of non-contradiction, other beings have natural necessity to order their finiteness and unidirectionality of action. It is the negative constructor of selection in this cosmology. It may create the structure of deficiency whereby the orders of being are successively endowed with greater degrees of self-contradiction, although this is impossible to prove. Even the Son must create out of natural necessity. Though the Son is a perfect image of the Father's intentionality, that intentionality includes that the Son know "not all things absolutely; there being some secret purposes, the knowledge of which the Father has reserved to himself alone" (*CD* XIV, p. 317). Book III reveals that the Son finds out after he has created

Adam and Eve that they will fall. He presumably did not know that one-third of the angels would fall when he created them. The Son does not foreknow his self-sacrifice for man. He reasons it out on the basis of what his Father tells him and of what he knows about his Father's nature. There is no indication that he knows before his Father tells him that his self-sacrifice will not yield one hundred percent redemption of mankind. Heretical as it may seem, it is the Son's lack of absolute knowledge — specifically the knowledge of evil — that is the deficiency he communicates to his creatures. The Tree of Knowledge of Good and Evil is the perfect objective correlative of the Son's incomplete knowledge. No matter that angels and humans would be better off without their fallen knowledge; they are created with a deficiency that will compel a number of them, statistically dependent on the hierarchical rank of their species, to seek to possess the knowledge of evil they do not have. How much greater than anyone else's must be the probability of Eve's fall, considering both the generic deficiency of the Son and the specific deficiency of Adam communicated to her.

Non-contradiction in God enmeshes creation in a web of fatality composed of natural necessity, disproportions among orders of being, and failed intentions. Adam and Eve are most apt to lose their orientation within the orders of being because between them and God is a greater disproportion than between God and the angels. The disproportion between Adam and Eve themselves is greater than that among rankings within the angelic hierarchy, for the masculine angels do not procreate one another nor do they ideationally conceive of one another.[53] The intentional component of Adam's idea of Eve — his wish — was not for someone inferior to him, as Eve is:

> Among unequals what society
> Can sort, what harmony or true delight?
> Which must be mutual, in proportion due
> Giv'n and receiv'd; but in disparity
> The one intense, the other still remiss
> Cannot well suit with either, but soon prove
> Tedious alike. Of fellowship I speak
> Such as I seek, fit to participate
> All rational delight.
>
> (VIII.383–91)

He wished for the classical friend, an equal. What he got is someone whose inferiority to him lies in the disparity between her remiss self-control and her intense self-containedness. Though she is Adam's kind, Eve's capacity for self-contradiction embodies Adam's perception of the disproportion both between himself and the animals and between himself and God. She must incorporate, as the conceptual component of her formal cause, both the defect and the remedy for the defect that was Adam's conception of his problem of aloneness and its solution. Every time Adam regards her, he is confronted with his original idea—defect and remedy (wish)—and so he continues to be troubled by his sense of disproportion between himself and the other:

> Or Nature fail'd in mee, and left some part
> Not proof enough such Object to sustain,
> Or from my side subducting, took perhaps
> More than enough; at least on her bestow'd
> Too much of Ornament, in outward show
> Elaborate, of inward less exact.
>
> (VIII.534–39)

Adam's understanding is already more experienced than it was when, some moments after his creation, he gave God his correctly reasoned justification for a companion. At first he does not understand the implications of the truths he unhesitatingly enunciates. He unreflectingly accepts two gifts from God—life and Eve—without knowing what he has accepted (as he later realizes, X.743, 888–96). After a few days in Eden and with Eve his understanding is confused by the particularities of observable phenomena. He begins to notice how literally Eve manifests his single imperfection, but he grasps at several explanations, all involving nature, to account for the disproportion between his own remiss 'higher knowledge' and her intense loveliness. He no longer knows the single, abstract truths he once knew. It is the same way with his understanding of the stars. In Book IV he understands how the stars fill a purpose and place in the harmonious cosmos (660–88). By Book VIII he is asking Raphael "How Nature wise and frugal could commit / Such disproportions" (26–27) between the tiny, motionless earth and the huge, numberless stars revolving at great speeds and at great distances around earth. Eve, too, progresses from her ontologically correct contentment in Adam's superiority (IV.440–48) to her reasoning that she cannot be happy if she is not endowed with a capacity to resist Satan equal to Adam's (IX.322–26). Before they have taken a bite of one forbidden apple, their perception of the disproportions in macrocosm and microcosm has shifted from confidence in the order of things to perplexity and, in Eve's case, to disbelief.

Raphael warns Adam, and Adam passes the warning on to Eve, that God and nature left nothing deficient. As for the disproportions, either they are mere appearances (the stars) behind which lie God's unfathomable purposes, or they are real and are designed as tests of self-knowledge (God and Adam, Adam and Eve). Disproportions are not deficiencies: Eve is not deficient, she is *less exact*. It is here, in the language of an inscrutable cosmic equation, that physics is defeated by metaphysics, that Milton's poetic believability breaks down under the weight of the whole structure of deficiency in *Paradise Lost*. When there are so many other fruits to eat, not eating the forbidden fruit is the easy prohibition Adam says it is—until the meddling intellect (of the reader as well as the characters) ceases to regard the disproportions as rational. There is an insurmountable gap between God's complete self-sufficiency and man's self-deficiency. The more images that God creates, the more evidence that he is perfect without them. A logical consequence of the gap between God and man is that human beings find it more natural to cling to those second selves that complete their deficiencies than they do to cling to a God to whose perfection they can add nothing. Adam chooses the bond of nature (IX.956), or natural necessity, over God, thus failing to realize God's intentions for him.

## III

Above all, the history of natural necessity is the tragedy of failed intentions. Insofar as God does create, natural necessity regulated by non-contradiction does pertain to him. His option of choosing not to create is irrevocably consigned to pure possibility. Having willed his intentions to create angels and mankind, he too must live with their failure. The numbers of damned angels and mortals represent a portion of his infinite substance that is irretrievably lost to him, having "become in the power of another party" (*CD* XV, p. 25). He cannot uncreate them; he cannot even reduce them to Chaos, for then they would not have knowledge of their punishment. The structure of deficiency—the diminution of intention in effect—is visible even among the already fallen. Satan's intention to ruin all mankind will not be fulfilled, for something under less than half of them will be saved. Sin, like Eve, is the objectification of inward deficiency. She represents Satan's lust for Godhead. First as a terror-inspiring goddess in Heaven, then as Satan's incestuous mate, and finally as the foul hag who keeps Hellgate, Sin is at once an accurate image of Satan's lack of virtue and simultaneously a vast diminution of his wish to be God. As we have seen, creation and redemption turn out to be a diminution of the Son's intentions.

There is a corollary to the structure of deficiency: authors must fall with their works, must themselves diminish with the failure of their intentions. Creation is a system of wish-fulfillment, God the agent who actualizes wishes, good and bad. Natural necessity not only diminishes intentions but also dictates that their authors do not fully understand what it is that they have wished. The independent existence of an author's wish unfolds the secret implications of the lack in him that called the wish into being; that is, it unfolds the full implications of his own destiny. Adam instantly understands that Eve's fall is synonymous with his resolution, or intention, to die. When the Son learns that man will fall and incur the death penalty, he, too, intends his fall from divinity into mortality. Satan's self-image, Sin, degenerates without his awareness of her change. At Hellgate, he denies authorship of her, unwilling to believe that his glorious attempt at overthrowing God could look so foul as she does. He gradually comes to realize that Sin's degeneration is his destiny:

> O foul descent; that I who erst contended
> With Gods to sit the highest, am now constrain'd
> Into a Beast, and mixt with bestial slime,
> This essence to incarnate and imbrute,
> That to the highth of Deity aspir'd.
>
> (IX.163–67)

Milton does not shirk the implication for God of natural necessity, that what he wills is his own fate. Milton presents him as a God responding to the actions of his creatures, rather than as initiating action. Thus, with the irony of someone who knows that he brought it on himself, God tells the angels that he will create mankind to fill the gap left by the fallen angels and to show Satan that his power is not diminished by their fall. In short, God, too, creates in order to remedy a deficiency. God's 'fall' is a fall from the self-sufficient, solitary God, free to create or not, whose attributes are indistinguishably unified while he has only himself to consider, into the Creator-God whose attributes are in danger of becoming mutually exclusive and contradictory because he must provide for beings other than himself, and whose free agency is now constrained to go on creating and re-creating because he cannot uncreate. He now needs the principle of non-contradiction to hold himself together internally, and he needs the Son to hold himself together externally, to save his appearances, and he needs mankind, the appearances which are to be saved. God's 'fall' into contradiction and his rescue by the Son are duly noted in the angels' hymn of praise to the Son:

> Hee to appease thy wrath, and end the strife
> Of Mercy and Justice in thy face discern'd,
> Regardless of the Bliss wherein hee sat
> Second to thee, offer'd himself to die
> For man's offense.
>
> (III.406–10)

Had it succeeded, Satan's plan to ruin mankind would have been the only possible perfect revenge on God. Satan wanted to force God to "with repenting hand / Abolish his own works" (II.369–70). Non-contradiction is put to the test in Book III when God appeals to the Son to rescue him from the hateful siege of contraries made by the attributes of justice, goodness, and will upon his omnipotence. The Son and the poet both undertake to defend God's integrity with the principle of non-contradiction:

> wilt thou thyself
> Abolish thy Creation, and unmake,
> For him, what for thy glory thou hast made?
> So should thy goodness and thy greatness both
> Be question'd and blasphem'd without defense.
>                                                   (III.162–66)[54]

Adam, with his customary penchant for enunciating truths the frightening implications of which he does not understand, also knows God's weak spot and presumes upon it by way of rationalizing his intention to disobey God:

> Nor can I think that God, Creator wise,
> Though threat'ning, will in earnest so destroy
> Us his prime Creatures, . . .
>     . . . so God shall uncreate,
> Be frustrate, do, undo, and labor lose,
> Not well conceiv'd of God, who though his Power
> Creation could repeat, yet would be loath
> Us to abolish.
>                                                   (IX.938–40, 943–47)

It is small comfort that God will not and cannot commit the evil act of uncreating what he has created. To scrap his plans for the final All-in-All would contradict his will. Therefore, the human race must go on propagating itself through God's various modes of re-creation until Hell's numbers are full. God's creativity is both profuse and wasteful. How much more economical would be God's ways and means if he had the power to revoke a decree or to abolish Satan or even Adam and Eve. Instead, through the principle of non-contradiction, he is responsible for the origin of evil on the cosmological level where natural necessity, the repetition of non-contradiction in the finite being, establishes the structure of deficiency in created things.

That structure of deficiency is also the formal cause of tragedy. With the exception of God, who knew before he actualized them that his intentions would fail, Milton's analysis of original sin applies to the system of wish-fulfillment in *Paradise Lost*: "At any rate it [original sin] was the consequence of sin, rather than sin itself; or if it were sin, it was a sin of ignorance; for they expected nothing less than that they should lose any good by eating the fruit, or suffer harm in any way whatever" (*CD* XV, p. 199). The fall from sufficiency is the Aristotelian paradox of hamartia, the tendency within a character innately noble to make an error of judgment. Everyone, including God, misses the mark; everyone loses something; everyone is tragic. The structure of deficiency and the progressive degeneration it effects are not the results of the evil choices that God's creatures make. On the contrary, they are the mechanics of creation, operating before the Fall in 'good' choices, involving everyone in collective *hamartia*. Collective *hamartia* produces divine tragedy; we can be sure that God does not relish his panoramic spectacle of the past, present, and future failures of his intentions. It is true that non-contradiction does not limit God to the particular effects that he produces, but it does bind him to the effects which he does produce.

There is such necessary disproportion between God and anything that he creates that creation itself is a fall—if not technically for God, then for the creature, beginning with the Son, the first of creatures, and on down. The Son communicates his essential deficiency of knowledge to all his creatures, which they will experience as an inability to realize their wish for their proper good. How influenced was Milton by Gabriel Biel I do not know, but their thought is similar:

> Biel's anthropology indicates that he views the tragedy of man as centered in a lack of knowledge which is not primarily explained as a result of his fall and loss of original justice, but as a natural consequence of his status as creature. . . . [We] meet in Biel's anthropology a dangerous approximation of fall and creation. Though the unbridgeable gulf between creator and creation is not symbolized in a neo-platonic sense by a sinful, sensual body which hinders the mind in its efforts to reach God, it is nevertheless man's created condition as revealed in his epistemological limitations that frustrates his efforts to know God. (Oberman, pp. 67–68; see also note 6)

Biel and Milton share the sense of a tragic flaw in creation itself and, along with Robert Holkot, the belief that in an absolute sense the self-sufficient God has no need of creatures but that in a self-ordained sense the Creator-God is obliged to his creatures:

> The justification of the sinner is preceded by a spontaneous act of attrition. For this reason, there seems to be a certain

justice in the infusion of grace. Similarly, on the part of God, justice seems to be present, since He has, in some way, made Himself a debtor to the penitent by the commitment that thou mayest be justified in thy works, and prevail when thou art judged. God promised this so that He could bestow forgiveness on penitent sinners. And thus, when one examines the justification of the sinner, one finds there are on both sides—on God's and on man's—actions based on justice.

\* \* \*

Although we are like clay in comparison to God one cannot by any means apply the analogy in every respect to man. Nor is the analogy totally correct, because there is no covenant between the potter and the clay; and even assuming that there could be such a covenant, the potter could very well break it without abrogating the Covenant law. But God cannot break His pact with man without the Covenant being destroyed. Nor can the clay [like man] either partially or fully merit anything from the potter.

Now, one should deal with this issue reverently rather than with cold logic. [Holkot, *Lectures on the Wisdom of Solomon*, Chapter III, Lecture 35, *Forerunners*, pp. 146, 149–50.]

One solution to the contradiction between the self-sufficient God and the God who creates is to divide him up into a before and an after, either logically or temporally or both. Thus God has the untrammeled will and power not to have created or to have created beings other than the ones he did create, but once having created, the contingent will of God has subjected itself to equally contingent laws (Oberman, p. 46). In spirit, Milton is in sympathy with the pre-Reformation and Reformation theologians who adopt this strategy, but I am not at all sure that formally he agrees with their tactics. For Milton, non-contradiction is a principle of consistency so rigorous that Milton's God does not require a before-and-after division, particularly if one interprets non-contradiction as gently coercing God's will and power on behalf of his goodness with an "argument . . . that such diversified, multiform, and inexhaustible virtue [matter] . . . should not remain dormant within the Deity" (Oberman, p. 21). Milton has no solution to the contradiction between the self-sufficient and the creator God, or between the creature sufficient to have stood though free to fall. Rather, his tactic is to call attention repeatedly to the contradiction as the source of energy which fuels the creative activity, divine and human.

Involved in the contradiction is a cosmic equation of enormous numbers which, could it be known to man, would mathematically express the uniform law of non-contradiction which drives contradiction through contradiction to contradiction. It would mathematically express the matrix of space-time and God's creation of the orders of being within it. In this equation, the relations of one thing to another would be mathematically equivalent to the verbal forms '(not) less than' and 'more than' (as Satan appears not "Less than Arch-Angel ruin'd," and as the Son's love is "nowhere to be found less than Divine," and as Eve is inwardly "less exact," and as Adam feels Nature took from him "More than enough," and as Moloch argues "More destroy'd than thus / We should be quite abolisht and expire"). Above all, it would express natural necessity and the conservation of sin. But it is a finite equation and could not express God. And, what is more vital to the created beings who contemplate the statistical failure rate of their species, the equation could not express free will although free will expresses it. The equation itself is forbidden knowledge. Man searches for it in vain, for natural necessity insures that his search for it will result in knowledge less than he seeks, and more than he bargained for. Still, Milton's verbal approximations of the equation both reflect and mock the seventeenth century's faith that natural law is uniform and mathematical.

As for non-contradiction, while it is the law expressed by the equation, it is so exclusively within the precincts of God's incomprehensible being that it is easily lost sight of by the creatures who must toil within the rounds of a natural necessity that impels them through *hamartia* into tragedy. Milton deliberately calls attention to non-contradiction because his justification of God rests on it. This cosmic Catch-22 renders God a blameless victim of the law and man a culpable victim, to whom God gives the grace to overcome it if he will. God must confront the consequences of his decrees and actions through all eternity. Human individuals, on the other hand, have the freedom of uncreating, of renouncing "Thir own both righteous and unrighteous deeds" (III.291–92). That is a freedom which Adam would not exercise; he would not renounce Eve. We are assured that there will be a multitude of those who will exercise their freedom against the compulsion of natural necessity. God's grace enables the wish for salvation to be fulfilled, but the desire to be saved is metaphysically and physically unaccountable. It is an individual mystery. That desire is also the paradox of the Christian individual, for its achievement realizes the highest aspiration of his individualism, which is to merge with the mystical body of Christ. In the bare fact of religious experience being a living contradiction within the individual, Milton was not so very far from Luther. His explication of the contradiction, however, would have provoked Luther to even harsher means of refuting him than he applied in *The Bondage of the Will* against Erasmus's *A Diatribe Concerning Free Choice*.

## Notes

1. Citations are to *Paradise Lost*, ed. Merritt Y. Hughes (New York: The Odyssey Press, 1962).
2. "The function of repetition is to render the structure of the myth apparent. . . . And since the purpose of myth is to provide a logical model capable of overcoming a contradiction (an impossible achievement if, as it happens, the contradiction is real), a theoretically infinite number of slates will be generated, each one slightly different from the others." Claude Lévi-Strauss, *Structural Anthropology*, trans. Claire Jacobson and Brooke Grundrest Schoepf (Garden City, New York: Basic Books, 1963), p. 226.
3. Raphael's "God made thee perfet, not immutable" (V.524) is redundant and contributes no new information to the myth.
4. John Calvin, *Institutes of the Christian Religion*, Vol 2., trans. Henry Beveridge (Grand Rapids: Wm. B. Eerdmans Pub. Co., 1970), pp. 210–11.
5. *Institutes of the Christian Religion*, trans. Ford Lewis Battles, ed. John T. McNeill, Vol. 20, *The Library of Christian Classics* (Philadelphia, Pa., 1960), pp. 292–93.
6. "PREDESTINATED; that is, designated, elected: proposed to himself the salvation of man as the scope and end of his counsel. Hence may be refuted the notion of a preterition and desertion from all eternity, in direct opposition to which God explicitly and frequently declares, as has been quoted above, that he desires not the death of any one, but the salvation of all; that he hates nothing that he has made; and that he has omitted nothing which might suffice for universal salvation." *De Doctrina Christiana*, ed., with trans. of Charles R. Sumner, by James Holly Hanford and Waldo Hilary Dunn, in *The Works of John Milton*, Vols. XIV-XVII, gen. ed. Frank Allen Patterson (18 Vols., New York, 1931–38), XIV, p. 103. All references in the text to Milton's *Christian Doctrine* cite this edition; book and page numbers are given parenthetically in the text.
7. On the issue of whether or not man can contribute anything to his salvation, Milton is closer to the fourteenth-century pre-reformation disciples of William of Ockham than he is to Luther or Calvin. Though without grace man is helpless, God's grace enables man to reach out to God as to a friend:

   > Likewise it is clear why the doctors call grace a habit, although it is not acquired but infused. Grace accomplishes in the soul something similar to the effects of a naturally acquired habit, although in a far more perfect fashion than an acquired habit. . . .

But grace elevates human power beyond itself, so that acts which had been turned by sin toward evil or inward toward one's self now can be meritoriously redirected against the law of the flesh and toward God. Grace leads, assists, and directs in order that man may be prompted in a way which corresponds with divine charity. And thus, grace weakens the remaining power of sin, not—as many doctors say—because it forgives or wipes out sins, but because it strengthens human power. (Gabriel Biel, "The Circumcision of the Lord," trans. Paul L. Nyhus, in *Forerunners of the Reformation: The Shape of Late Medieval Thought Illustrated by Key Documents*, ed. Heiko Augustinus Oberman [New York: Holt, Rinehart and Winston, 1966], p. 171.)

See also the quotation from Holkot below. Future references to pre-Reformation theologians cited from this edition are given parenthetically in the text as *Forerunners* with page numbers.
8. *Lectures on Romans*, Chapter 7, trans. Jacob A. O. Preus, in *Luther's Works*, Vol. 25, ed. Hilton C. Oswald (Saint Louis: Concordia Publishing House, 1972), pp. 331, 336, 340.
9. "That to the highth of this great Argument / I may assert Eternal Providence, / And justify the ways of God to men" (*PL* I.24–26). "Justify" smacks of "justification." Properly speaking, justification only applies to man. In Reformation theology man is justified by faith; he is justified *to God*. The implication that God needs to be justified *to men* alerts the reader at the outset of *Paradise Lost* not to expect orthodoxy. "Assertion" alludes to Luther's "An Assertion of All the Articles of Martin Luther Condemned by the Latest Bull of Leo X [*Assertio omnium articulorum M. Lutheri* . . .]." Martin Luther was asserting his articles of faith against the Pope. Against whom was Milton asserting Eternal Providence? Against Luther and other Reformers he disagreed with. By echoing key terms of the Protestant Reformation Milton is expressing his dissatisfaction with its theology. It is bad theology, he implies, to take refuge in the incomprehensibility of God's judgment with respect to the justice of predestining humans to damnation, as Luther does here: "Let us take it that there are three lights—the light of nature, the light of grace, and the light of glory, to use the common and valid distinction. By the light of nature it is an insoluble problem how it can be just that a good man should suffer and a bad man prosper; but this problem is solved by the light of grace. By the light of grace it is an insoluble problem how God can damn one who is unable by any power of his own to do anything but sin and be guilty. Here both the light of nature and the light of grace tell us that it is not the fault of the unhappy man, but of an unjust God; for they cannot judge otherwise of a God who crowns one ungodly man freely and apart from merits, yet damns another who may well be less, or at least not more, ungodly. But the light of glory tells us differently, and it will show us hereafter that the God whose judgment here is one of incomprehensible righteousness is a God of most perfect and manifest righteousness. In the meantime, we can only *believe* this, being admonished and confirmed by

the example of the light of grace, which performs a similar miracle in relation to the light of nature" (*The Bondage of the Will* in *Works*, Vol 33, p. 292). Luther wrote *The Bondage of the Will* in response to Erasmus's *A Diatribe Concerning Free Choice*, which Erasmus had written to counter Luther's rejection of free will in his *Assertio*.

Recourse to God's incomprehensibility on a matter so vital as salvation earned Milton's scorn. He explains that he wrote his Christian doctrine because he was dissatisfied with all previous expositions of it: "But in fact I decided not to depend upon the belief or judgment of others in religious questions for this reason: God has revealed the way of eternal salvation only to the individual faith of each man, and demands of us that any man who wishes to be saved should work out his beliefs for himself. So I made up my mind to puzzle out a religious creed for myself by my own exertions, and to acquaint myself with it thoroughly. In this the only authority I accepted was God's self-revelation, and accordingly I read and pondered the Holy Scriptures themselves with all possible diligence, never sparing myself in any way." *The Christian Doctrine* in *Complete Prose Works of John Milton*, Vol. VI, trans. John Carey, ed. Maurice Kelley (New Haven: Yale University Press, 1973), p. 118.

10. C.A. Patrides, *Milton and the Christian Tradition* (Oxford, 1966), p. 214.
11. Heinrich Heppe, *Reformed Dogmatics Set Out and Illustrated from the Sources*, trans. G.T. Thomsom, rev. and ed. Ernst Bizer (London: George Allen & Unwin, 1950), pp. 166–67. Heppe's survey of Reformation theology contains a wealth of excerpts from Reformed writings; Maurice Kelley uses him frequently to annotate Milton's *Christian Doctrine* in the Yale *Complete Prose Works*.
12. C. A. Patrides, assessing the influence of the Book of Revelation upon Milton's historicism, finds this similarity: "The Johannine vision, as Thomas Brightman summarily observed in 1615, 'sufficiently furnish[s] thee with the Historyes of the world from the first beginning of it to the last end.' Concurrently viewed as 'the majestick image of a high and stately Tragedy,' the Apocalypse displays within the context of a 'celestiall Theater' the creative and redemptive thrusts of God in opposition to—and, eventually, in triumph over—the forces of Antichrist defined as 'the cumulative mystery of iniquity rampant in the postlapsarian world' (above, p. 212)." "'Something like Prophetick strain:' apocalyptic configurations in Milton," *The Apocalypse in English Renaissance Thought and Literature*, eds., C.A. Patrides and Joseph Wittreich (Ithaca: Cornell University Press, 1984), p. 231.
13. Man is responsible for making his terrible history and man is free at any time to change his history for the better. Not only human history but divine and satanic histories are balanced, like a massive top, on the fine point of man's free will. That humans, save those fit though few, do not realize or appreciate how crucial they are to the cosmos was the cause of Milton's wrath in his prose tractates. Yet, he must also have thought that man's pivotal position was unfairly burdensome, for he emphasized reforming people rather than punishing them, or, as Patrides observes in another context: "Milton went out of his way to oppose the relentless

emphasis of the Apocalypse on implacable retribution by introducing into all the eschatological visions of *Paradise Lost* (III, 323–38; X, 635–9; XI, 900–1) a decisive and recurrent element of lenity. . . . The catalogue of woes that are to befall the human race (XI, 477–90) was grim enough in the first edition of *Paradise Lost*; yet Milton amended it in the second edition by adding to the horrors detailed (ll. 485–7). Even so, the terminal point of history in the epic is not preceded by the massive and devastating calamities set forth in the Apocalypse at such epidemic lengths, and, it should be admitted, ever so lovingly. Not vengeance but the fulfillment of God's promises and the beatific vision beyond history are what appealed to Milton most" (*The Apocalypse in English Renaissance Thought and Literature*, p. 216).

14. See Aristotle, *Metaphysics*, trans. Hippocrates G. Apostle (Bloomington, Ind: Indiana University Press, 1966), 1027a, pp. 105–06.
15. *De Divinatione Per Somnum*, in *The Basic Works of Aristotle*, ed. Richard McKeon (New York: Random House, 1966), 463b, p. 628.
16. The probability of one-half assumes an infinite amount of time in which to turn up identical numbers of odd and even. The very fact that time is finite (apart from its formulaic relationship to X number of sinners) may also account for the larger number of damned, which then becomes a function of statistical probability given a limited amount of time in which to play out the numbers game.
17. *Anatomical Exercises on the Generation of Animals*, trans. Robert Willis in *Great Books of the Western World*, Vol 28, ed. in chief, Robert Maynard Hutchins (Chicago: Encyclopædia Britannica, Inc., 1952), p. 399. For a brief survey of genetic theory in the Renaissance and seventeenth century see Hans Stubbe, *History of Genetics*, trans. T.R.W. Waters (Cambridge, Mass: MIT Press, 1972), pp. 68–76.
18. "For though in nature nothing really exists beside individual bodies performing pure individual acts according to a fixed law, yet in philosophy this very law and the investigation, discovery, and explanation of it is the foundation as well of knowledge as of operation. And it is this law, with its clauses, that I mean when I speak of *Forms*, a name which I the rather adopt because it has grown into use and become familiar." Francis Bacon, *The New Organon*, in *Francis Bacon: A Selection of His Work*, ed. Sidney Warhaft (New York: Macmillan, 1985), p. 377. "And inquiries into nature have the best result when they begin with physics and end in mathematics" (*ibid.*, p. 384). ". . . to inquire the Form of a lion, an oak, of gold; nay, of water, of air, is a vain pursuit: but to inquire the forms of sense, of voluntary motion, of vegetation, of colours, of gravity and levity, of density, of tenuity, of heat, of cold, and all other natures and qualities, which, like an alphabet, are not many, and of which the essences, upheld by matter, of all creatures do consist; to inquire, I say, the true Forms of these, is that part of metaphysique which we now define of. . . . for knowledges are as pyramids, whereof history is the basis. So of natural philosophy, the basis is natural history; the stage next the basis is physique; the stage next the vertical point is metaphysique. As for the vertical point, *opus quod operatur Deus à principio usque ad finem*, the

summary law of nature, we know not whether man's inquiry can attain unto it." *The Advancement of Learning*, ed. G. W. Kitchin (London: Everyman's Library, 1973), II.7, pp. 95–96.

19. Westfall, pp. 89, 88; the quotation is from Boyle's *Free Inquiry into the Vulgarly Received Notion of Nature.* That God's general providence and his particular providence are contradictory is Boyle's intuition of the primal contradiction in God between his self-sufficiency and his creativity, which I shall discuss in section II below.
20. Patrick Grant, *Literature and the Discovery of Method in the English Renaissance* (London: The Macmillan Press, Ltd., 1985), pp. 15–16. The Medievals "saved the appearances" of the multiform phenomena by codifying them into a model which gets "everything in without a clash ... by mediating its unity through a great, and finely ordered, multiplicity" (C. S. Lewis, *The Discarded Image* [Cambridge, Eng: Cambridge University Press, 1971], p. 11).
21. Not by the *laws of generation*, but by the *act of begetting*. However, in light of what Milton goes on to say about the power of matter, Sumner may have been correct in interpreting *cum gignendo* as signifying the natural law of heredity concomitant on begetting rather than the begetting itself.
22. Sumner added this phrase for clarification; the words are not in Milton's text.
23. *Indicta*, past participle of *indīcō*: to proclaim, appoint; to impose, enjoin, inflict. "The power which had been appointed to, or imposed on, matter." Sumner's "communicated to" is too weak to convey the magisterial force of God's will when he delegated one of his powers to matter.
24. The Yale edition of *The Christian Doctrine* refers us to Milton's *Art of Logic* via W. C. Curry (*Complete Prose Works*, p. 322, n. 72). "In the order of nature matter follows the efficient cause, and is a kind of effect of the efficient cause; for the efficient cause prepares the matter so that it will be ready to receive a form. Inasmuch as the efficient cause is that which first moves and matter is correspondingly that which is first moved, the efficient is called the active principle and matter the passive principle. This definition of matter is virtually the same among all writers. The definition says that matter is a *cause*; for an effect exists by the influence of its matter" (trans. Walter J. Ong, S.J., in *Complete Prose Works of John Milton*, Vol. VIII, ed. Maurice Kelley [New Haven: Yale University Press, 1982], p. 230). "The *Christian Doctrine*, then, is more consistent than orthodox treatises and is in closer agreement with Aristotle in this detail than with conservative Christian belief" (William B. Hunter, "The Power of Matter" in *The Descent of Urania: Studies in Milton, 1946–1988* [Lewisburg: Bucknell University Press, 1989], p. 142.
25. René Descartes, *Discourse on Method and Meditations on First Philosophy,* trans. Donald A. Cress (Indianapolis: Hackett Pub. Co., 1980), pp. 24–25.
26. Descartes could have told Satan, even more definitively than Abdiel does, why it is absurd to think he is self-begotten: "But if I were derived from myself, I would not doubt, I would not hope, and I would not lack anything whatever. For I would have given myself all the perfections of

which I have some idea; in so doing, I would be God!" (*Meditations on First Philosophy*, p. 75).
27. So did Milton, though, according to Hunter, "with the principle of life already established, Milton could make little use of this second act of creation by God. Perhaps this is why he does not stress this climactic moment, for man could, of course, have sprung from the earth as did the animals. Biblical authority, however, demanded the intrusion; Milton could not overlook the detail no matter how extraneous it was to his system" "(The Origin and Destiny of the Soul," *The Descent of Urania*, p.117). Hunter traces Milton's *élan vital* of living things to the central concept of the Hermetica that energy constantly circulates in the universe and is replenished by the sun (pp. 126–132).
28. Ralph Cudworth, "The Digression concerning the Plastick Life of Nature, or an Artificial, Orderly and Methodical Nature," in *The Cambridge Platonists*, ed. C. A. Patrides (Cambridge, Mass.: Harvard University Press, 1970), p. 322. Cudworth's "Digression" is taken from his *The True Intellectual System of the Universe* (1678). Fifty years before Cudworth published his "Digression," William Harvey used the term "plastic power" as a synonym for the vital principle of generation: "The egg also seems to be a certain mean; not merely in so far as it is beginning and end, but as it is the common work of the two sexes and is compounded by both; containing within itself the matter and the plastic power, it has the virtue of both, by which it produces a foetus that resembles the one as well as the other" (*Animal Generation*, p. 384). Milton does not represent nature as being the unconscious drudge that Cudworth and More conceive it to be; nature is aware of Eve beginning and of Adam completing the act of Original Sin (IX.782–84, 1000–1004).
29. Henry More, *Philosophical Poems, 1647*, A Scholar Press Facsimile (Menston, England: The Scholar Press, Ltd., 1969), p. 346. For discussions about the impact of the theory on the seventeenth-century learned community see Robert A. Greene, "Henry More and Robert Boyle on the Spirit of Nature," *Journal of the History of Ideas* 23 (1962), pp. 451–74, and William B. Hunter, Jr., "The Seventeenth Century Doctrine of Plastic Nature," *Harvard Theological Review* 43 (1950), pp. 197–213. Milton consigns to the Limbo of Vanities "All th' unaccomplisht works of Nature's hand, / Abortive, monstruous, or unkindly mixt, / Dissolv'd on Earth" (III.455–57).
30. Ellen Goodman, "Sway and Subjection: Natural Causation and the Portrayal of Paradise in the *Summa Theologica* and *Paradise Lost*" in *Milton and the Middle Ages* (Lewisburg: Bucknell University Press, 1982), p. 82.
31. "Yet in *Paradise Lost* the prohibition is not set in the abstract nature that Milton's insistence on its arbitrariness implies. The prohibition instead finds its place at the head of a visible creation which, as we have seen, swarms with powers in process—a creation not without apparently magical properties. The Tree of prohibition is therefore distinguished by its very blankness: it stands as the sole abstract sign in a world that otherwise forms for Adam and Eve a series of concrete or qualitative signs,

a world the various items of which taken together serve as a symbol of God's abundant goodness. . . . the prohibition . . . marks the fruit of the Tree off as radically *different* . . .". Christopher Kendrick, *Milton: a Study in Ideology and Form* (New York and London: Methuen, 1986), p. 199. Kendrick argues that the Tree is a manifestation of a predestinary ethical grid which in turn is a manifestation "of the predestinary God of early Protestantism" in which Milton believed, "even as his dynamic sense of the subject, his sense of personal vocation, forced Arminianism upon him" (p. 123). Kendrick's allegation flies in the face of Milton's explicit denunciation of predestination in *The Christian Doctrine* and certainly deserves more convincing evidence for it than a citation to Max Weber's *The Protestant Ethic and the Spirit of Capitalism* (p. 229, n. 41).

32. Though Harvey recognized that parents can pass on their virtues to some of their offspring, he believed that "their descendants, once or twice removed, however, unless they have come of equally well-bred parents, gradually lose this quality; according to the adage, 'the brave are begotten by the brave,' " (*Animal Generation*, pp. 455–56).

33. Though the theoretical parts of *Animal Generation* seem ludicrous to us today, Harvey believed he was a pathfinder in biology and that his main problem was finding words to name phenomena which had never been described before: ". . . such is the abundance of matter and the dearth of words. But if he would have recourse to metaphors, and by means of old and familiar terms would make known his ideas concerning the things he has newly discovered, the reader would have little chance of understanding him better than if they were riddles that were propounded; and of the thing itself, which he had never seen, he could have no conception. But then, to have recourse to new and unusual terms were less to bring a torch to lighten, than to darken things still more with a cloud: it were to attempt an explanation of a matter unknown by one still more unknown, and to impose a greater toil on the reader to understand the meaning of words than to comprehend the things themselves. . . . Wherefore, courteous reader, be not displeased with me, if, in illustrating the history of the egg, and in my account of the generation of the chick, I follow a new plan, and occasionally have recourse to unusual language" (pp. 336–37).

34. It is instructive here to contrast Milton's biological theology with that of a twentieth-century interpreter of Reformed dogmatics, Herman Hoeksema. Both poet and theologian have a strong feel for the genetic conservation of sin in humanity and for the naturally evolutionary thrust of it as well. Hoeksema believes in God's predestination of individuals; Milton does not. This crucial difference in their theology has divergent consequences for their biology and for the role that biology plays in human history. Adapting modern science to Reformed theology, Hoeksema interprets evolution as the emergence of sin from its primitive ancestor Adam into the fully developed "Man of Sin": "Adam's sin is the root of all sin, and from that root the complete horror of sin will become manifest through the development of the race. But the race must first develop itself in connection with the development of the entire earthly creation. And thus every tribe and every nation and also every person, each one according to

his own character, gift and talent, time and circumstances, means and powers, contributes his own actual sin to fill the measure of iniquity . . .". Herman Hoeksema, *Reformed Dogmatics* (Grand Rapids, Mich., 1966), pp. 279–80.

The evolutionary concepts held by Hoeksema and Milton have this in common: there is no principle of natural selection for salvation, because, as Hoeksema says, sin is an "active lack," not one "that will be remedied in the way of gradual development" (p. 248). The conservation of sin eliminates the unfit from salvation, and the final state of mankind is not the emergence of a higher species proceeding from a primitive or defective stock: ". . . for since it cannot be that a cause is worse than its effect in the same category, i.e. that anything should be contributed to a second thing, by that which the supposed giver does not itself possess, it is sufficiently clear that rational nature, being the product of something different, could not have arisen from a brute, but only from an intelligent nature" (Heppe, p. 48). The fourteenth-century nominalist John of Mirecourt's exception to Aristotelian causality is rare; he did not think it self-evident "that a thing cannot as a total cause produce something nobler than itself, or that it is impossible for something to be produced which is nobler than anything which now exists." Frederick Copleston, S.J., *A History of Philosophy*, Vol. 3, pt. 1 (Garden City, N.Y., 1963), p. 141. In Hoeksema's predestinated universe, before the foundations of the world were laid, God had already picked the people who are to be saved from the mass of humanity uniformly damned. Sin is free to evolve new forms and varieties of itself—the more the better—until it reaches the evolutionary end product in the Man of Sin, which is history's teleology and its termination date. On the cosmic scale there is no conflict between nature and grace, because human history is not free if it (1) is the result of natural law and (2) is the record of the acts of predestinated individuals of whom the elect do experience the conflict without affecting "the development of the race." Hence, Hoeksema categorically denies that anything in the earthly creation is the result of "repair work" (p. 240), and sees, rather, an uninterrupted evolution of sin towards its predestinated terminus.

35. Milton's God recapitulates the contradiction inherent in St. Thomas' God, whom Arthur O. Lovejoy analyzes in "Necessity and Self-Sufficiency in the Thomistic Theology: A Reply to President Pegis," *Philosophy and Phenomenological Research* 9 (1948–49), 71–88.

36. Anton C. Pegis, "Principale Volitum: Some Notes on a Supposed Thomistic Contradiction," *Philosophy and Phenomenological Research* 9 (1948–49), 60. Pegis' rejoinder to Lovejoy in this article (51–70) and his subsequent "Autonomy and Necessity" in the same volume (89–97) are excellent semantic "double-think," but they fail to dispel the obvious contradiction that Lovejoy so clearly elucidates.

37. Unless God's knowledge is divided in some way, as between the necessary knowledge he has of himself and the free knowledge he has of created things (Heppe, p. 72), then as *actus purus* he "wills whatever He understands. By His understanding (far otherwise than the creature!) He forms the essences of things and so cannot not will them" (Heppe, p. 84).

Milton's impulse toward unitive law resulted in his assertion that God's and man's thought processes are homologous to the extent that they both can understand what they do not will (but not the converse).

38. A. S. P. Woodhouse, "Notes on Milton's Views on the Creation: The Initial Phases," *Philological Quarterly* 28 (1949), 223.

39. John Reesing, "The Materiality of God in Milton's *De Doctrina Christiana*," *Harvard Theological Review* 50 (1957), 172. As long as God creates *ex nihilo*, the change from potency to actuality pertains only to the creature (Heppe, p. 194). In order to reconcile God's immutability with a matter *ex deo* in Milton's theology, Walter Clyde Curry resorts to the Thomistic distinction between substance as incommunicable *essence* and substance as communicable *suppositum* (*Milton's Ontology, Cosmogony and Physics* [Lexington, Ky.: University of Kentucky Press, 1957], pp. 184–85). Reformed dogmatists consider the idea of the *suppositum* irrelevant (Heppe, p. 63), but do follow St. Thomas in defining the relationship between man's limited perfections and God's infinite perfections as analogical and equivocal in concept (Heppe, pp. 60–61). For a discussion of St. Thomas' concept of analogy see: George P. Klubertanz, S.J., *St. Thomas Aquinas on Analogy* (Chicago: Loyola University Press, 1960); Hampus Lyttkens, *The Analogy between God and the World* (Uppsala: Lindequitska bokhandeln, 1953); and Ralph M. McInerny, *The Logic of Analogy* (The Hague: Martinus Nijhoff, 1961). In Milton's system, however, the relationship of God to the world is not merely one of analogy, or even the nominalist unity in concept, but some sort of unity in kind, because Milton holds no substantial distinction between matter and spirit, and matter is inherent in God.

40. The Thomistic argument is repeated by Protestant theologians who do not perceive that there is a contradiction between such statements as "No perfection was added to God by the creation of the world, [before God created the world] God had been sufficient and blessed in Himself and had need for nothing," or "Necessity or need did not move Him to create the world, because He needs nothing," and such statements as "There are no outward impelling causes (if one may indeed use this expression of God). The divine goodness is inward; the good diffuses and communicates itself," "The impelling cause of the creation of things was God's immense goodness joined to His supreme wisdom, which He willed to communicate and by communicating to manifest, because the good is communicative of itself," or simply the general acceptance of the Augustinian-Thomist position that "His goodness [is] the cause of His will" (Heppe, pp. 194–95). Reformed dogmatists insist more strongly than medieval Catholics on God's free will, but they also fall into the trap of predicating God's goodness as an attribute which of itself is communicative of itself, as though God's goodness were an attribute of his unconscious mind.

41. See William Barrett, *Irrational Man* (Garden City, New York: Doubleday Anchor Books, 1962), pp. 98–99 and pp. 69–146.

42. Christian theologians have had centuries of practice at extricating Christian dogmas, beliefs, tenets from charges of contradiction. The way to avoid contradiction is to redefine the supposed contraries so that they do

not conflict. In his proof that no reprobate is ever a member of the Catholic Church, Jan Hus must explain how Peter's denial of Christ and Paul's persecution of him did not put Peter and Paul into the contradictory state of being both righteous and unrighteous. Hus distinguishes between the grace of predestination and present grace. According to the former Peter and Paul remained righteous while according to the latter they were, for the time, unrighteous. Since their righteousness and unrighteousness did not refer to the same kind of grace, they were not in a state of contradiction (Jan Hus, "The Church," *Forerunners,* pp. 222–24). The strategy of medieval theologians to define away contradictions was not always practiced by the Reformers, as we saw in the case of Luther above.

43. Johannes Wollebius, *Reformed Dogmatics,* ed. and trans. John W. Beardslee III (New York: Oxford University Press, 1965), p. 40. In his *Life* of Milton, Milton's nephew Edward Phillips describes a typical Sunday afternoon in his uncle's school: "The Sunday's work was, for the most part, the reading each day a chapter of the Greek Testament, and hearing his learned exposition upon the same (and how this savored of atheism in him, I leave to the courteous backbiter to judge). The next work after this was the writing from his own dictation, some part, from time to time of a tractate which he thought fit to collect from the ablest of divines who had written of that subject: Amesius, Wollebius, &c., *viz. A perfect System of Divinity,* of which more hereafter" (Hughes, p. 1030). Maurice Kelly in the Yale edition of Milton's *Christian Doctrine* cites numerous allusions to Wollebius (see the Index, *Complete Prose Works,* pp. 862–63).

44. Marcia L. Colish, *The Mirror of Language* (New Haven, Conn: Yale University Press, 1968), pp. 110–11.

45. It follows that I cannot accept Edward Said's structuralist contention that in *Paradise Lost* "words are endless analogies for each other" but never signify reality or truth and point rather to an "ontology of nothingness" at the center of the poem. "*Abecedarium culturae*: structuralism, absence, writing," *TriQuarterly* 20 (1971), 34–35.

46. A.B. Chambers, "Chaos in *Paradise Lost,*" *Journal of the History of Ideas* 24 (1963), 69.

47. On the resemblance of Milton's metaphysics to that of degenerative cosmologies see Curry, Ch. 2, particularly pp. 60–63. As Curry points out, Milton "having derived matter directly from God . . . proceeds—with apparently no consciousness of philosophical contradiction—to consider it the *first* step in the process of an historical creation" (p. 75).

48. Charles M. Coffin, "Creation and the Self in *Paradise Lost,*" ELH 29 (1962), 14–15.

49. The contradictory signals sent out by such schizophrenic natures pose problems of interpretation and reciprocity for others. Satan's soliloquy in Book IV (ll.32–113) illustrates the problem of the finite creature's impotence in giving a gift to the Person Who Has Everything. One motive for his rebellion was the feeling that he could not repay God for his favors. Satan's pride, of course, prevented him from looking for the easy way to meet his obligation, simple gratitude. Satan also contends that God hid his power from the angels, thus tempting them to rebel (I.637–42), an

argument which implies that the bad angels interpreted God's kindness toward them as weakness. The problem of interpretation is real, especially in an hierarchical chain of communication from the top down, and originates as much with the attributes of the superior person to be interpreted as with the evil disposition of the inferior interpreters to misinterpret. See also Kendrick, *Milton: A Study in Ideology and Form*, p. 113.

50. According to Kathleen Swaim, Raphael's pedagogy in the central books of *Paradise Lost* is intended to move Adam from passive acceptance of God's bounty to active participation in it. Consequently, she interprets Raphael's scientific disquisition on the earth, the sun and stars as analogically referring to man and the Son: "The small, fruitful, potentially good earth images Adam and humanity. The sun manifests deity and images specifically the Son. Receiving his beams invigorates good; without such a target for his influence as human spirit, that Son too is barren and unactive.... In his initial speech in Book 4, Adam expressed the view that humanity cannot perform 'Aught whereof [God] hath need' (418–19).... In pointing to the sun's barrenness, its absence of effects and activity, Raphael is developing, even reversing this tenet. If God does not need humanity's effects in an absolute sense, Milton's deity is at least susceptible to human influence in revising and fulfilling his design" (*Before and After the Fall: Contrasting Modes in Paradise Lost* [Amherst: University of Massachusetts Press, 1986], pp. 77–78).

51. In *Milton and Science* (Cambridge, Mass: Harvard University Press, 1956), Kester Svendsen provides a quotation from Ester Sowernam (the pen name of an early-seventeenth-century feminist) to illustrate the old notion that Eve is made from Adam's imperfection because of the rule of causation that "*Quicquid efficit tale, illud est magis tale*" (p. 184).

52. *Space, Time, and Deity*, Vol. I (New York, 1966), pp. 262–63 and 205 respectively. Compare similar statements in Heppe, p. 66.

53. On the issue of angelic sexuality Milton is ambiguous. Spirits can assume whatever shape they wish (*PL*, I.423–31); Raphael admits that they have a way of making love, but not that there is a spiritual sexuality. Adam, who has presumably seen angels only in masculine form—and they do all have masculine names—thinks angels are masculine: "O why did God, / Creator wise, that peopl'd highest Heav'n with Spirits Masculine, create at last / This novelty on Earth . . ." (X.888–91).

54. Mine and the angels' interpretation of the Son's rescue of God from contradiction are, of course, to be denied by the orthodox: "although mercy and righteousness produce different effects, they are in no wise contrary, nor as contraries have they a place in God, nor can they be distinguished in the mind in turn" (Heppe, p. 97). However, I am pleased to note such a distinguished critic of Milton as Michael Lieb tackling head on the Son's shocking words to his Father: "Consider the implications of the Son's challenge. Warning his Father that if His Decree is not executed in a manner consistent with His promise of mercy, the Son charges that his Father's actions would render Him defenseless against whatever justifiable accusations (either in the form of questioning or outright blasphemy) His

actions might provoke. One senses in the challenge that the Son himself would be foremost among the reprobate in excoriating the Father, should the Father fail to heed His Son's warning. . . . In an epic that purports to justify the ways of God to men, Milton creates a circumstance in which the very theology upon which that justification is founded threatens to undermine its own cause. . . . If Milton writes incendiary drama, it is because the theology of his poem must be constantly testing itself, constantly subjecting itself to challenges of the most extreme sort" (*The Sinews of Ulysses: Form and Convention in Milton's Works* [Pittsburgh: Duquesne University Press, 1989], pp. 91–92).

# 5

## *Money of the Mind: Dialectic and Monetary Form in Kant and Hegel*

## Marc Shell

According to Plato and Hegel, dialectic comprises two related ways of thinking, the *division* of a whole into parts and the *generation* of a whole from partial hypotheses. These dialectical methods are exemplified and informed by monetary representation and exchange. Plato, for example, argues that most men unwittingly divide up the conceptual and political world in which they live by a kind of division that is formally identical with money changing. His dialogues show how the dialectical relationships of the whole Idea (the One) to its special parts (the many) differ from the relationships of a coin of large denomination to the coins of smaller denomination into which it may be changed. They show how monetary differs from dialectical differentiation.[1] Plato stresses that ignoring or relying uncritically on deceptive interconnections between economic and linguistic categories (rather than taking them into account) renders the intellectual disease of which they are symptomatic more difficult to diagnose and more politically dangerous. In the thought of such modern philosophers as Arthur Schopenhauer[2] and Immanuel Kant[3] there is still some unquestioned dependence on formal relationships between division and money changing.

Plato argues that dialectical generation, or the production of the whole from partial hypotheses, may be connected with monetary processes in the same way as dialectical division. Socrates, for example, is said to deposit in his interlocutors partial falsehoods or likenesses of the whole Idea that the god has deposited with him. These seminal parts are homogeneous with the Idea in the same way that monetary interest is homogeneous with its principal or that a child is homogeneous with its progenitor.[4] Socrates' maieutic art ensures that from these likenesses are generated, by a series of intellectual births and rebirths from the minds of his interlocutors, intellectual offspring ever more like the Idea. (In the same way the hypotheses figured on the divided line approach the Idea ever more closely.) Thus Socrates husbands the Idea as if he were a midwife, and he draws intellectual hypotheses out of and to the Idea as if he were a banker drawing out compound interest from a financial deposit or hypothec.[5]

Greek dialecticians thus articulate the relationship of genuses with species in terms of monetary differentiation and elucidate intellectual hypothesizing in terms of monetary hypothecation. That articulation, as we shall see in this essay, involves tropologies of division and hypothesizing that are similar to (and which perhaps influenced) the tropologies of adequation (*adequatio*) and sublation (*Aufhebung*) proposed by Kant and Hegel. In Hegelian dialectic, for example, differentiation (division) and hypothesizing similarly involve the generative potential of parts (hypotheses and antitheses) and the absolute whole. They involve the mutual cancellation of two partial *Hypotheses* in polar opposition to each other, and their incorporation and transcendence by a third. This transcendence, Hegel implies, is the sublative cashing in (*Aufhebung*) of an already canceled or anulled financial bond, or exhausted *Hypothek*.[6] The moderns—Kant and Hegel—shift dialectic, as we shall see, away from the Platonic division of the Ideal One toward the cancellation (*Aufhebung*) of things to zero. The modern movements from division to sublation and from One to none, however, do not eradicate the 'economics' in dialectic. The modern concept of sublation, indeed, seems to express the historical fact of the internalization of economic form in philosophy.

## *Suppression and Adequation in Kant*

In *An Attempt to Introduce the Concept of Negative Quantities into Mundane Wisdom* (1763), Kant discovers suppression (*Aufhebung*) to zero in Newtonian physics and in credit economics.[7] Kant considers two kinds of opposition. Logical opposition is contradiction, affirming and denying something about a single subject. (Such affirmation and denial, as Kant says, are of no consequence: *nihil negativum repraesentibile*.) Real opposition, on the other hand, arises when two predicates of a single subject are opposed, but without logical contradiction. Real opposition occurs, for example, when a single body is pulled in different directions by two forces so that one force tends to suppress (*aufheben*) the other.[8] One direction in which the body is pulled may be called 'negative' and the other 'positive,' but these words are meaningful only when the directions are taken in relation to each other.[9]

The principal example of nonphysical suppression that informs Kant's concept of negativity is mutual suppression by credit and debt. (The example is not surprising; the opposition of positivity to negativity was first 'discovered' by Brahmagupta when he studied the unique interaction of credit and debt in the monetary economy of India in the seventh century A.D.)[10] Throughout *The Concept of Negative Quantities*, Kant refers to "negative" debt and "positive" credit as real opposites. In this way he allies *Aufhebung* with a zero sum:

> A person who owes a debt to another person of 100 florins must find this sum. But suppose that the same person is owed 100 florins by another. The latter is then held as reimbursing the former. The two debts united form a ground [*Grund*] of zero. There is no money to give and no money to receive.[11]

In economics, as in physics, the zero is supposed to be a relative nothing, the final result of *Aufhebung*. In Kant's thinking, an *Aufhebung* is the cancellation to zero, or stasis, of a debt (*Aktivschuld*) by a credit (*Passivschuld*) when both *Schulden* are "predicates belonging to a single subject and are quantitatively equal to each other." The *Grund* is zero.

Kant seems to generalize this notion of reciprocal exchange infinitely.[12] In *The Concept of Negative Quantities*, he applies the notion of mathematical negativity and reciprocity to psychology, to the estimation of the total values of pleasure and displeasure, to crime and punishment, and so on. For Kant, the sum total of such opposites is or should be zero. The concept of zero and of negativity is thus crucial to Kant's studies of morality and human intentions. Numerical mathematization informs the Categorical Imperative of his later works on morality. And in *Perpetual Peace* (1795) the notion that different forces cancel each other informs a modern political theory of the balance of powers in which, as in Adam Smith's economics, a cunning historical ruse is seen to balance out and perfect the separate tendencies of individuals, larger groups, or nations. The end of this historical balance is a mutual cancellation, which becomes a dynamic equilibrium that is supposed to move history forward.[13] The theory of negative quantities, which began by associating equation with mutual suppression, ends with a metaphysical and political justification of the liberal free-market system.

Plato tried to show how opposites, such as pleasure and pain, participate in each other as species of one genus or as parts of a single unity. Kant, however, tries to show that such opposites mutually suppress each other to zero. The Being of unity in Plato, then, is replaced by the *Grund* of a relative zero in Kant.

This replacement, which relies on a theory of equilibrium or equation, affects the Kantian theory of truth. The Platonic conception of truth is connected with the one way to One (*alētheia*). The Kantian conception of truth, however, is connected with the double way of equation toward zero. In the *Critique of Pure Reason* (1781; second edition, 1787), for example, Kant adopts the Thomist definition of truth as the equation or adequation of *intellectus* and *res*.[14] He assumes as granted "the nominal definition of truth, that it is the agreement (*Übereinstimmung*) of knowledge with its object."[15] Thus he associates logical truth with an adequation implying the existence of two things that are (in some essential way) adequate or equal to each other. As a matter of course, an equal subtracted, or lifted up (*aufgehobene*), from an equal leaves zero.[16] The tropic movement toward zero is essential to the concept of truth as adequation.

Kant argues that the general logic of truth can be either analytic or dialectic. Analytic logic is a negative touchstone that touches properly only the form of truth or that tests only whether our knowledge contradicts itself. General logic, however, has "no touchstone for the discovery of error as concerns . . . the content." Kant criticizes the "dialecticians" who believe that general logic can be treated as "an *organon* for the actual production of at least the semblance of objective assertions." He argues that "dialectic" is a logic of illusion, and that "dialecticians" do not understand that "logic teaches us nothing whatever regarding the content of knowledge, but lays down only the formal conditions of agreement with the understanding," and that "since these conditions can tell us nothing at all as to the objects concerned, any attempt to use this knowledge as an instrument [*Werkzeug*] or organon which professes to extend and enlarge our knowledge can end in nothing but mere talk. . . ." Kant thus argues that the formal laws of logic cannot provide such adequation; knowledge is nothing more than the combinatory activity of the understanding.[17] In Kant, then, the *Grund* of a relative zero becomes, like Being itself, a kind of unknowable source.

Plato argued that the universe is subject to government by number, and he recognized a general similarity between number (*numerus*) and coined money (*nummus*): the theory of number and the theory of coined money concern both symbols (numbers as numerals [*Zahlen*] and the inscriptions in ingots) and things (numbers as groups of things [*Anzahlen*] and the ingots themselves), which the symbols represent as, or homogenize into, one genus. Kant distinguishes his from the

Platonic position by an elaborate disengagement of the intellectual *Zahl* from the *Anzahl* of things.[18]

The Kantian concept of truth, however, is relative to another numerical concept, the zero obtained from discourse about economics and physics. In *The Concept of Negative Quantities*, Kant argues that the *Grund* of being is associated with an equation that is the mutual cancellation (*Aufhebung*) to zero of opposite and real (i.e., not logically contradictory) objective forces, such as physical attraction and repulsion or monetary debt and credit. In *The Critique of Pure Reason*, he argues similarly that truth is associated with the adequation of *intellectus* and *res*, and refers the relationship or affinity of subject with object to a transcendental *Grund*.[19] (Note, however, that credit and debt, of which he wrote in *The Concept of Negative Quantities*, are homogeneous, and that the knower and the known, of which he writes in the *Critque of Pure Reason*, are heterogeneous.) In his theory of truth, then, Kant both uses *Aufhebung* (as adequation) and decries dialectic (which would confirm the truth of objective assertions). That *Aufhebung* is crucial both to the zero in the adequation of analytic logic (which is confined to mere forms) and to the zero in real equation (which may consider quantities and forces of objects) suggests, however, an unavoidable problem in the Kantian critique of dialectic. As it happens, the Kantian relationship between *Aufhebung* and truth is one of the problems with which the dialectician Hegel takes issue.

## *Against Formalism*

Hegel criticizes the infinite generalizations of wayward Kantian systems of reciprocities like those of Friedrich Wilhelm Joseph von Schelling and Johann Gottlieb Fichte. In *The Phenomenology of Mind* (1807), for example, Hegel attacks the formalism of Schelling: "The predicate may be subjectivity or objectivity, or again magnetism, electricity, and so on, contraction or expansion. . . . With a circle of reciprocities of this sort it is impossible to make out the real fact in question."[20]

According to Hegel, Kant's formalism of real opposites degenerates with Schelling into a schematizing system of pseudoclassification or pseudodifferentiation like the system of labeled boxes in a merchant-grocer's stall. Schelling employs mathematical relations, such as "$0 = 1 + 1 - 1 + 1 - 1 \ldots$," to define his notion of differentiation and cancellation (*Aufhebung*).[21] Hegel, in his *History of Philosophy*, claims that for Schelling all difference is only quantitative, as is money in its role as measure, and he makes his famous assertion that philosophical "difference must really be understood as qualitative."[22] Similarly, in *Faith and Knowledge* (1802), Hegel attacks the formalism of deduction in Fichte as "nothing but a transformation of signs, of the *minus* sign into *plus* sign." He mocks Fichte's formalism, as presented in his *Vocation of Man* (1800), by an ironic observation that "an empty money-bag is a bag with respect to which money is already posited, to be sure, though with the *minus* sign; money can immediately be deduced from it because, as lacking, money is immediately posited."[23] Hegel thus accuses post-Kantian formalists of a tendency to differentiate among the things of the world as though thinking were merely double-entry bookkeeping.

This accusation informs Hegel's discussion of "the opposition of Being and Nothing" in his *Logic* (1812–16). Here Hegel offers a critique of the Newtonian physics that (as he argues) Kant incorporated wholesale into his philosophy, and he makes a related attack on Kant's ontology and theory of the creditability of Being, or on Kant's attempt to demonstrate the impossibility of the Cartesian and Leibnizian proofs of the existence of God.[24] In the *Critique of Pure Reason*, Kant compared the actual and potential worths of certain monies (*Taler*) and pretended that Descartes had argued that because we have the idea of God He must exist in the same way that if we have the idea of money it can be spent. Kant wrote that "the attempt to establish the existence of a supreme being by means of the famous ontological argument of Descartes is merely so much labor and effort lost; we can no more extend [*reicher werden*] our stock of [theoretical] insight by mere ideas [*Ideen*], than a merchant can better his position by adding a few noughts [*Nullen*] to his cash account."[25] Hegel criticizes Kant's supposed demonstration of the impossibility of the ontological argument by ridiculing his identification of "ideas to be extended" with "noughts to be cashed in." Hegel, for whom the possibility of ontology is crucial, argues that "what above all has made successful the Kantian critique of the ontological proof of the existence of God is without doubt the example which Kant added to make it more striking." He argues at length that a coin is different from God; in terms of the attachment of predicates to subjects, they operate differently.[26]

## Sublation and the Modus Tollens

Hegel's position against formalism accounts for his redefinition of *Aufhebung*. In Hegel *Aufhebung* is not 'suppression,' as it is in the Kantian definition, but rather 'sublation.' In the *Logic*[27] Hegel defines his new meaning for *Aufhebung* with a reference to the Ciceronian pun, "Tollendum esse Octavium," which may be translated as "Octavian is to be raised/rased." (*Sublation*, the term I use to translate Hegel's *Aufhebung*, is derived from the Latin verb *tollo, tollere, sustuli, sublatum*.) In the Latin pun *tollere* has two of the three meanings of *Aufhebung* in Hegelian dialectic. It means 'keeping or preserving' and 'making to cease or to finish,' but it does not mean 'qualitatively transcending,' the third meaning of *Aufhebung*, which Hegel usually has in mind.[28]

In his reworking of *Aufhebung* Hegel criticizes Kant's dismissal of arguing by the *modus tollens* and Kant's consequent limitation of the boundaries of human knowledge. Kant, in his discussions of contradiction in the *Critique of Pure Reason* and in his *Logic* (1800), defined the *modus tollens*, which he associates with *Aufhebung*, as one mode of reasoning which "proceeds from consequences to their grounds." For Kant, the *modus tollens*, or apagogic mode, is "the mode of conclusion according to which the consequence can only be a negative and indirectly sufficient criterion of the truth of cognition." (Compare 'If A then B; not-B, therefore not-A' with 'If A then B; B, therefore A.') If we allow this definition to stand unqualified (as Hegel does not), then it is common sense to distrust the *modus tollens* because, as Kant notes, it is "only negative."[29]

For Kant the *modus tollens* is "permissible only in rhetoric and in those sciences in which it is impossible mistakenly to substitute what is subjective in our representations for what is objective, that is, for the knowledge of that which is in the object." Nevertheless Kant does allow one use of hypotheses "in the domain of pure reason." One may use hypotheses, he says, "for the purpose of defending a right not in order to establish it." In this case,

> We must always look for the opposing party [which we may attack by using hypotheses] in ourselves. For speculative reason in its transcendental employment is *in itself* dialectical; the objections which we have to fear lie in ourselves. We must seek them out, just as we do in the case of claims that, while old, have never become superannuated, in order that by annulling [*Vernichtigung*] them we may ground [*grunden*] a permanent peace [*ewigen Frieden*].[30]

Only in argument where the opposing party is "ourselves" does Kant hold that dialectical hypotheses are tolerable to pure reason.

Hegel seeks to extend the territory within which to allow annulment by the *modus tollens* and by dialectic. He does so by reinstating and adopting Thomas Aquinas's conception of the *modus tollens*, or *sublatio*, as mediation between opposites.[31] Hegel introduces a new *modus tollens* (the dialectical *Aufhebung*), which becomes his principle mode of argument.

## Checkers and Checks

Sublation in Hegelian dialectic comprises both the cancellation or equation of opposing forces to a relative zero, as it does in Kant, and the transcendence of opposites, as it does in J. C. Friedrich von Schiller.[32] The presentation of Hegel's theory, moreover, associates logical procedures, such as cancellation and transcendence, with uniquely monetary ones. If Hegel conceives of money as a purely quantitative measure (as opposed to, say, a commodity with value in its own right), then the association of logic with money may be symptomatic of, and may even inform, problems in his notion of *Aufhebung*. Thus locating "the logical place of money"[33] in Hegelian dialectic helps to situate the "quality" of Hegelian *Aufhebung*.

In this section I shall consider three traditions on which Hegel draws, traditions in which *Aufhebung* is associated with counting, exchange, and interest.

1. In its initial stages Hegel's intellectual method is similar to the arithmetic of contemporary German accountants. In German states in the eighteenth century, most merchants did their accounts by manipulating tallies or checkers on a board. (In Hegel's time the English chancellor of the exchequer still used this method; compare figures 1, 2, and 3.) In reckoning, "the tallies or counters used for working out problems on a board were 'picked up' [*aufgehobene*] when dealt with; thus if one was picked up from either side, the result that remained was unaffected."[34] The money token, or checker, was canceled without changing the total. The cancellation of the opposing part became a partial means toward indicating the one whole.

The historical transition from reckoning with this checkerboard to figuring with Arabic numerals, algorithm, and the sign for nought (the cipher '0') was a significant turning point in Western thought.[35] (See figure 4.) The new 'algebra' of double-entry bookkeeping had been 'discovered' by ninth-century Arabs who needed an efficient method to calculate inheritance shares. Their discovery influenced analysis of simple and dialectical opposition. Al-Khowārazmi's *Concise Calculation of Restoration and Confrontation* was, "in effect, a new way of solving equations, first by 'restoring' normalcy to an equation by bringing its negative terms up to a positive value through addition, a process which was repeated on the other side of the equation; and second by 'confronting' similar and congruent terms on either side of the equation and eliminating them."[36] This way of using equation and adequation to zero especially intrigued thinkers who lived during the transition from the old system of accounting to the new one. Among these thinkers were Shakespeare, who lived during a period of rapid economic and financial development in Elizabethan England,[37] and

*Figure 1. Illumination, the Court of the Exchequer. England, circa 1450. An usher stands on the table, apparently speaking; in the foreground is a square cage, grated and barred, behind which are two prisoners; there are two large, iron-bound chests, suggestive of treasure. From G. R. Corner, "King's Bench, Common Pleas, and Exchequer, at Westminster,"* Archaeologia; or Miscellaneous Tracts Relating to Antiquity, *vol. 39 (1868).*

*Figure 2. Pen and ink sketch, the Court of the Exchequer. Drawn during the reign of Henry IV (1367–1413). At the center is the square checkerboard. In the Red Book in the Chief Remembrancers Office, Four Courts, Dublin. From James F. Ferguson, "A Calendar of the Contents of the Red Book of the Irish Exchequer,"* Proceedings and Transactions of the Kilkenny and South-East of Ireland Archeological Society, *vol. 3: 1854–55 (Dublin, 1856).*

Kant and Hegel, who lived in economically and financially backward, although philosophically advanced, states.

2. Discussion about the relationship between economic theory and philosophy in Hegel's time was largely centered on the issues of changing money and redeeming monetary notes. Kant, in "What is Money?" (1797), discusses money as an intellectual concept or rational form.[38] Fichte, in his "Theory of the Right of Exchange" (1800), presents an argument by which the withdrawal of money from a bank account and the drawing of conclusions from logical forms may

*Figures 3a and 3b. Counter, front and back. Nuremberg, early seventeenth century. (British Museum)*

be allied. "The form," writes Fichte, "is the draft [*Trasse*]."[39] The works of economic theory that Fichte adapts to idealist philosophy — Carl Grattenhauer's *Procuration in Exchange* (1800), for example, and Gottlieb Hufeland's *Protestation in Exchange* (1799) — were themselves adapted to economic theory from works of idealist thinkers such as the Schlegel brothers and other "idealist transcendentalists."[40]

In *The Difference Between Fichte's and Schelling's System of Philosophy* (1801), Hegel criticizes Fichte's theory of exchange by zeroing in on his apparently innocent proposal that checks be cashable by the bearer only upon the bearer's signing his name and presenting a passbook or identity card.[41] (Fichte believed that such signing would avoid counterfeiting.) Hegel harshly criticizes the "closed" medieval money system that Fichte proposes.[42] Hegel rarely treats problems of reforming the monetary system[43] or of defining the "aura" of monetary tokens in a particular culture;[44] even more infrequently does he make such treatments an occasion for defining the logical place of money per se; yet, in his critique of Fichte, he emphasizes the connection between the logical problem that in Fichte's system of philosophy "the intellect is bound to fall into the making of endless determinations" and the economic dilemma that "in Fichte's state [with its complex series of state-issued passbooks] every citizen will keep at least half a dozen people busy with supervision, accounts, etc., each of these supervisors will keep another half dozen busy, and so on, ad infinitum, [with the result that] the simplest transaction will cause an infinite number of transactions."[45]

Hegel would transform the "financial" procedure of Fichte's

138  Intimate Conflict

*Figure 4.* Vignette, the old and new arithmetic. *A comparison of calculation by the counting-board and by Arabic numerals. From Gregor Reisch,* Margarita Philosophica *(Freiburg, 1503). (George Arents Research Library, Syracuse University)*

*Figure 5. Emergency money. Rheinhausen, 1921. The inscription in the bottom border reads: HEB' MICH GUT AUF UND LOS' MICH NIEMALS EIN!! (Preserve me and never redeem me!!). Not an official issue, but a private one (Scherzschein, or "joke note") issued by a Kollegenschaft ("group of colleagues") in Rheinhausen. (Museum des Deutschen Bundesbank)*

formalist logic into a unique and powerful process of philosophic cancellation and redemption. In eighteenth-century commercial discourse and practice, a canceled (*aufgehobone*) bond or note still had positive value as a receipt or discharge from debt. (Henry C. Brokmeyer uses *cancel* in both financial and logical senses to translate *aufheben* in his translations of Hegel's works on logic.)[46] In Hegelian dialectic the nought of cancellation (*Aufhebung*) is, like this bond, both null and positive. (Although *Aufhebung* can denote 'cashing in a bond,' it can also denote 'preservation' and hence 'not cashing it in.' Thus the inscription in the bottom border of the emergency money depicted in figure 5 cleverly opposes *Aufhebung* as 'preservation of the banknote' to *Einlösung* as 'cashing it in': "Heb' mich gut und lös' mich niemals ein!!") In Hegel the nought that is the bond is neither simple negativity, as in Kant, nor apparently simple unity, as in Plato; rather the bond ought to be cashed in, with interest, by the appropriate teller. This 'tally-man' is the dialectician.[47]

3. That the cashiered bond to be cashed in (*aufgehobone*) is interest bearing brings us to another traditional association of *Aufhebung* with money—its connection with the institution of monetary interest. The use of *Aufhebung* to mean 'to collect interest of the monetary kind' is as old as the fourteenth century.[48] This is one of

its principal meanings in the works of Martin Luther.[49] In such writers as Schiller, Goethe, and Hegel, the collection of monetary interest is extended conceptually to include 'interest of the spiritual or intellectual kind.'[50]

In Hegelian, as in Platonic, dialectic, economic hypothecation informs intellectual hypothesizing: a monetary *hypothec* (or principal) from which interest is drawn is like a philosophical hypothesis from which a deduction is drawn, and just as mature bonds are homogeneous with the sums of their principals and interests, so dialectical syntheses are, in a way, homogeneous sublations of their hypotheses. In Socrates' exposition of dialectic in the *Republic*, this apparent homogeneity between hypotheses and Idea poses no problem, since there is mythic leap from the partial hypotheses to the Idea figured on his divided line. In Hegel (and in the later dialogues of Plato), however, theory has to confront directly the problem of homogeneity and heterogeneity, of sameness and difference, that motivates every dialectical process.

## *The Difference*

*Sub-lation* is connected grammatically with *dif-ference*. *Tollo, tollere, sustuli, sublatum* borrows its principal parts from *fero, ferre, tuli, latum*. Thus Hegelian *Aufhebung*, associated with the Ciceronian and the Thomist *sublatio*, has the same conceptual relationship to the German proverb 'Aufgeschoben ist nicht aufgehoben' ('Deferral is not doing away with') that the *modus tollens* has to the Latin witticism 'Quod differtur non aufertur' ('Deferral is not removal').[51] Such grammatical connections and puns, of the kind that Hegel has in mind when he refers us (in his *Logic*) to the dictionaries, suggest the logical connection between *Aufhebung* and *Differenz* that motivates Hegelian dialectic.

This connection between sublation and difference is also apparent in Hegel's consideration of the concept of truth. Kant, as we have seen, relies on a definition of truth in which the *intellectus* is supposed to become "adequate" to the *res*: the pertinent difference between them is annulled (becomes nought) as they become 'equal' to each other. Hegel, however, argues in the *Phenomenology* that truth does not involve "the rejection of the discordance, the diversity, like dross from pure metal, nor, again, does truth remain detached from diversity, like a finished article from the instrument [*Werkzeug*] that shapes it. Difference itself continues to be an immediate element within truth as such, in the form of the principle of negation."[52] Thus Hegel attacks those who reject dialectical negation or mediation in philosophy.

Hegel himself begins with illusion and negation. "The system of the experience of the spirit," he writes in the *Phenomenology*, "deals only with the negative appearance [*Erscheinung*] of the spirit, a spirit that gains its truth only by finding itself in absolute dismemberment" and then "looking the negative in the face and abiding with it."[53] Hegel explains the need to focus on negativity by emphasizing the distinction between negativity and the ordinary conception of falsehood. This distinction is summarized by Hegel's description of the process of the generation of truth. "Dissimilarity [*Ungleichheit*; of knowledge with its substance] is dissimilarity which is an essential moment. Out of this differentiation [*Unterscheidung*] their identity comes, and this resulting identity is truth."[54] This relationship between negativity (or nonidentity) and truth, which Hegel posits against nondialectical thinkers such as Kant, is the way by which phenomenology (the 'logic of illusion') becomes logic.

Throughout his writings Hegel is careful to distinguish his concept of truth from mathematical and monetary relations. In the *Phenomenology*, for example, he insists that "true and false are [not] among the determinate thoughts which are considered immobile separate essences, as if one stood here and the other there, without community, fixed and isolated. Against this view, one must insist that truth is not a minted coin [*ausgeprägte Münze*] which can be given or pocketed ready-made."[55] In a fragmentary essay of 1793, Hegel had already claimed that the conventional use of syllogisms and other logical exchanges constituted a deceptive intellectual currency, and he tried to distinguish "authentic wisdom" from the "inauthentic" knowledge of "mere argument [*Räsonnement*]."

> Wisdom does not begin from the concepts with a "mathematical method," and arrive at what it takes for truth through a string of syllogisms [*Schlussen*] like Barbara and Baroco—it has not purchased its conviction at the general market where they give out knowledge to everyone who pays the fair price, nor would it know how to pay for it in the current hard cash [*in blanker Münze*] that gleams on the counter—it speaks rather from the fullness of the heart.[56]

The syllogistic inferences that the pietistic young Hegel singles out for special attention—Barbara and Baroco—are associated with the *modus tollens* and with the problems of negativity and differentiation in general.[57]

In dismissing the traditional use of syllogistic inferences, Hegel would raise himself above (and/or erase) the conventional distinction between the genuine and the counterfeit. It is Hegel's conviction in the *Phenomenology* that "counterfeit instead of genuine coin may doubtless have swindled individuals many a time . . . but in the knowledge of that inmost reality where consciousness finds the direct certainty of its own self, the idea of [such] delusion is entirely baseless."[58] Hegel argues that truth cannot be separated from falsehood any more than an instrument can be separated from the finished product that it helped to make. The two parts of being are interrelated in a way different from that of oil and water in a heterogeneous mixture. "The false," writes Hegel, "is no longer something false as a moment of the true."[59]

The motive force of the *Phenomenology* is the inequality or dissimilarity that obtains in consciousness between the Subject and the Substance.[60] This negative force allows Hegel's system (and also, as Marx suggests, the systems of the Greek atomists)[61] to begin, by arguing *modus tollens*, with a consequential falsehood.

> A so-called fundamental proposition or first principle of philosophy, even if it is true, is yet none the less false just because in so far as it is merely a fundamental proposition [*Grundsatz*], merely a first principle. It is for that reason that it is easily refuted. The refutation consists in bringing out its defective character; and it *is* defective because it is merely the universal, merely a principle, the beginning. If the refutation is complete and thorough, it is derived and developed from the nature of the principle itself, and not accomplished by any other counter-assurances [*Versicherungen*] and chance fancies.[62]

The refutation of a first and false principle is both positive and negative. That the truth must always be realized in this form is expressed in the idea that "represents the Absolute Spirit—the grandest conception of all."[63] This absolute, alone and without the counter-assurances of a credit economy, replaces both the Kantian zero and the Platonic One, which Hegel discusses as the two major precursors to his dialectic.

## *Putting Hegel Down*

The remarkable tension in Germany between the development of thought and that of material production—and, I think, of financial reckoning, or calculation[64]—helps to explain the German philosophers' fascination with the relationship between money and ontology, and it elucidates the influence of the economists James Steuart and Adam Smith on Kant and Hegel.[65] Monetary theory ties together symbol and commodity, as well as universal and particular, in a knotty conception of the relationship between thought and matter. (Thus Hegel, in *The Philosophy of Right* [1821], presents a theory of money, and of the contemporary problem of paper money in particular, which involves the dialectic of symbol and commodity.)[66] Tension between the development of thought and that of material production, however, does not explain away dialectic. My reference to historical contexts—for example, the development at the same time and place of both coined money and Greek dialectic, Brahmagupta's discovery of dialectical negativity in the credit economy of India, and Al-Khowārazmi's discovery of algorismic algebra among a people uniquely concerned with inheritance shares[67]—is not meant to put dialectic down to material conditions. Even when historically accurate and inclusive, such observations differ from, and may even obscure the way toward, accounting thoughtfully for idealist dialectic.

Ideology, or the study of the expression of the connection between spirit and matter, generally focuses, as does Heinrich Storch in *Course of Political Economy* (1815), on the relationship between "internal goods [*biens internes*] or elements of civilization" and "material goods, components of material production."[68] (It includes consideration of how the material interests of a particular class are expressed or promoted through religion and philosophy: Jean-Jacques Rousseau in his *Discourse on the Origin and Foundations of Inequality among Men* [1755], for example, studies how the dogmas of the priests support the institution of private property;[69] David Hume, in *A Treatise on Human Nature* [1739], interprets property as a "species of causation";[70] and Moses Hess, in *Twenty-One Sheets from Switzerland* [1843], associates the "estrangement" of all the physical and mental senses, which he remarks in modern European civilization, with capitalist ways of "having" and "alienating" properties.)[71] Within a decade of Hegel's death, many students of ideology concentrated their focus on specifically monetary 'alienation': the reactionary Wilhelm Schulz in *The Movement of Production* (1843),[72] for example, and the radical Moses Hess, who, in his remarkable "On the Essence of Money" (1844), initiated a systematic study of spiritual money (*geistiges Geld*) rather than material money, money of the person rather than money of the purse.[73]

In "On the Essence of Money," Hess considers the interrelations between money, language, and German philosophy, arguing that in German thought "God is merely idealized capital, and heaven the theorized merchant world" and suggesting that "theological and philosophical speculation will cease only with the cessation of commercial speculation, and only then will religion give way to genuine politics."[74] Karl Marx, adopting Hess's words and arguments,[75] attempts to state some of the general and supposedly necessary similarities between negativity and monetary alienation that would help to explain such tropes as *adequatio* and *Aufhebung*. In his sweeping "Critique of Hegelian Dialectic and Philosophy as a Whole" (1844), Marx attempts to do to Hegel what Hegel did to Kant, or, rather, he attempts to do more. "[Hegelian] logic," writes Marx, "is mind's coin of the realm [*das Geld des Geistes*], the speculative or thought value of man and nature—their essences grown totally indifferent to all real determinateness, and hence their unreal essences."[76] And, in an afterword to *Capital*, Marx explains that "with [Hegel, the dialectic] is standing on its head" and that he is trying "to turn [the dialectic] right side up again."[77]

If Marx's attempt literally to put down[78] Hegel were to prove wholly appropriate, it would have to outdo Hegel in the same way Hegel began to outthink traditional logic. In his *System of Ethical Life* (1802–3), Hegel had already defined money as a middle term that makes for "the indifference of all labor,"[79] and in his *First Philosophy of Spirit* (1803–4), he called money an abstraction of need and labor that makes for a "monstrous system," or "life of the dead body" which requires "continual dominance and taming like a beast," a taming that Hegel's State would accomplish much as would Marx's communist society.[80] And, following in the wake of Kant and Fichte, Hegel tried, in his *Philosophy of Right* (1824–25), to explain money as one expression of reason.[81]

This study of *Aufhebung* in Kant and Hegel is not the place to settle the Marxist claim to have surpassed philosophy. As that claim appears in "The Critique of Hegelian Dialectic and Philosophy as a Whole," in *Capital*, and elsewhere, however, it is certainly misleading. Thus many thinkers, following what they interpret to be Marx's lead but ignoring the significance of the differences between the kinds of oppositions and sublations that we have considered, assert that "mind's coin of the realm" plays no part at all in their own thinking. They fail even to inquire whether some money of the mind, like that which they suppose to pervade Hegelian logic, participates in their own supposedly superior dialectics.[82] Marx's critique of Hegel may fail to acknowledge Hegel's critiques of Kant and Fichte, but it does warn that the thinking which fails to account for or even to encounter its own internalization of economic form remains insensitive to a sting that goads thought into becoming philosophy and, perhaps, into surpassing it.

## Notes

1. On the relationship between division (*diairēsis*) and money changing in the Platonic dialogues (in which both the intellectual process and the financial one are signified by *kermatidzein*), see Jakob Klein, *A Commentary on Plato's Meno* (Chapel Hill, N.C., 1965), p. 81. See also Seth

Benardete, "Eidos and Diairesis in Plato's *Statesman*," *Philologus* 108 (1963): 212; and Marc Shell, *The Economy of Literature* (Baltimore, 1978), pp. 21–62.
2. "Every *general* truth is related to special ones as gold to silver in so far as we can convert it into a considerable number of special truths that follow from it, just as gold coin can be turned into small change" (Arthur Schopenhauer, "On Logic and Dialectic," in *Parega and Paralipomena: Short Philosophical Essays*, trans. E. F. J. Payne [Oxford, 1974], 2:21).
3. Immanuel Kant sometimes considers even the idea of virtue, which Socrates in the *Meno* seems to conflate with the One, in terms of money changing. "All human virtue in exchange is fractional currency," says Kant. "He is a child who takes it for genuine gold [*ächtes Gold*].—But it is better to have fractional currency [*Scheidemünze*] than to have no medium in circulation: fractional currency can be changed for cash money [*baares Geld*], albeit with considerable loss" (*Immanuel Kant's Anleitung zur Menschen- und Weltkenntnis, nach dessen Vorselungen im Winterhalbjahre 1790–91*, in *Immanuel Kants Menschenkunde*, ed. Fr. Ch. Starke [Hildesheim, 1976], p. 82).
4. For Plato's analogy from intellectual offspring both to animal offspring (*tokos*) and to monetary interest (*tokos*), see Plato, *Republic* 507, 509, 534.
5. In English as in Greek, *hypothec* (from *hupothēkē*, literally "deposit") and philosophical *hypothesis* (from *hupothēsis*) are cognate. On Socrates' divided line, see Shell, *The Economy of Literature*, pp. 39–45.
6. In German philosophy the association of *Hypothek* with *Hypothesis* is suggested by the discussions of both words in Johann Georg Walch, *Philosophisches Lexicon*, 4th ed. (Leipzig, 1775; rpr. Hildesheim, 1968).
7. Kant, *Versuch, den Begriff der negativen Grössen in die Weltweisheit einzuführen*, in *Werke in zehn Bänden*, ed. Wilhelm Weischedel (Darmstadt, 1968), 2:775–819. Unless otherwise noted, references to Kant's *Werke* are to this edition. The relation between this *Versuch* and other of Kant's works is a theme of Susan Meld Shell, *The Rights of Reason: A Study of Kant's Philosophy and Politics* (Toronto, 1980); and Hans Saner, *Kant's Political Thought: Its Origins and Development*, trans. E. B. Ashton (Chicago, 1973).
8. "In its mathematical sense [*Aufhebung*] is used of magnitudes which reduce each other to zero [or which] mutually annul or suppress each other, and therefore become indifferent to their equation" (W. T. Harris, "Note," in *Hegel: Selections*, ed. J. Loewenberg [New York, 1929; rpr. 1957], p. 102).
9. Some thinkers on the left ignore the significance of the distinction that Kant makes between logical and real opposition. Lucio Colletti ("Marxism and the Dialectic," *New Left Review* 93 [September-October 1975]: pp. 3–30) suggests that this distinction is necessary to understanding "the relationship between Marxism and science." The distinction also pertains to the historical development of dialectic from Plato to Marx and to thinking about the relationship between money and commodity, as well as about the oppositions between and contradictions within social classes.
10. H. G. Zeuthen (*Geschichte der Mathematik im Alterum und Mittelalter*

[Copenhagen, 1896], esp. p. 280) argues that the Indians invented negative numbers by observing an economy of debts and credits. See J. Ruska ("Zur ältesten arabischen Algebra und Rechenkunst," *Sitzungsberichte der Heidelberger Akademie der Wissenschaften Philosophische-historische Klasse* [1917], 2 Abhandlungen, esp. pp. 35, 49, 60–61, 104, 109–10, 113–14) on Indian sources of Greek 'algebra'; and Morris Kline (*Mathematical Thought from Ancient to Modern Times* [New York, 1972], p. 185), who notes that the "first known use [of negative numbers] is by Brahmagupta about [the year] 628."

11. Kant, *Versuch*, in *Werke*, 2:784; cf. 2:785–89.
12. On a similar generalization of the concept of reciprocal exchange, see Gregory Vlastos, "Equality and Justice in Early Greek Cosmologies," *Classical Philology* 42 (July 1947): 173–74.
13. Kant, *Zum ewigen Frieden*, in *Werke*, 9:191–251. The transformation of "mutual cancellation" into "dynamic equilibrium" is already treated in Kant's cosmological *Allgemeine Naturgeschichte und Theorie des Himmels* (1775), in *Werke*, 1:219–400.
14. For Plato, see the ironic Socrates' etymological explanation of truth (*alētheia*) as "the wandering way of the god" (*theia alē*) (*Cratylus* 421b). For Thomas Aquinas, see his *Questiones disputatae de veritate*, question 1, art. 1. Aquinas borrows the phrase *adequatio res et intellectus* from Isaac Israeli (ca. 855–955).
15. Kant, *Kritik der reinen Vernunft*, A 58 = B 82; translated as *Immanuel Kant's Critique of Pure Reason*, trans. Norman Kemp Smith (London, 1933), p. 97. (For references to the *Kritik*, numbers preceded by A refer to pages of the first edition [Riga, 1781] and numbers preceded by B refer to pages of the second edition [Riga, 1787].) The 'object' in question is the object of knowledge, not the thing-in-itself.
16. The connection between 'equation' and *Aufhebung* is commonplace in German mathematical discourse. Thus Andreas Reyher, in a widely used textbook (*Arithmetica oder Rechen-Büchlein* [Gotha, 1653; 4th ed., 1657], p. 72) writes: "Wie die grosse gebrochnene Zahlen in Kleinere *gleichgeltende* zu reduciren, *auffzuheben* oder zu bringen."
17. Kant, *Kritik*, A 60–61 = B 85–86; trans. Smith pp. 98–99. I do not consider, for the time being, transcendental logic.
18. On "the calculating character of modern times" and the Kantian conception "of the world as a huge arithmetical problem," see Georg Simmel, *The Philosophy of Money*, trans. T. Bottomore and D. Frisby (London, 1978), esp. pp. 443–46.
19. Kant, *Kritik*, A 57–64 = B 82–88; trans. Smith, pp. 97–101.
20. Hegel, *Phänomenologie des Geistes*, in *Werke*, 20 vols. (Frankfurt, 1970), 3:48–49. Unless otherwise noted, references to Hegel are to this edition. Translations of the *Phänomenologie* are from the translation by J. B. Baillie (*The Phenomenology of Mind* [New York, 1967], here p. 108). I have also consulted the translation of the preface by Walter Kaufmann (*Hegel: Texts and Commentary* [New York, 1965]).
21. Joseph L. Esposito (*Schelling's Idealism and Philosophy of Nature* [Lewisburg, Pa., 1977], esp. pp. 178–85) suggests that Hegel misunder-

stands Schelling and is confused about the relationship between quantity and quality. Esposito notes that "Schelling's Absolute first *appears* as simple (absolute) indifference, as [Lorenz] Oken . . . had interpreted it, and progressively moves toward greater differentiation. . . . However, this differentiation is not, in fact, conceived as *real*. . . . To explain this Schelling would use the . . . mathematical relation $[0 = 1 + 1 - 1 + 1 - 1]$. Hegel prefers to characterize this motion of cancellation [*Aufhebung*] as 'the life of the Concept,' but for Schelling this metaphor and all those involving 'movement' [which] Hegel uses [are] deceptive" (p. 180; see F. W. J. von Schelling, *Sämmtliche Werke*, 14 vols., ed. K. F. A. Schelling [Stuttgart, 1856–61], 2: 41).

22. Hegel, *Vorlesungen über die Geschichte der Philosophie*, in *Werke*, 20:440–54; translated as *Lectures on the History of Philosophy*, trans. E. S. Haldane and F. H. Simson (London, 1896), 3:512–45.

23. Hegel, *Glauben und Wissen*, in *Gesammelte Werke*, ed. Hartmut Buchner and Otto Pögeler (Hamburg, 1968), 4:391–92; translated as *Faith and Knowledge*, trans. W. Cerf and H. S. Harris (Albany, N. Y., 1977), p. 159.

24. Hegel, *Wissenschaft der Logik*, in *Werke*, 5: 88–92; translated as *Science of Logic*, trans. W. H. Johnston and L. G. Struthers (London, 1929), 1: 98–102. See Hegel, *Jenenser Logik, Metaphysik und Naturphilosophie aus dem Manuskripte*, ed. G. Lasson (Leipzig, 1923); and *Enzyklopädie der philosophischen Wissenschaften im Grundrisse, Erster Teil: Die Wissenschaft der Logik*, in *Werke*, 8: 135–37.

25. Kant, *Kritik*, A 630 = B 658; trans. Smith, p. 507. Compare Kant's quite different *Der einzig mögliche Beweisgrund zu einer Demonstration des Daseins Gottes* (1763), in which he relies on the theory of *Aufhebung* presented in his essay on the concept of negative quantities (1763). Kant writes: "Das Dasein ist gar kein Prädikat, und die Aufhebung des Daseins Keine Verneinung eines Prädikats, wodurch etwas in einem Dinge sollte aufgehoben werden" (in *Werke*, 2: 642).

26. Hegel, *Enzyklopädie*, in *Werke*, 8: 135. See the ironic remark in Hegel's 1831 revision of the *Wissenschaft der Logik* (originally published 1812) "that man should raise himself to this abstract generality in his mind, so that, in fact it becomes a matter of indifference to him whether the hundred dollars . . . are or are not" (*Wissenschaft der Logik* [*Werke*, 5:91], trans., Johnston and Struthers, 1:101). Hegel does not consider in what sense monies, such as *Taler*, may differ in respect to "predication," not only from God but also from other things. In his discussion of this section of Hegel's *Logik*, Charles Taylor (*Hegel* [Cambridge, 1975], pp. 246–52) misconstrues Hegel's understanding of quantity by misinterpreting his "100 *Taler* [units of money]" as "100 units [of anything]."

27. Hegel, *Logik*, in *Werke*, 5:114; trans. Johnston and Struthers, 1:119–20.

28. In a letter to Cicero, D. Brutus writes that "Labeo Segulius . . . told me . . . that Caesar [i.e., Octavian] himself had made no complaint at all about you, except as to the remark which he said you had made 'that the young man should be praised, honoured and *immortalized* [*tollendum*]' " (in Cicero, *Letters to his Friends*, trans. W. Glynn Williams, 3 vols. [Cambridge, Mass., 1929], vol. 2, p. 479, 11.20). From Velleius Paterculus

(Oxford Classical Text, ed. R. Ellis [Oxford, 1898], 2.62), it would seem that *tollendun* was to have a double meaning like the one that Hegel ascribes to it, but D. R. Schackleton (*Cicero: Epistulae ad Familiares* [Cambridge, 1977], 2:541) suggests that such a meaning would have been 'forced.' See *Suetonius*, trans. J. C. Rolfe, 2 vols. (Cambridge, Mass., 1913), 1: 137.

29. Kant, *Kritik*, A 790–91 = B 818–19; trans. Smith, pp. 625–26. And Kant, *Logik*, in *Kants gesammelte Schriften*, ed. Konigliche Preussische Akademie der Wissenschaften (Berlin, 1923), 9: 1–150, esp. sec. 7; translated as *Logic*, trans. Robert Hartman and Wolfgang Schwartz (Indianapolis, 1974), pp. 57–58. On the *modus tollens*, see note 57.

30. Kant, *Kritik*, A 777 = B 805; trans. Smith, pp. 617–18. Kant's attitude to the *modus tollens* may be compared with his Newtonian suspicion of hypotheses: "Everything . . . which bears any manner of resemblance to an hypothesis is to be treated as contraband [*verbotne Ware*]; it is not to be put up for sale even at the lowest price, but forthwith confiscated immediately upon detection" (Kant, *Kritik*, A xv; trans. Smith, p. 11). According to Aristotle, there are other proofs by refutation of hypotheses (*anairoumenon hypothēsin*) (Aristotle, *Eudaimonean Ethics* 1222b; see also *Sophistical Refutations* 177a).

31. In his consideration of whether evil destroys good entirely, Thomas Aquinas writes that "the good which is directly opposite to an evil is wholly made away with [*tollitur*], as we have said, but other goods are not wholly made away with [*tollentur*]" (*Summa Theologiae*, 1a.48.4). Related examples of the way the Hegelian concept of *Aufhebung* militates against that of Kant include his discussion of giving and receiving hypothecs or deposits (*Phänomenologie*, in *Werke*, 3:316–23; trans. Baillie, pp. 446–53) and his refutation of the Kantian reciprocity theory of crime and punishment: "The annulment [*Aufhebung*] of the crime is retribution [*Wiedervergeltung*] in so far as (a) retribution in conception is an "injury of the injury," and (b) since as existent a crime is something determinate in its scope both qualitatively and quantitatively, its negation as existent is similarly determinate. This identity rests on the concept, but is not an equality between the specific characteristics of the crime and that of its negation; on the contrary, the two injuries are equal only in respect of their implicit character, i.e., in respect of their 'value' " (*Philosophie des Rechts*, in *Werke* 7: 192; translated as *The Philosophy of Right*, trans. T. M. Knox [Oxford, 1952], p. 71).

32. J. C. Friedrich von Schiller (*Über die ästhetische Erziehung des Menschen in einer Reihe von Briefen* [Letters on the Aesthetic Education of Man], letter no. 18, in *Sämmtliche Werke* [Munich, 1962], 5: 625) writes that "beauty unites [the] two opposed states and thus sublimates [*aufhebt*] the opposition. But because both states remain eternally opposed to each other, they cannot be united in any other way than by being sublimated." See also Schiller's use of *Aufhebung* in letter no. 20, where he observes that "the scales balance when they are empty; but they also balance when they contain weights" (Schiller, *Sämmtliche Werke*, 5: 633).

33. See Bruno Liebrucks, "Über den logischen Ort des Geldes," *Kantstudien*

61 (1970): 159–89; and Alfred Sohn-Rethel, *Warenform und Denkform* (Frankfurt, 1971).
34. See Johann Eisenhut, *Ein künstlich Rechenbüch auff Zyffern, Linien und Walschen Practica* (Augsburg, 1538), G 2b. On the synonymity of *Aufhebung* with *elevatio* in the discourse of German accountants, see Karl Menninger, *Kulturgeschichte der Zahlen* (Königsplatl, 1934), p. 265. According to Felix Müller ("Zur Terminologie der ältesten mathematischen Schriften in deutscher Sprache," *Abhandlung zur Geschichte der mathematischen Wissenschaften* 9 [1899]: 319), the meaning of *aufheben* in mathematical discourse derives from its significance in the commercial discourse of accounting with reckoning pennies.
35. For an early comparison of calculation by checkerboard (abacus) and by algorithm, see Gregor Reisch, *Margarita Philosophica* (Freiburg, 1503). Reisch includes a vignette depicting the opposition between the old and new arithmetic (figure 4).
36. Muhammad al-Khowārazmi, *The Concise Calculation of Restoration and Confrontation*, composed in Baghdad ca. A.D. 825; the quotation is from F. E. Peters, *Allah's Commonwealth: A History of Islam in the Near East 600–1100 A.D.* (New York, 1973), pp. 334–35. For the connection with inheritance, see *The Algebra of Mohammed ben Musa*, ed. and trans. F. Rosen (London, 1831), esp. p. 2; and S. Gandz, "The Algebra of Inheritance," *Osiris* 5 (1938): 319–91.
37. On the significance of the old and new arithmetic in Shakespeare's plays, see Henry W. Farnam, *Shakespeare's Economics* (New Haven, Conn., 1931), esp. pp. 108–14.
38. Kant, "Was ist Geld?" in *Die Metaphysik der Sitten*, in *Werke* 7: 400–404; translated as *Kant's Philosophy of Law*, trans. W. Hastie (Edinburgh, 1887), pp. 125–29.
39. Fichte, "Theorie des WechselRechts" in *Gesamtausgabe*, ed. Reinhard Lauth and Hans Gliwitzky (Stuttgart, 1979), 2.5.211. On the specifically German *Trasse*, or 'bill of exchange' (see Italian *tratta*), see Alfred Schirmer, *Wörterbuch der deutschen Kaufmannssprache* (Strasbourg, 1911), p. 193.
40. Carl Grattenhauer, *Ueber die Wechselprocura* (Berlin, 1800), pp. 12 and 16; see Gottlieb Hufeland, *Primae lineae doctrinae de protestione cambiali* (Jena, 1799).
41. Hegel, *Differenz des Fichte'schen und Schelling'schen Systems der Philosophie*, in *Werke*, 2:84–86; translated as *Differenz (The Difference Between Fichte's and Schelling's System of Philosophy*, trans. W. Cerf and H. S. Harris [Albany, N.Y., 1977], pp. 146–47). Hegel here refers to Fichte's *Grundlage des Naturrechts nach Principien der Wissenschaftlehre* (1797); in *Sämmtliche Werke*, ed. I. H. Fichte, 8 vols. (Berlin, 1845–46), 3:292.
42. See Fichte's *Der geschlossene Handelsstaat* [The Closed Commercial State] (1800), in *Sämmtliche Werke*, 3: 387–513.
43. There are some exceptions. See, for example, Hegel, *Über die englische Reformbill* (1831), in *Werke*, 11:84–87. Karl Rosencranz (*Georg Wilhelm Freidrich Hegels Leben* [Berlin, 1844; rpr. Darmstadt, 1971], p. 61) notes that Hegel did a study of the finances of Berne during the 1790s. See what

is probably Hegel's first publication, his anonymously published German translation of J. J. Cart's *Lettres confidentielles* (*Vertrauliche Briefe über das Vormalige staatsrechtliche Verhältnis des Wadtlandes* [*Pays de Vaud*] *zur Stadt Bern* [Frankfurt, 1798]). Hegel's introduction to this translation is included in *Dokumente zu Hegels Entwicklung*, ed., T. Hoffmeister (Stuttgart, 1936; rpr. Stuttgart, 1974), pp. 247–57.

44. On coinage in Rome, however, see Hegel, *Vorlesungen über die Philosophie der Religion*, in *Werke*, 17:169–70; and Hegel, *Aphorismen aus Hegels Wastebook* (1803–6), in *Werke*, 2: 544.
45. Hegel, *Differenz*, in *Werke*, 2:84–86; trans. Cerf and Harris, *Differenz*, pp. 146 and 148.
46. I thank the Missouri Historical Society for making the still unpublished manuscript of Brokmeyer (1828–1906) available to me.
47. For the role of the tally (*Tale*) in Fichte's understanding of absolute knowledge, see Fichte, *Darstellung der Wissenschaftlehre* (*Aus dem Jahre 1801*) (in *Sämmtliche Werke*, 2:17–18): "Beyond all knowing, according to our present representation, freedom and being come together and permeate one another, and only this intimate permeation and identification of the two into a new being brings about knowing—now truly in the form of knowing—as an absolute *Tale*."
48. For example: "Die vff gehabene czinse" (*Meissner Urkunde von 1398*) in Lorenz Diefenbach and Ernst Wülcker, *Hoch- und nieder-deutsches Worterbuch der mittleren und neueren Zeit* (Basel, 1885) p. 103. See the English *raise*, which can mean "to collect (rents or other charges)" (*Oxford English Dictionary*, s.v. "Raise," v., 25).
49. For *Aufhebung* in Martin Luther as "the collection of interest and of fees for indulgences," see the German writings of Luther in the Jena edition, pt. 1 (Jena, 1564), 195a, 298b, and pt. 2 (Jena, 1563), 263b. See too Luther's use of "gleich aufheben mit einem" to mean "beide theile fahren lassen, auf eine linie zu stehn kommen" (Luther, pt. 5 [Jena, 1575], 340a; discussed by Jacob and Wilhelm Grimm, *Deutsches Wörterbuch* [Leipzig, 1854–1960], s.v. "Aufheben," 10) and his use of *aufheben* to mean "aufheben und behalten" ("to pick up and to lay aside for future use"). Keith Spalding (*Dictionary of German Figurative Usage* [Oxford, 1952], s.v. "Aufhebung") discusses Luther, pt. 1, 40a, together with Luther's translations of Matt. 14:20, Matt. 16:9, Mark 6:43, and Luke 9:17.
50. For Schiller, see his letter to Goethe (August 17, 1797): "Mit meinem Protégé . . . habe ich freilich wenig Ehre aufgehoben" (*Schillers Werke*, Nationalausgabe, ed. L. Blumenthal and B. v. Weise [Weimar, 1977], 29:117–18). For the argument that *Aufhebung* in Schiller's letter is to be connected with collecting interest or rent, see *Trübners Deutsches Wörterbuch* (Berlin, 1939–57), s.v. "Aufhebung." Compare Goethe's use of *einwechseln* in Johann Peter Eckermann, *Gespräche mit Goethe* [Conversations with Goethe], ed. E. Beutler (Zurich, 1948), pt. 2: December 6, 1829.
51. For the German proverb, see Georg Büchmann, *Geflügelte Worte, der Zitatenschatz des deutschen Volkes* (Berlin, 1927), p. 436; for the Latin witticism, see Arnobius, *Commentarii in Psalmos Davidis*, p. 36.

52. Hegel, *Phänomenologie*, in *Werke*, 3:41; trans. Baillie, p. 99. One *topos* that Hegel attacks—that wisdom is like a pure metal (usually gold)—informs much of the Western tradition in philosophy and mathematics. See for example, François Vieta, *In artem analyticem isagoge*; in *Francisci Vietae opera mathametica*, ed. F. Van Schooten, (Leyden, 1646), p. 1. A few thinkers, however, do argue that truth cannot be separated from falsehood in the same way that gold can be separated or refined from dross. Jakob Boehme, for example, relies on the images of alchemy, but does not believe in the complete separation of the false from the true; and G. W. von Leibniz, in his crucial essay on truth argues that "distinct notions," while they are like those unreliable ones that "assayers [*Docimastae*] have of gold," are hardly sufficient for understanding "cognition, truth and ideas." On Boehme, see Hegel, *Vorlesungen über die Geschichte der Philosophi*, in *Werke*, 20. For Leibniz, see his *Meditationes de cognitione, veritate et ideis* [*Reflections on Knowledge, Truth and Ideas*], in *Philosophischen Schriften*, ed. C. J. Gerhardt, 7 vols. (Berlin, 1875–90; rpr. Berlin, 1960), 4:423.
53. Hegel, *Phänomenologie*, in *Werke*, 3:25; trans. Baillie, p. 93.
54. Ibid., in *Werke*, 3:40; trans. Baillie, p. 99.
55. Ibid., in *Werke*, 3:40; trans. Baillie p. 98.
56. Hegel, Fragment: "Religion ist Eine . . . ," in *Werke*, 1:25; translated as "Religion is One," in H. S. Harris, *Hegel's Development* (Oxford, 1972).
57. "Barbara" indicates the mood AAA in the first figure of syllogisms, M———P / S———M // S———P. "Baroco" indicates the mood AOO in the second figure of syllogisms, P———M / S———M // S———P. The proper names are mnemonic devices from a hexameter verse that aids the student to remember the nineteen "valid" syllogistic modes. See Wilhelm T. Krug, *Allgemeines Handwörterbuch der philosophischen Wissenschaften* (Leipzig, 1832), s.v. "Schlussmoden." All second figures, including Baroco, must have a universal major, premises opposed in quality, and a negative conclusion; they are thus associated with the *modus tollens*. Second figures, such as Baroco, may seem to be reduced to (or exchanged for) first figures, such as Barbara.
58. Hegel, *Phänomenologie*, in *Werke*, 3:408, trans. Baillie, p. 570.
59. Ibid., in *Werke* 3:41; trans. Baille, p. 99. See Heraclitus, Fragment 67, in Hermann Diels, *Die Fragmente der Vorsokratiker*, 5th ed. (Berlin, 1934), with additions by Walter Kranz; and Marc Shell, *The Economy of Literature*, esp. pp. 53–54.
60. Hegel, *Phänomenologie*, in *Werke*, 3:22–23; trans. Baillie, p. 85.
61. Karl Marx, *Differenz der demokritschen und epikureischen Naturphilosophie*, in Karl Marx and Friedrich Engels, *Werke*, ed. Institut für Marxismus-Leninismus beim ZK der SED (Berlin, 1956–68), Ergänzungsband, pt. 1, pp. 257–375. (Hereafter this edition of Marx and Engels will be referred to as MEW.) Marx, like Hegel (*Phänomenologie*, in *Werke*, 3:27; trans. Baillie, p. 97), allies this kind of negation with negation in the systems of Leucipidus and Democritus.
62. Hegel, *Phänomenologie*, in *Werke*, 3:27; trans. Baillie, p. 85.
63. Ibid., loc. cit.

64. Hegel, for example, ignores the calculus introduced by Leibniz and Newton (of whose physics he offers nevertheless a scathing attack in the second part of the *Logik*, in *Werke*, 6) and thus sidesteps problems in probability theory and in moral arithmetic (later to become econometrics). These problems, however, ought properly to have influenced both his understanding of infinitesimal smallness (and the naught) and infinite largeness, and his theory of opposition and difference.
65. On Adam Smith and Hegel, see Guy Planty-Bonjour, "Introduction," in Hegel, *La Première Philosophie de l'esprit*, trans. G. Planty-Bonjour (Paris, 1969); P. Chamley, *Économie politique et philosophie chez Steuart et Hegel* (Paris, 1963); and Jean Hyppolite, *Genèse et structure de la Phénoménologie de l'esprit de Hegel* (Paris, 1946), 2:382.
66. Like Adam Smith and Kant, Hegel argues that "money is not one particular type of wealth amongst others, but the universal form of all types so far as they are expressed in an external embodiment and so can be taken as 'things' " (Hegel, *Philosophie des Rechts*, in *Werke*, 7:467; trans. Knox, pp. 194–95). Hegel also insists that "a bill of exchange . . . does not represent what it really is—paper; it is only a symbol of another universal—value. . . . Money represents any and every thing, though since it does not portray the need itself but is only a *symbol* of it, it is itself controlled by the specific value [of the commodity]. Money, *as an abstraction*, merely expresses this value" (Hegel, *Philosophie des Rechts*, ed. Eduard Gans, in Hegel, *Sämtliche Werke: Jubilämausgabe in zwanzig Bänden*, ed. Hermann Glockner [Stuttgart, 1964], 17:119; trans. Knox, p. 240. See Hegel, *Philosophie des Rechts, nach der Vorlesungsnachschrift von H. G. Hotho, 1822/23*, in *Vorlesungen über Rechtsphilosophie, 1818–31*, ed. Karl Heinz Ilting, 6 vols. (Stuttgart, 1973), 3:234–43. In the *Rechts-, Pflichten- und Religionslehre für die Unterclasses* (1810 ff.) (in *Werke*, 4:240), Hegel discusses money as *die allgemeine Ware* and as "abstract value."
67. There are many other instances, for example, "the modern sign of . . . equality [which was] first used in [a book] of [Robert] Recorde that is dedicated to the 'governors and the reste of the Companio of Venturers into Moscovia' with the wish for 'continualle increase of commodities by their travell' " (Robert Recorde, *The Whetstone of Witte* [London, 1556]; see Simon Stevin, *De thiende* [Leyden, 1585; facsimile rpr., The Hague, 1924]). The position that mathematics follows trade is expressed by Edgar Zilsel ("The Sociological Roots of Science," *American Journal of Sociology* 47 [January 1942]: 547), who argues that the "classical mathematical tradition . . . could be revived in the sixteenth century because the new society had grown to demand calculation and measurement." See also Alexander Koyré, *Newtonian Studies* (Cambridge, Mass., 1965), pp. 5–6.
68. Henri Storch, *Cours d'économie politique, ou Exposition des principes qui déterminent la prosperité des nations*, ed. with notes by J.-B. Say (Paris, 1823), 3:217. Among the analogies between spirit and matter adduced by Storch is the one that "internal goods are susceptible of being accumulated like wealth, and of forming capitals that can be used in reproduction" (3:236). See Karl Marx, *Theorien über den Mehrwert*, MEW, 26.1:258;

translated as *Theories of Surplus Value*, trans. Emile Burns (Moscow, 1975), 1:286.
69. Jean Jacques Rousseau, *Discours sur l'origine et les fondements de l'inégalité*, in *Oeuvres complètes* (Paris, 1959), 3:111–223.
70. David Hume, *A Treatise on Human Nature*, ed. L. A. Selby-Bigge (Oxford, 1888 and 1896), pp. 310 and 505–6.
71. Moses Hess, *Einundzwanzig Bogen aus der Schweiz*, pt. 1 (Zurich, 1843), p. 329. Hess suggests that in modern society "an object is 'ours' only when we have it—when it exists for us as capital or when it is directly eaten, drunk, worn, inhabited, etc."
72. Wilhelm Schulz (or Schulz-Bodmer), *Die Bewegung der Production* (Zurich, 1843).
73. Moses Hess, "Über das Geldwesen," in *Philosophischen und sozialistischen Schriften: 1837–1850*, ed. Auguste Cornu and Wolfgang Monke (Berlin, 1961), p. 346. See Jean-Joseph Goux's discussion (*Les Iconoclastes* [Paris, 1978], p. 162) of the "merchant teleology of reason."
74. Hess, "Über das Geldwesen," pp. 337 and 347.
75. On Marx's use (some say 'plagiarism') of Hess's work on money, see Georg Lukács, "Moses Hess und die Probleme der idealistischen Dialektik," *Archiv für die Geschichte des Sozialismus und der Arbeiterwegung*, ed. Carl Grunberg, 12 (1926): 108, 124, 138; Edmund Silberner *Moses Hess: Geschichte Seines Lebens* (Leiden, 1966) esp. pp. 191–92; and Elisabeth de Fontenoy, *Les Figures juives de Marx* (Paris, 1973), esp. pp. 61–65.
76. Marx, "Kritik der Hegelschen Dialektik und Philosophie überhaupt," MEW, Ergänzungsband, pt. 1, p. 571; translated as "Critique of the Hegelian Dialectic and Philosophy as a Whole," in Marx, *The Economic and Philosophic Manuscripts of 1844*, trans. Martin Milligan (New York, 1964), p. 174 (adapted). Elsewhere Marx allies money with mind by way of an ironic restatement of Mephistopheles' offer of twenty-four horses' legs to Faust in Goethe's *Faust* (1824–27): "I am *stupid* [*geistlos*]," states Marx's version of Faust, "but money is the *real mind* [*Geist*] of all things and how then should its possessor be stupid?" (Marx, *Ökonomisch-philosophische Manuscripte* (1844), MEW, Ergänzungsband, pt. 1, p. 564; trans. Milligan, p. 167).
77. Marx, *Das Kapital*, MEW 23:27; translated as *Capital*, trans. S. Moore and E. Aveling (New York, 1967), 1: 20. On Marx's inversion of Hegel's position, see Louis Althusser, "On the Young Marx" and "Contradiction and Over-Determination," in *For Marx*, trans. Ben Brewster (New York, 1970).
78. As 'picking up' is one literal translation of *Aufhebung*, so 'put-down' is one literal translation of *hypothēsis* ('hypothesis').
79. Hegel, *System der Sittlichkeit*, in Hegel, *Schriften zur Politik und Rechtsphilosophie*, ed. G. Lasson (Leipzig, 1918), p. 478; translated in Hegel, *System of Ethical Life (1802–3)* and *First Philosophy of Spirit (1803/4)*, trans. H. S. Harris and T. M. Knox (Albany, N.Y., 1979), p. 154.
80. Hegel, *Philosophie des Geistes* (Jenaer Systementwürfe I), ed. Klaus Düsing and Heinz Kimmerle, in *Gesammelte Werke* (Hamburg, 1975), 6:324; trans. Harris and Knox, p. 249. That one prerequisite for the advancement of

enlightened learning is the transcendence (*Aufhebung*) of private property was already the argument of Carl Wilhelm Frölich, *Über den Menschen und seine Verhältnisse* (1792), ed. Gerhard Steiner (Berlin, 1960), esp. the section about the "Aufhebung des Privateigentums" (pp. 84–107).
81. Hegel, *Philosophie des Rechts, nach der Vorlesungsnachschrift K. G. v. Griesheims 1824/25*, in *Vorlesungen über Rechtsphilosophie*, 3:229. See *Vorlesungen*, 3:230 on "Geistiges Eigentum."
82. For example, Louis Althusser (*Essays in Self-Criticism*, trans. Grahame Lock [London, 1975], pp. 178–79), asserts a clear boundary between "the category of origin [that gives] classical bourgeois philosophy . . . from Descartes to Kant . . . the means of *guaranteeing* its ideas" and genuine "dialectic." "When you reject the category of origin as a philosophical issuing bank," writes Althusser, "you have to refuse its currency, too, and put other categories into circulation: those of the dialectic." Althusser admits that Hegel and Marx not only "refuse[d]" but "transformed and reintroduced . . . the use and guarantee of the categories of Origin and Subject," yet he does not observe, in their reformation of Kant's "issuing bank," a money of the mind like the one that informs his own purportedly "self-critical" thinking and that his own financial troping—philosophical "circulation," for example—helps to indicate.

# 6

# *Metaphor as Contradiction: A Grammar and Epistemology of Poetic Metaphor*

## Brian G. Caraher

*The contrast between sense (a signified which is atemporal or nonspatial insofar as it is a sense, a content) and its metaphorical signifier (a contrast already at work within the element of sense to which metaphor completely belongs)\* is sedimented (another metaphor) by the whole history of philosophy. And this is so without taking into account the fact that this divergence between sense (signified) and the senses (sensible signifier) is declared through the same root (sensus, Sinn). One might, like Hegel, admire the generosity of this stock and interpret its hidden sublation speculatively and dialectically...*
                Jacques Derrida, "White Mythology"[1]

The topic of metaphor has been a variously and sometimes vigorously debated issue. I would like to address the question of metaphor by drawing attention to two modern British writers on the subject. Both had hoped to settle philosophical unrest about metaphor and to lay the groundwork for successful analyses of the operation of metaphor in language as well as in literature. However, their work is

---

\* This complex structure carries with it a number of confusions. Some of them can be avoided by the distinction proposed by I. A. Richards between the metaphorical vehicle and metaphorical tenor. A meaning (produced by the "co-presence of the vehicle and tenor") is "to be clearly distinguished from the tenor" (*The Philosophy of Rhetoric*, p. 100).

badly in need of reconsideration, especially when seen in the light of recent uses of the term *metaphor* by certain philosophers and literary theorists in France and the United States.

First I will examine the implications of two interrelated problems that arise in a grammar of poetic metaphor: (1) the insufficiency of grammatical types alone to account for the process of metaphor; and (2) the need to assume an extra-syntactic context as the way toward achieving explanatory adequacy. A grammar of poetic metaphor, consequently, is bound up with the cognitive import of metaphors; and the method of analyzing metaphors must take the whole process of metaphor, ideational as well as syntactic, into account. In the second part of the essay, I will explore the epistemology informing this contextualized grammar of poetic metaphor. I outline the operation of poetic metaphor and its relation to human perceptual capacities and describe the whole process as the interaction of two opposed or contradictory thoughts or mental events. In the third part of the essay I discuss a highly influential mode of objection to such an epistemology of poetic metaphor.[2]

# I

In *A Grammar of Metaphor* Christine Brooke-Rose concerns herself with developing a "grammatical approach" to metaphor for the English language and its literature, and she maintains that a "grammatical analysis" of metaphors allows comparative studies of the nature of metaphoric relationship.[3] She concentrates primarily on English poetry from Chaucer to Dylan Thomas but gives examples to show that this type of analysis can be applied to language generally. For example, she notes a change from a predominance of noun-metaphors in Old English to a predominance of verb-metaphors in fourteenth-century Middle English; the impact of Norman French and Latin grammar are cited as influences responsible for this change (*GM*, 1–3). In general defense of this grammatical approach to metaphor, Brooke-Rose states: "Most modern studies of metaphor, from Aristotle to the present day, have been concerned with the idea-content rather than with the form: what is the mental process involved in calling one thing another? Now metaphor is expressed in words, and a metaphoric word reacts on other words to which it is syntactically and grammatically related. The effect of this interaction varies considerably according to the nature of this grammatical relationship" (*GM*, 1). This attention to the form of metaphor, to the verbal interaction that produces metaphor, is a very welcome advance over previous poorly developed attempts at the linguistic analysis of metaphor, attempts either too brief and superficial or which consisted of random and pointless tabulations.[4]

However, with this attempt at grammatical analysis of metaphor serious problems arise, foremost of which is that the verbal interaction that produces metaphor cannot be distinguished from other types of verbal interaction. Casting aside any analysis of idea-content or extra-syntactic dimensions of metaphors, Brooke-Rose claims that "any identification of one thing with another, any replacement of the more usual word or phrase by another, is a metaphor" (*GM*, 17). This claim makes it very difficult to distinguish metaphor from metonymy and synonymity. Purportedly, these three terms designate different types of verbal interaction, and generally rhetoricians and stylists attempt to discriminate among them in formulating definitions and analyses. However, Brooke-Rose's grammatical analysis fails to offer careful distinctions. Specifically, if one word or phrase becomes metaphoric by replacing "the more usual word or phrase," how then are we to redefine or meaningfully distinguish metonymy and synonymity from metaphor? All three verbal processes can be said to replace "the more usual word or phrase by another."

An example that encapsulates this situation is provided by some verbal replacements that can be executed on the phrase 'in his youth.' This phrase can be synonymous with 'in his prime' or 'in his early years.' The three phrases 'in his flower,' 'in his bloom,' and 'in his spring,' though, offer three metaphors, with 'flower,' 'bloom,' and 'spring' replacing the more usual word, 'youth.' Yet 'flower' and 'bloom' are themselves synonyms, and the phrases 'in his flower' and 'in his bloom' can be analyzed as synonymous with one another. The phrase 'in his spring,' already recognized as a metaphor, stands in metonymic relation to the phrases 'in his flower' and 'in his bloom.' That is, the latter two phrases suggest or are conceptually associated with the former; they are *metonyms* or associational substitutions for the former.[5] As can readily be seen, three different types of verbal interaction are manifested by the same syntactic structure. Not only metaphor, as Brooke-Rose contends, but metonymy and synonymity as well can be grammatically analyzed as the "replacement of the more usual word or phrase by another."

The way in which Brooke-Rose avoids confronting this analytic dilemma in *A Grammar of Metaphor* raises a second problem. Throughout her analysis of metaphor into grammatical types, she repeatedly makes statements such as "the metaphor is assumed to be clear from the context or from the reader's intelligence" (*GM*, 24). There is a continual *assumption* that the *recognition* of a metaphoric verbal interaction is indeed dependent on something that is extra-syntactic. This assumption keeps the problem of distinguishing metonymy and synonymity from metaphor from intruding on Brooke-Rose's grammatical analysis of metaphors. The clear implication would be that our human capacity to recognize a metaphor appears grounded elsewhere than in understanding purely grammatical relationships. This is *not* to say, however, that variation in the *effect* of metaphors fails to correspond in large measure to variation in the types of grammatical relationship. But it *is* to say that the context of a metaphor and the reader's ability to see and understand that context are the primary factors in recognizing metaphors and in distinguishing metaphor from other types of verbal interaction such as metonymy and synonymity. To speak otherwise would be to deny that at least three different kinds of verbal interaction can make use of the same grammatical types without being confused by linguists, grammarians, or even ordinary speakers.[6]

I. A. Richards is the second writer on metaphor I would like to discuss, and his book *The Philosophy of Rhetoric* addresses directly the problem of context and its relation to verbal interaction. Though not a linguist, Richards is serious about his claim to be considering "how words work in discourse."[7] He clearly rejects, however, the axiomatic and analytic way of proceeding that characterizes Brooke-Rose's study of metaphor. To theorize about the linguistic behavior called metaphor, or even rhetoric in general, Richards states that a context theory of meaning is essential (*PR*, 32–36). He is not as thorough on the notion of context as some other writers,[8] but he does show how important this notion is to metaphor and to language in general.

In contrast to some recent theorists, Richards opens *The Philosophy of Rhetoric* by noting that there is no positive or proper meaning for a word; what we take as the proper meaning for a word is actually "the constancy of the contexts that give [a word] its meaning" (*PR*, 11).[9] Richards also notes that theorists who assume a positive or proper meaning for a word are in error but that their error is made possible by the fact that "the conditions governing" the meanings of many words "are so constant that we can disregard them" (*PR*, 10). Richards targets primarily Husserl, Carnap, and the logical atomists or positivists, but this observation also applies to Saussure and other linguists who depend upon the relation of 'signifier' to 'signified.' In Richards's analysis, words do not represent, denote, or signify certain meanings. Rather, they function to bring a variety of contexts into play—depending upon the other words with which they are interacting. These contexts operate as our 'recognitions' or 'laws of response' and govern the behavioral significance and meaning ascribed to a particular verbal interaction (*PR*, 36).

The analyzable grammatical characteristics of verbal interactions are acknowledged as crucial co-participants in the meaning of any given piece of discourse, but it is also important to recognize that Richards stipulates two other co-participants in this meaning. In addition to the dimension of the verbal interaction, any given piece of discourse is also characterized, first, by an "over-determination" or "multiplicity" of meaning and, second, by our "fabric of conventions." Since there is no single positive or proper meaning for a word, phrase, or piece of discourse apart from the meanings that are governed by the context, discourse in general is characteristically "over-determined" (*PR*, 35). Contradictions, paradoxes, and ambiguity are normal features of discourse, and the context theory of meaning will turn this "multiplicity of meaning" to advantage rather than attempt to refine or purify determinations as is done in logical languages (including semiotics) and in natural and technical sciences.[10] Also, the context theory of meaning must govern the use and interactions of appropriate conventions that get called into play from our rather extensive "fabric of conventions." In exploring the problem of meaning "we re-discover that the world—so far from being a solid matter of fact—is rather a fabric of conventions, which for obscure reasons it has suited us in the past to manufacture and support" (*PR*, 41–42). It is true that Richards allows these last two characteristics of discourse to recede into the background during his analysis of the action of metaphor. However, it does remain clear that meanings ascribed to any specific verbal interaction involve the cooperative interchange of grammar, conceptual over-determination, and socio-linguistic conventions.

Now, if we were judging the operation of metaphor in discourse by only the grammatical types of which it makes use, we would be back at the point where we started: how do we meaningfully distinguish metaphor from metonymy and synonymity in grammar? With Richards, though, the interaction of words that yields a metaphor does so by calling up contexts for the reader or listener that help him or her to recognize the metaphor and to see and judge the way in which the metaphor operates within a possible multiplicity of meaning and appropriate speech conventions.[11]

Indeed, Richards contends that metaphor is not purely "a verbal matter, a shifting and displacement of words":

> Fundamentally it is a borrowing between and intercourse of *thoughts*, a transaction between contexts. *Thought* is metaphoric, and proceeds by comparison, and the metaphors of language derive therefrom. To improve the theory of metaphor we must remember this. And the method is to take more note of the skill in thought which we possess and are intermittently aware of already. (*PR*, 94)

At this point Richards introduces his two famous technical terms—namely, the *tenor* and the *vehicle*. These two terms are supposed to be the "method" by which we can "improve the theory of metaphor" (*PR*, 94), but the history of their use since their introduction has actually gone against the grain of Richards' initial deployment.[12] These terms were supposed to name "the two ideas that any metaphor, at its simplest, gives us" (*PR* 96). For: "In the simplest formulation, when we use a metaphor we have two thoughts of different things active together and supported by a single word, or phrase, whose meaning is a resultant of their interaction" (*PR*, 93).

In formalist literary criticism, however, 'vehicle' has been taken to mean the figure, image, or device used in place of the usual word or phrase; and the 'tenor' has been taken as the meaning, idea, or thought-element of the metaphor. Philip Wheelwright, for example, takes 'vehicle' to be "the imagery or concrete situation described" and 'tenor' to be "the ulterior significance that [the imagery] suggests to the responsive imagination."[13] This formalized construction of Richards' two terms implies that the tenor alone carries the thought or meaning of the metaphor and that the vehicle is present and active as a mere substrate. Wheelwright's construction lacks Richards's sense that there are two interacting yet different thoughts involved in a metaphor. Richards's terms unfortunately lend themselves quite easily to this misleading interpretation; ironically, Richards's own attempt to improve the method of study of metaphor encourages a view of metaphor he would rather discourage. In her brief assessment of Richards's approach, Brooke-Rose also notes that "the very terms" tenor and vehicle "destroy" the interaction Richards seeks to stress (*GM*, 9). The problem, then, is to arrive at a method of talking about metaphor that does not depend upon Richards's technical terms. This method, though, should account for the fact that the conceptual recognition of a metaphor takes shape within a context and that a metaphor has at least "two thoughts of different things active together."

A short example will help to illustrate. A representative poem by Bashō can put the preceding discussion of Richards in better focus.

> A black crow
> Has settled himself
> On a leafless tree,
> Fall of an autumn day.[14]

At first, before generic and contextual considerations come into full play, the poem appears as a somber evocation of a natural event. There seems no elaborate conceit or substitution other than an abrupt yet easily accepted juxtaposition of the crow's settling on a tree and the coming of the season of leafless trees. A particular event functions, then, as a synecdoche of the more general action of an autumn day. Metaphorically, that is, a particular event evokes the general. However, the poem demands the recognition that it operates within a specific genre of poems, namely, *haiku*. The writing and reading of *haiku*, moreover, traditionally call up certain contexts that govern conventional meanings of the poems. This does not mean what has been said so far about Bashō's poem or its metaphor is in error. It means simply that, considered within its generically appropriate context, the poem can say more to its readers. We may get this sense from a certain 'over-determination' of meaning in the poem, such as the blackness and emptiness of the crow, the tree, the autumn fields the crow would be scavenging for some sign of food, and so on. Or we may get this sense that something more is at work through our awareness of such lyric conventions as the bird's being a poetic *persona*. However, all this multiplicity of sense would remain speculation without cognizance of the conditions that govern the full range of meaning available to a *haiku* poem. In general, and without discussing the crucial historical qualifications of the problem, the *haiku* writer happens upon an event or image in nature that in its terseness and precision works to focus his or her mind (and the reader's) clearly on the natural phenomenon and show how an act of mind can accord with a natural event. Thus, the context of Bashō's poem is the attempt to bring an act of mind into agreement with a natural event without the natural event's appearing to be simply the device or image that the mind uses to express itself.[15]

Readers know by convention that a *haiku* poet, as well as more familiar lyricists in the English language, can take as a *persona* the figure of a bird. Bashō has chosen a particularly unassuming and unlikely *persona*—the black crow. This scavenger of nature, however, has composed and poised himself alone and meditatively on a barren tree. Set apart from his labors and his fellows, it is as if he could diffuse himself into the entire season and temperament of autumn. Darkness, emptiness, and a sense of melancholy carry through from the solitary crow to the leafless tree, to the dwindling season. Bashō's poetic act of mind, moreover, suggests that the observer of nature can be an otherwise undistinguished scavenger who in solitary, meditative posture recognizes how his darkness and melancholy correspond to the darkness and melancholy of the season. Thus the autumn day shares the poet's desire to settle or to fall down into himself: both nature and human being seek solitary composure and repose.[16]

In this *haiku* the act of attending to a somber natural event gives rise to a metaphoric process. The natural event, brought to attention in a particular mood, carries over into and expresses an act of mind. The natural event may be called the 'vehicle' and the mood of the poet the 'tenor,' as long as Richards's initial senses of the terms are kept in focus. For the metaphor to work here, "two thoughts of different things" are made "active together": the natural event maintains its precision and distinctiveness while at the same time its human counterpart carries the mind into a metaphoric relation with the natural event. This natural event (or even the noun *crow*), however, is neither a substitute for nor a conduit of the act of mind. The particular posture of the "black crow" stands as a clearly perceived phenomenon that, at the same time as it is being perceived as a natural event, also enters into a metaphoric relation with the human act of mind responsible for such exacting perception. Thus I would like to claim that we have a poetic metaphor where a natural element and a human element are co-active in producing themselves as corresponding thoughts or cognitions. Neither element acts alone as the sole idea, thought, or meaning of that metaphor.

## II

This conjunction of "two thoughts of different things"—of a natural and a human element—in the process of metaphor is not a new idea. Paul Ricoeur and Christine Brooke-Rose both make note of its appearance in classical rhetoric (although the terms employed in such classical texts as Aristotle's *Rhetoric*, Quintilian's *Institutio Oratoria*, Donatus' *Ars Grammatica*, and Bede's *De Schematibus et Tropis* are usually 'inanimate' and 'animate' rather than 'natural' and 'human'[17]). Similar paired terms also appear in some recent work in the linguistic theory of metaphor. Derek Bickerton (see note 4), for example, indicates that metaphors usually involve transfers between the members of such binary categories as "Abstract and Animate (*time passes, prosperity grows, hopes wither*, etc.)" and "Animal and Human (persons are *rats, lions, bears, monkeys*, etc.)."[18] A clear inference emerges that analysis of metaphor appears inextricably bound up with the idea-content of metaphors produced within the interaction of two contrasting categories of experience.

It is my contention that, for poetic metaphor, the cooperative yet contrasting categories of the human and the natural can be found to describe best the two broad areas of experience of which every metaphor is a co-active product. This claim is made on the basis of the example from the work of Bashō; but it is a hypothesis that garners the support of an insistent and traditional (though variegated), mode of philosophical thought about metaphor. This claim, moreover, can be tested against a variety of poetic examples. Take, for instance, the unexpected yet resonant metaphor that wells up within the speaker's confessional discourse in Sylvia Plath's "Tulips":

> And I am aware of my heart: it opens and closes
> Its bowl of red blooms out of sheer love of me.[19]

An unwelcome gift of red tulips eventually elicits an act of generosity on the speaker's behalf: a metaphoric interaction and co-active exchange of human "heart" and natural "blooms" in the midst of attempts to ward off such self-subsuming transfers. The purportedly involuntary and natural action of the flowers responding to light and environment helps recognize and articulate the action of the human heart starting to respond to its own self-engendering rhythms. Another example of poetic metaphor can be garnered from Louise Glück's "All Hallows"—a lyric that evokes a rural Halloween, a harvested countryside, and the summoning of a displaced earthly spirit:

> Even now this landscape is assembling.
> The hills darken. The oxen
> sleep in their blue yoke,
> the fields having been
> picked clean, the sheaves
> bound evenly and piled at the roadside
> among cinquefoil, as the toothed moon rises:
> 
> This is the barrenness
> of harvest or pestilence.
> And the wife leaning out the window
> with her hand extended, as in payment,
> and the seeds
> distinct, gold, calling
> *Come here*
> *Come here, little one*
> 
> And the soul creeps out of the tree.[20]

From the first line, from the passive voice construction of the verb "assemble," the subtle, metaphoric interaction of human and natural elements seems intimated. The "landscape is assembling" in the composure of evening light, but it assembles as well because it bears the signs and markings of human work: yoked teams of oxen, ordered sheaves, and a moon wearing a singularly focused face for collecting what is ripe for the hungry months and mouths of winter ("the toothed moon"). Yet a final moment of assembly needs its metaphor too. The seeds of the harvest, held out toward the assembled landscape in a human palm, summon the fearful "soul" of natural things to come out of hiding on the evening of All Souls. The seeds speak with human voice and pathos; they ask the childlike soul of the barren landscape to accept themselves as restitution for the human work of harvest. In response, "the soul creeps out of the tree"—a metaphoric action that simultaneously contrasts and blends the categories of the human and the natural. The seeds of restitution, of course, will renew the process of natural growth and human harvest the following year.

Again, the opening line of Dylan Thomas's "The Force That Through the Green Fuse Drives the Flower" posits a natural force insistently welling through the green stem of a flower only to place that notion in metaphoric exchange by the next half-line—"Drives my green age."[21] The slender sheath of the human body is yet another "fuse," its youth metaphorically "green" and sharing the same relentless "force" that propels the growth of natural things. Or consider Edward Lear's delightfully playful verse, "The Nutcrackers and the Sugar-Tongs," with its network of nominative and verbal metaphors built upon the conceit that two instrumental extensions of human hands can take it upon themselves to talk, walk, and ride horses as though they could be real actors ("Shall we try? Shall we go? Do you think we are able?") among "blue hills and green meadows."[22] Even the commonplace metaphors of such "nonsense verse" ("Our legs are so long, so aptly constructed") toy with various possibilities of metaphoric exchange between the artifacts of a domesticated world and the desires of escape into a world of natural beings and forms. Though the grammatical conditions governing meanings of a verbal interaction such as poetic metaphor cannot be universally determined, as I. A. Richards points out, the nature of a metaphor's "two thoughts of different things active together" can be said to turn upon the transfer taking place between a human and a natural element.

A problem might arise concerning the type of transfer occurring between human and natural elements in the process of poetic metaphor. Are these "two thoughts of different things" *co-active* or does the metaphorical transfer always move in one direction, either from the natural to the human or vice versa? Richards's terms, 'tenor' and 'vehicle', might again encourage a misleading interpretation here. The vehicle, as perhaps characteristically a natural event, could be taken as the core or kernel of a metaphor, while the tenor, perhaps always a human element, could be understood as something that follows after or tenuously surrounds the real core of the metaphor. A formalist or even an objectivist theory of metaphor will tend toward this interpretation. Perhaps, too, the natural vehicle may be idealized as that which offers itself up, sublimates itself to a higher function, the human tenor. Idealist and essentialist theories of metaphor appear to follow this mode of metaphorical transfer.[23] However, Richards's initial deployment of his technical terms indicates that neither the tenor nor the vehicle has any absolute position vis-à-vis the other term. They comprise co-active ideas mutually supported by the same word or phrase in a piece of discourse. So also will my analysis of these co-active ideas as the interaction of a human and a natural element be understood; neither counterpart will be privileged.

To be more convincing on this point, is it possible to have a metaphor in which the 'vehicle' is a human event and the 'tenor' a natural element? If so, the position would be strengthened that the "two thoughts" made "active together" in a poetic metaphor are indeed equally and inseparably co-active. That is to say, neither the human nor the natural element, just as neither tenor nor vehicle, is to be pre-emptorily accorded a privileged or anterior status in an epistemology of poetic metaphor. Instead they would be recognized as mutually determined and determining.

One example is Ezra Pound's brief lyric, "In a Station of the Metro." This poem concisely juxtaposes a myriad of human faces in an underground railway station with petals flowering against a dark, natural background:

> The apparition of these faces in the crowd;
> Petals on a wet, black bough.[24]

This highly revered imagist poem poses a sharply rendered visual scene, but it should not be forgotten that the lineaments of this scene factor solely upon a visual metaphor that puts human faces and natural flowers, underground platform and darkened tree limb, into co-active perceptual exchange. Moreover, human "faces in the crowd" comprise a 'vehicle' for the appearance or perception of a 'tenor' glimpsed with conciseness and precision: "Petals on a wet, black bough." The strong visual rendering of the metaphoric exchange in the poem pivots upon an event characteristic of modern urban life playing the role of vehicle.

William Wordsworth's figures of the Cumberland Beggar and Leech-Gatherer provide additional, even more subtle, examples.[25] From the perspective of Wordsworth's two participant-narrators, these two old men are isolated from the community of humankind (the world of 'usefulness') and, under this aspect of isolation, each assumes the appearance of something utterly other—blank, helpless, mute, like stones or beasts. Each shows forth the threat of 'uselessness'[26] and solitary silence that lies on the other side of human bonds. The "aged Beggar" sits "in the sun . . . surrounded by those wild unpeopled hills . . . and [eats] his food in solitude" (ll. 1, 12-15). Unlike other human beings, he eats in neither shade nor shelter and without companions and conversation. The Beggar seems to take on properties of the "low structure of rude masonry" upon which he sits (l. 3). And when he walks,

> His staff trails with him; scarcely do his feet
> Disturb the summer dust; he is so still
> In look and motion, that the cottage curs,
> Ere he has passed the door, will turn away,
> Weary of barking at him.
>
> (ll. 59–63)

The Beggar is scarcely animate as he passes through the villages. The Leech-Gatherer also reveals this aspect of estrangement from the human world when he abruptly appears to the participant-narrator of "Resolution and Independence" as "a huge stone" and then in turn "like a sea-beast":

> I saw a Man before me unawares:
> The oldest man he seemed that ever wore grey hairs.
> As a huge stone is sometimes seen to lie
> Couched on the bald top of an eminence;
> Wonder to all who do the same espy,
> By what means it could thither come, and whence;
> So that it seems a thing endued with sense:
> Like a sea-beast crawled forth, that on a shelf
> Of rock or sand reposeth, there to sun itself.
>
> (ll. 55–63)

Thus the two old men appear utterly separated from the ordinary community of humankind, and in this state of isolation their humanity becomes the vehicle for perceiving a tenor taken from the natural world. The most striking quality of the tenor, moreover, is how it stands in contradictory relation to its vehicle—how it makes the human show itself in the aspect of its opposite, of its counterpart, the natural.

The experience of these poems, however, does not conclude with this contradictory display of the inhuman or nonhuman or the otherness of nature in the guise of the human. Even though the Cumberland Beggar and the Leech-Gatherer are marginal or boundary cases of the human, they are nonetheless human, and their humanity insists upon itself even as they are being experienced as something utterly other than human. In the case of the Cumberland Beggar, the narrator participates in and articulates for the reader the precise and particularizing vision that is the Beggar's:

> On the ground
> His eyes are turned, and, as he moves along,

> *They* move along the ground; and, evermore,
> Instead of common and habitual sight
> Of fields with rural works, of hill and dale,
> And the blue sky, one little span of earth
> Is all his prospect.
>
> (ll. 45–51)

This narrow and exacting "prospect" isolates the Beggar's form of vision from the wider prospects of communal humankind, yet it is also the isolation of something very human—the capacity to notice, to single out, to isolate, to see, to participate in, and perhaps even to enjoy—no matter how minutely or insignificantly. This capacity finds a fitting complement in the centrality that the Beggar's lonely and periodic appearances assume in the villagers' capacity to remember and continue their record of "past deeds and offices of charity" (l. 90). These human capacities come to the fore while the Beggar is witnessed *as* something other than human, is seen *as* something other than what the narrator or the villagers can recognize as seeing and acting like themselves. But the Cumberland Beggar is, after all, like them; he can show forth a nonhuman aspect only because the human mode of apprehension is capable of isolating a thing from its wider prospect of interaction and significance. The participant-narrator and the poem's readers are able to see the Cumberland Beggar as the nonhuman or the natural because we share with the Beggar the form of seeing that for him has become so narrowed. Under the pressure of perceptual isolation, a human vehicle can take on an aspect of the natural world as well as vice versa. The figure of the Cumberland Beggar, therefore, comprises a metaphor of the inseparable relation of the natural and the human for our human form of seeing. I believe a similar consideration of the Leech-Gatherer in "Resolution and Independence" could also be made, especially observing the fact that the old man does speak "With something of a lofty utterance drest— / Choice word and measured phrase, above the reach/ Of ordinary men" (ll. 94–96) and the recognition that there exists "so firm a mind" (l. 138) in something that resembles a "sea-beast" (l. 62).

The crucial thing to be pointed out, I believe, is the cognitive functioning of metaphor.[27] The nonhuman appearance of the Cumberland Beggar is a contradiction, but not a contradiction in the logical sense, where one statement opposes or denies the truth-claim of another. It is a contradiction in the experiential or existential sense of the word—a person, a thing, or a situation that contains or is composed of contrary or contradictory elements. In seeing the "aged Beggar" as utterly separate and nonhuman, his person yields two contradictory elements. The experience of metaphor here exhibits a contradiction, a contradictory display. However, in this experience of metaphor as a contradiction, readers can also experience or glimpse the source of such contradiction. Quite expressly, it is a feature of our human mode of apprehension to fuse together, to *con-fuse,* what we call the human and the natural in order to achieve any form of seeing at all. Consequently, we are already in a state of contradiction when we perceive a contradiction, and it is this prior state that produces or composes a particular contradictory perception. The perceptual incongruity of seeing the Cumberland Beggar or the Leech-Gatherer as nonhuman entities is structured by our general perceptual capacity, which confuses within a single experience the human and the natural for us. The contradictory elements of a particular poetic metaphor, that is, are themselves founded upon a human perceptual capacity marked by contradiction, an incongruous fusing together of human and natural realms or categories.[28] The unavoidable reciprocity of this state of cognitive affairs is dramatically brought home when we see a marginal and rather unlikely perceiver like the Cumberland Beggar *as* a poetic metaphor of our human mode of perception.

As I have argued, it is possible to have a metaphor in which the vehicle is a human and the tenor a natural element. The examples of "In a Station of the Metro" and the Cumberland Beggar have shown that I. A. Richards's initial senses of the terms 'vehicle' and 'tenor' as "two thoughts" made "active together" can still be understood as describing two equally co-active elements in the experience of poetic metaphor. Indeed, poetic metaphor cannot be said to privilege or intend systematically one of its elements over the other. Human and natural, tenor and vehicle, do not pair off into rigorous asymmetrical dichotomies. They are terms of modest analytical convenience that help factor out the co-active elements of poetic metaphors, which may in one instance present a natural element as vehicle and a human element as tenor and in another instance present a natural element as tenor and a human element as vehicle.

However, the example of the Cumberland Beggar has carried the argument further and shown that the co-active elements of a metaphor are indeed co-active in a particular way. Two elements stand opposed or contradictory to one another, because our perceptual capacity itself appears rooted in contradiction. In order to see distinctly the melancholy and lonely composure of a black crow in autumn or the isolation and estrangement of a silent Beggar, a perceiver has already confused inextricably in the one experience human and natural aspects or elements. Likewise, feeling the capacity of the heart to attend to its own rhythms lovingly seems intimately confused with the unwanted generosity of a "bowl of red blooms." Poetic metaphors compose intimately contradictory recognitions of our human capacity to see, feel, and understand that which is not ourselves but upon which our very human powers of cognition and recognition generously, naturally, entirely depend. Analysis can help distinguish to some critical satisfaction the co-active elements of metaphoric experience, yet particular experiences of poetic metaphors keep pointing us back toward the generative matrix of perceptual contradiction.

An avenue is now open for seeing ways in which metaphor, metonymy, and synonymity—which in the discussion of Brooke-Rose's *A Grammar of Metaphor* were recognized as sharing the same grammatical types—differ conceptually from one another. Instead of a contradictory exchange between two elements as in metaphor, the contiguity of two elements or attributes characterizes metonymy. The nature of this metonymic relationship has been explored most notably by Roman Jakobson (see note 3). For example, the metonymic association between the words *hut* and *thatch* is best described as semantically contiguous; one word is conceptually associated with or suggests the other. Metonymic associations embrace grammatical substitutions among words and phrases that are semantically interdependent and conceptually approximate. It is possible to locate weaker metaphors and similes on a conceptual continuum leading from the process of metaphor at one end to the process of metonymy at the other. Metaphors can be said to lose force or brisk instructive power once they begin to gravitate toward analogy, comparison, and approximation. Synonymity, in the meantime, involves a more or less equivalent or similitudinous exchange between the meanings and uses of two words or phrases in ordinary discourse. For example, the words and phrases 'hut,' 'hovel,' 'shack, 'cabin,' and 'one-room wooden shelter with a thatched roof' are syntactically and semantically similitudinous. In contrast, 'burrow' is a word that does not belong in this series of synonyms because semantically it stands in a contrastive or contrary relation to the word 'hut'; animals dig out and inhabit burrows, whereas humans construct huts. 'Hovel' is a synonym for 'hut,' but 'burrow' is a metaphor. (I relate similitude, which is often associated with metaphor, to an entirely different process.) Synonymity comprises the linguistic operation for broadening expressive power and achieving fineness of expressive nuance.

## III

To accept my cognitive claim concerning metaphor as contradiction is not to conclude that metaphor (or rhetorical figuration generally) becomes the metaphysical error that Jacques Derrida and

Paul de Man have maintained it can be. Derrida's notion of 'metaphoricality' and de Man's peculiar uses of the 'trope' of 'metaphor' and the 'text' of 'rhetoric' collectively point to an ambivalence supposedly latent in the concepts 'metaphor' and 'rhetoric.'[29] The terms double back upon themselves because, in the search for absolutely authoritative forms of knowledge, Derrida and de Man detect inevitable duplicity in the figural language of philosophical and literary texts. According to them, literary use of and intellectual dependence upon figural language purportedly conceal the mutual self-destruction or deconstruction that takes place between the structure and the signification of every trope. The meaning that is supposed to be communicated by a trope such as metaphor they see as already anticipated by the structure of the trope. Thus, the use or the performance of figural language is exposed as redundant and illusory. The structure of every trope, moreover, signifies one of several fundamental oppositions—such as inner *versus* outer or space *versus* time—that are associated with a suspect literary or philosophical tradition. Presumably, the decoding of rhetorical language (deconstruction) dispels the illusion fostered by naive readers that meaning is constructed or achieved in discourse. Such rhetorical reading exposes a code of static oppositions that purports to constitute discourse, static oppositions grounded in nothing but the very discourse from which they emerge. The operation of figural language thus actually masks conceptual paralysis, a rigorous loss of meaning ordained and predetermined by the duplicitous nature of 'metaphor' and 'rhetoric'.

For both Derrida and de Man, irony is the tool for deconstructing the illusion of coherence and continuity that figural language weaves over its own paralysis. Both the condition of illusion and the strategic use of irony to expose the condition toward which figural language tempts us find their pretext in Nietzsche's "On Truth and Falsity in Their Ultramoral Sense." Nietzsche asserts that "truths are illusions of which one has forgotten that they *are* illusions; worn-out metaphors which have become powerless to affect the senses."[30] The unrelentingly passionate and rigorously analytic tool of ironic wit and reasoning deconstructs the duplicitous impulses and metaphors to which we are heir. Nietzsche's use of irony to reveal the lies beneath human impulses, metaphors, and truths as well as Derrida's and de Man's use of irony to unmask the duplicitous and ungrounded status of metaphor and rhetoric, however, conceal another mode of irony.

On the one hand, deconstructive irony is a tool of thought, of intellection or reflectivity; it studies and appraises constructions of thought *according to the law of contradiction*.[31] If a construction of thought disobeys this law in an attempt to establish a coherent figure or a conceptually consistent discourse, deconstructive irony faults the construction by rendering it impossible or undecidable—that is, by rending it at its 'rational' seams. Derrida, for example, strives to do precisely this task in "White Mythology" by detecting contradictory conceptual fault lines that philosophical discourse concerning metaphor from Aristotle onward seeks to obscure within its own unexamined metaphorics.[32] However, deconstructive irony cannot explain the existence of the ungrounded status of metaphor and rhetoric. It merely demonstrates the illusion of coherence and consistency that a discourse is capable of constructing. What deconstructive irony fails to articulate comprises another mode of irony—indeed, one that functions according to a different principle than the law of contradiction.[33]

I propose to call this other mode of irony experiential or aesthetic irony. Aesthetic irony *exhibits the contradiction* that structures aesthetic experience—namely, the simultaneous separating and blending of the experiencer and the experienced, human agents and phenomena. We are not able to probe behind aesthetic irony in some radically skeptical or deconstructive manner. Moreover, the notion of aesthetic irony may be a way of conceptualizing the source of that "mode of poetic knowing," of "discovering power," that Walker Percy attributes to "the cognitive dimension of metaphor." Percy notes that this dimension of metaphor "is usually overlooked" because cognition is all too often not identified with poetry and "poetic knowing." Quite persuasively, Percy argues that the peculiarities and function of metaphor constitute "a special case of that mysterious 'error' which is the very condition of our knowing anything at all." This "error" is "the act of symbolization" from which the categories of mental activity and the particular qualities of phenomena can be recovered, but only after the fact, only after they are discovered powerfully in a moment of aesthetic experience.[34] In other words, poetic metaphors provide a primary mode for our human experience of natural phenomena. Metaphors shape experience in advance of rational categories for experience and rules for the construction (and deconstruction) of discourses about experience and phenomena. A poetic metaphor yields a transgressively instructive error within current capabilities of human cognitive understanding from which we can learn by articulating and explaining the contradictory pathways of the errant recognition.

For example, Percy cites an ordinary yet extraordinarily rich metaphor from the American South of not so many years ago:

> In Mississippi, the coin record players, which are manufactured by Seeburg, are commonly known to Negroes as seabirds. . . .

> When the Mississippi Negro calls the Seeburg record player a *seabird*, it is not enough to say that he is making a mistake. It is also not enough to say that he is making a colorful and poetic contribution to language. It is less than useless to say that in calling a machine a bird he is regressing into totemism, etc. And it is not even accurate to say that he knows what the thing is and then gives it a picturesque if far-fetched name. In some fashion or other, he conceives the machine under the symbol *seabird*, a fashion, moreover, in regard to which we must be wary in applying the words "right" or "wrong," "poetic" or "discursive," etc. Certainly the machine is not a seabird and no one imagines that it is, whatever the semanticists may say. Yet we make a long cast and guess that in conceiving it as a *seabird*, the namer conceives it with richer overtones of meaning, and in some sense neither literal or figurative, even as being more truly what it is than under its barbarous title, Seeburg automatic coin record player.[35]

Percy collapses both racist and conventionally rationalist ways of dismissing or defusing the instructive force of this nominative metaphor that substitutes an unusual tenor garnered from the natural world for the name of a vehicle constructed to operate as a useful device within human communities. He clearly recognizes the conceptual overdetermination at stake in the verbal interaction ("the namer conceives it with richer overtones of meaning"). This errant, mistaken metaphor of the seabird/Seeburg wryly, succinctly puns on desires simultaneously expressed and curtailed within ordinary lives of Afro-Americans: the desire for flight, escape, liberation akin to the range of a seabird capable of leaving Mississippi landfall at will, and the constriction of such desires to machines, coins, records, and the few hours daily or weekly in which 'flight' is mediated by music and the companionship it makes. What appears arguably an error in language and cognition can function as a clue to experience. Metaphors indeed are errors that can disclose the experiential contradictions in which we dwell and by which our aesthetic experience and cultural desires achieve their shape.

In place of Walker Percy's notion of "error," however, I propose the more formal concept of aesthetic irony. Aesthetic irony functions, I would like to suggest, rather like Kant's Transcendental Aesthetic; the synthetic cognitions, such as poetic metaphors, constructed within the cognitive field of our experience resist radical skepticism because they embody the materials and motives that shape the possibility of experience and understanding for our human way of knowing.[36] The real service of deconstructive irony would be to collapse in dialectical fashion the romances and allegories that subvert, deny, or rewrite the experiential contradiction (Percy's "error") that is aesthetic irony. Indeed, aesthetic irony can be seen as a constitutive principle of aesthetic experience, while deconstructive irony functions as its regulative principle. The epistemological error and unwitting irony of Derrida and de Man would be their conflation, perhaps disfiguration, of two distinctive modes of irony.[37]

So to the contention that the concepts 'metaphor' and 'rhetoric' are metaphysical errors, I would counter that aesthetic irony establishes the realm of 'metaphoricality' as a fully inhabitable one for human beings.[38] The work of cognitive linguists such as George Lakoff and Mark Johnson has ably and amply demonstrated the conceptual primacy and effectivity of both everyday and poetic metaphors. Indeed, Lakoff's and Johnson's researches afford pragmatic inquiries into the contingencies of Western philosophical and literary critical speculations regarding the nature of metaphor. Metaphor is not so much a metaphysical error as an experiential and cognitive *gestalt* so basic to our ways of knowing that it makes no sense to imperil, however rigorously, its instructive recognitions.[39] The deconstructive specter of an absolute ground for a rigorously analytic mode of discourse is, I believe, a false and misleading ideal. In general, Derrida and de Man share this quest for an illusive ground for discursive constructions with the logical positivists. The latter seize upon it as a positive goal or *telos*, while the former are equally, and nostalgically, dependent on that illusion, even though their dependence is expressed in an obsessive deflation of all assertions.[40]

## IV

In conclusion, the examples of the Cumberland Beggar and the Leech-Gatherer have intimated that the incongruity witnessed in the experience of poetic metaphor is structured within our human perceptual capacity, one that characteristically confuses the human and the natural. Contradiction composes our perceptions, and metaphor provides an exemplary way of attending to the process that makes aesthetic experience possible. Yet what we glimpse in the experience of metaphor is not some absolute ground for metaphor whose mechanics happen to favor contradiction. Poetic metaphor offers its own activity as its necessary and sufficient ground. My distinction between aesthetic and deconstructive irony helps to support this claim.

## Notes

1. Jacques Derrida, "White Mythology: Metaphor in the Text of Philosophy," trans. F. C. T. Moore, *New Literary History* 6 (1974): 27–28. This essay originally appeared as "La mythologie blanche," *Poetique* 5 (1971): 1–52. The parenthetical phrase in Derrida's footnote is not found in the original French; it is apparently the translator's clarification or elaboration of Derrida's phrasing: "Le sens, le vouloir-dire [meaning] . . ." (16 n. 22). Another translation of the same essay can be found in Jacques Derrida, *Margins of Philosophy*, trans. Alan Bass (Chicago: University of Chicago Press, 1982), pp. 207–71; see especially p. 228.

    I am grateful to Irving Massey for his helpful reading of earlier versions of this essay. My thesis develops from earlier work in Brian Caraher and Irving Massey, ed., *Literature and Contradiction* (Buffalo: State University of New York, 1974). See also Irving Massey, *The Gaping Pig* (Berkeley: University of California Press, 1976), pp. 146–49.

2. Among the wealth of recent scholarship on the topic of metaphor in literature and philosophy, five incisive studies of the cognitive dimensions of metaphors should be cited. My argument here, however, will take the cognitive import of poetic metaphor in a different direction. See Paul Ricoeur, *The Rule of Metaphor: Multi-disciplinary Studies of the Creation of Meaning in Language*, trans. Robert Czerny (Toronto: University of Toronto Press, 1977); Eva Feder Kittay, *Metaphor: Its Cognitive Force and Linguistic Structure* (Oxford: Clarendon Press, 1987); Charles O. Hartman, "Cognitive Metaphor," *New Literary History*, 13 (1982): 327–39; Stephen David Ross, "Metaphor, the Semasic Field, and Inexhaustibility," *New Literary History*, 18 (1987): 517–33; and Richard Moran, "Seeing and Believing: Metaphor, Image, and Force," *Critical Inquiry* 16 (1989): 87–112.

3. Christine Brooke-Rose, *A Grammar of Metaphor* (London: Secker and Warburg, 1958), p. 3; subsequently referred to as *GM*, with page numbers in parentheses.

    It is difficult to make a clear and categorical distinction between metaphors in ordinary language and in literature. Neither Brooke-Rose nor any of the other writers I will discuss in this essay successfully draws this distinction. However, I would like to limit the field of generalization for my remarks to metaphors appearing in poetic texts—namely, what I call "poetic metaphor." I do this for convenience as well as to preclude the seemingly endless dilemma of 'live' versus 'dead' metaphors.

4. On p. 20, Brooke-Rose cites a number of previous attempts at linguistic analysis of metaphor, most of them dating from the late nineteenth and early twentieth centuries, with one dating from the thirteenth.

    Some more recent and more systematic work on the linguistic analysis of metaphor is represented by Jakobson's famous essay "Aphasia: The Metaphoric and Metonymic Poles," in Roman Jakobson and Morris Halle, *Fundamentals of Language* (The Hague: Mouton, 1971, 2nd rev. ed.), and by Tzvetan Todorov in "On Linguistic Synbolism," *New Literary History* 6 (1974): 111–34. Both Jakobson and Todorov assume that a rigorous analysis of discourse ("symbolic process" or "linguistic symbolism," respectively) will yield a precise location for metaphor within a system or network of binary linguistic oppositions. Extralinguistic and nonsystemic considerations are ruled out, although Todorov makes certain gestures toward historical and diachronic qualifications of his abstract and synchronic schemata (Todorov, 129–34). Umberto Eco ("Metaphor, Dictionary, and Encyclopedia," *New Literary History*, 15 [1984]: 255–71) and Michael Cabot Haley (*The Semeiosis of Poetic Metaphor* [Bloomington: Indiana University Press, 1988]) offer two versions of a semiotic theory of metaphor circumscribed by systemic models of signification and communication.

A very useful essay on the linguistic analysis of metaphor is Derek Bickerton, "Prolegomena to a Linguistic Theory of Metaphor," *Foundations of Language* 5 (1969): 34–52. Bickerton indicates the embedded and inescapable difficulties linguistic theories of metaphor derived from generative grammar and from semiology will encounter. As an alternative, he details a more adequate model for a semantic system and that system's processes of metaphor. Notably, this model calls for the recognition of a extralingual system of attribute-assignment specific to every natural language; this system, empirically observed, is neither rigidly synchronic nor exclusively diachronic.

5. This example is suggested by a simpler one—"man's prime as 'in full bloom'"—found in Aristotle's *Rhetoric* III, 11 (1411b) (Grube trans.). See Samuel R. Levin, "Aristotle's Theory of Metaphor," *Philosophy and Rhetoric*, 15 (1982): 24–46, for a conceptual exposition and defense of Aristotle's remarks on metaphor.

6. In "The Apprehension of Metaphor," *Language and Style* 14 (1981): 20–33, Timothy Crusius and W. Ross Winterowd attempt to move beyond Brooke-Rose's grammatical analysis of metaphors into a generative grammar of metaphor. They maintain "that in their deep structure, all metaphors are equitives, equational structures having the abstract form *A is B*" (p. 22). Their extensive analyses of nouns and nominative and adjectival phrases, though, still make it difficult to distinguish their "deep structure" for metaphor from predication as well as synonymity.

7. I. A. Richards, *The Philosophy of Rhetoric* (New York: Oxford University Press, 1965; orig. pub. 1936), pp. 5f; subsequently referred to as *PR*, with page numbers in parentheses.

8. Some of the most insightful and useful work in the area of context, linguistic behavior, and meaning has been carried out by Ludwig Wittgenstein, J. L. Austin, and John Searle in their various investigations of language-games and speech-acts. See especially John R. Searle, "Metaphor," in Andrew Ortony, ed., *Metaphor and Thought* (Cambridge: Cambridge University Press, 1979), pp. 92–123. Marcus B. Hester, *The Meaning of Poetic Metaphor* (The Hague: Mouton & Co., 1967), offers an analysis of imagery and metaphoric seeing in the light of Wittgenstein's theory of meaning as use.

9. When theorizing about symbolic and metaphoric dimensions of discourse, representational theories of meaning or signification postulate 'proper'

meanings for words or signs. As a number of commentators have noticed, this is a thoroughly suspect strategy. See Derek Bickerton, pp. 36–38 and Jonathan Culler, "Commentary," *New Literary History* 6 (1974): 220–22. Notably, in "White Mythology," Derrida develops, within his interpretation of Aristotle's passages on metaphor and rhetoric, a distinction between "proper" and "figurative" senses of words (46–55). As Culler notes (221), Derrida uses the distinction only in order to destroy it, to show the impossibility of "proper" senses or meanings of words. See Derrida, *Of Grammatology*, trans. Gayatri C. Spivak (Baltimore: Johns Hopkins University Press, 1976), pp. 270–80, for a similar deconstructive maneuver regarding proper sense and metaphor in the text of Rousseau.
10. For some related arguments, see Israel Scheffler, *Beyond the Letter: A Philosophical Inquiry into Ambiguity, Vagueness and Metaphor in Language* (Boston: Routledge & Kegan Paul, 1979).
11. Max Black has developed an "interaction view" of metaphor that is indebted to Richards' work. See Max Black, "Metaphor," *Models and Metaphors: Studies in Language and Philosophy* (Ithaca: Cornell University Press, 1962), pp. 25–47, and "More about Metaphor," in Andrew Ortony, ed., *Metaphor and Thought*, pp. 19–43.
12. Some forty years after the initial publication of *The Philosophy of Rhetoric* Richards discussed tenor and vehicle in terms compatible with his original introduction of them. See I. A. Richards, *Complementaries*, ed. J. P. Russo (Cambridge, Mass.: Harvard University Press, 1976), pp. 116–18.
13. Philip Wheelwright, *Metaphor and Reality* (Bloomington: Indiana University Press, 1962), p. 55. See also Laurence Perrine, "Four Forms of Metaphor," *College English* 33 (1971): 125–38.
14. Nobuyuki Yuasa, "Introduction" to Bashō, *The Narrow Road to the Deep North and Other Travel Sketches*, trans. N. Yuasa (Baltimore: Penguin Books, 1966), p. 26. Yuasa's introduction is quite informative, especially with regard to the historical development of *haiku* technique and aesthetics and Bashō's distinctive practice within and enrichment of this development.
15. Ibid., p. 33. In his introduction, Yuasa indicates at length in at least two places that Bashō's principle of poetic composition entails a feelingful interaction of self and object, internal and external, subjective and objective (pp. 33–34, 42–43). Thus, Bashō's conception of the process of poetic composition reflects the same context that governs the reading of the completed poem.
16. This situation should be distinguished from personification and the pathetic fallacy. Human attributes and emotions are not projected or displaced upon the black crow. The figure of the crow neither personifies the poet (or the poet's state of mind) nor shoulders the pathos of the human. The poetically rendered action of the bird figures forth co-actively the poetic act of composure; a metaphoric relation is enacted between a singular event in nature and the human who scavenges for embodiments of temporal repose.

In general John Ruskin's notion of the pathetic fallacy betrays an anxiety concerning the boundaries of fact and feeling, natural event and human pathos. Ruskin projects suspicion regarding poetic metaphors and their cognitive import and tends to privilege poetic similes and analogies. The latter kinds of figural speech declare clear lines of comparison and thereby maintain a sharper border between "the pure fact" and "habits of thought." See John Ruskin, "Of the Pathetic Fallacy," *Selections and Essays*, ed. F. W. Roe (New York: Charles Scribners Sons, 1918), pp. 114–30, especially pp. 122–23.

17. In a passage that argues against a conventional theory of metaphor, Paul Ricoeur notes an interesting peculiarity in classical rhetoric: "Est-ce par hasard si régulièrement revient, sous l'apparence d'un exemple, le transfert l'inanimé à l'animé?" (Is it an accident if regularly we receive, under the appearance of an example, the transfer of the inanimate to the animate?) Paul Ricoeur, *La metaphore vive* (Paris: Editions du Seuil, 1975), p. 366. I am grateful to Irving Massey for drawing my attention to this passage.

    Christine Brooke-Rose notes that the study of the relationship of animate and inanimate in the process of metaphor is the best of the alternatives to her linguistic approach to metaphor. In the first chapter of *A Grammar of Metaphor*, she divides the methods of writing on metaphor into two broad groups—the "philosophical approach" and the "linguistic approach." Generally speaking, the philosophical approach attends to the mental process of metaphor and analyzes by "idea-content" whereas the linguistic approach disregards such questions and "cut[s] right across these categories by considering the syntactic groups on which metaphor must, willy-nilly, be based" (*GM*, 3, 16). There are four subdivisions within the philosophical approach, and "the most constructive of the four main classifications by mental process is, from my point of view, that which concentrates on the animate-inanimate relationship, though it is barely developed. The verb metaphor animates, by transferring to an object an action not normally associated with it; and many noun metaphors, as I hope to show, have a strong element of activity and 'bring the thing before the eyes in action,' as Aristotle would say" (*GM*, 15).

18. Bickerton, pp. 50–51. The categories Bickerton describes apply to the processes of metaphor for the English language in general and not strictly to the appearance of poetic metaphors.

19. Sylvia Plath, *Ariel* (New York: Harper & Row, 1966), p. 12; *The Complete Poems*, ed. Ted Hughes (New York: Harper & Row, 1981), p. 162.

20. Louise Glück, *The House on Marshland* (New York: The Ecco Press, 1975), p. 3.

21. Dylan Thomas, *The Poems of Dylan Thomas*, ed. Daniel Jones (New York: New Directions, 1971), p. 77.

22. Edward Lear, *The Owl and the Pussy-Cat and Other Verses*, ed. Roberta Sewal (New York: The Mulberry Press, n.d.), pp. 33–35.

23. See, for instance, Irving Massey, "Two Types of Visual Metaphor," *Criticism* 19 (1977), especially p. 286, and Samuel T. Coleridge, *Notebooks* (New York: Pantheon, 1961), 2, entry 2441.

24. Ezra Pound, *Personae*, rev. ed. (New York: New Directions, 1990), p. 111.

25. William Wordsworth, "The Old Cumberland Beggar" and "Resolution and Independence," *Poetical Works*, ed. Thomas Hutchinson, rev. ed. Ernest

De Selincourt (London: Oxford University Press, 1936), pp. 443–45, 155–57. Citations will be made by noting line numbers in parentheses.

26. See line 67 of "The Old Cumberland Beggar," the first line of the narrator's injunction to and lesson for his audience: "But deem not this Man useless."
27. With regard to narratives and textual webs of metaphor, metaphors function within a narrative context by articulating through figures the forces or tensions that are subliminal or motive in that context. Arbitrary or context-free metaphors lack the power to move a potential experiencer because one is not led into an experience but merely shown ideas. Even the shock value or effect such an idea may have in conversation, for instance, depends upon setting some sort of situation for its exhibition. To go any further along these lines would require the development of a rhetoric of metaphor, a study of how metaphor helps shape discourses and narratives.
28. In a slightly different vein, the role of mental images in perception in Hume, Kant, Wordsworth, and others is argued by Mary Warnock, *Imagination* (Berkeley: University of California Press, 1976). Warnock discusses at length the intimate and inseparable connections between imagination and perception, images and percepts. One of her conclusions is that "imagination is our means of interpreting the world, and it is *also* our means of forming images in the mind. The images themselves are not separate from our interpretations of the world; they are our way of thinking of the objects in the world. We see the forms in our mind's eye and we see these very forms in the world. We could not do one of these things if we could not do the other" (p. 194).
29. Jacques Derrida, "White Mythology," p. 64 and pp. 47–74 in general; Paul de Man, "Semiology and Rhetoric," *Diacritics* III, 3 (1973): 27–33; de Man, "Action and Identity in Nietzsche," *Yale French Studies* 52 (1975): 16–30; de Man, "The Epistemology of Metaphor," *Critical Inquiry* 5 (1978): 13–30; and de Man, *Allegories of Reading: Figural Language in Rousseau, Nietzsche, Rilke, and Proust* (New Haven: Yale University Press, 1979), especially pp. 3–56, 103–131, 147–59.
30. Friedrich Nietzsche, "On Truth and Falsity in Their Ultramoral Sense," *Works*, ed. Oscar Levy (New York: Russell & Russell, 1964), II, p. 180.
31. See Jan Lukasiewicz on the principle of contradiction in Book Gamma of Aristotle's *Metaphysics*. He maintains that the principle of contradiction has "no logical worth" but yields instead "*a practical-ethical value*"; that is, it cannot get at first principles but it can keep us from making errors in thinking and argumentation. Jan Lukasiewicz, "On the Principle of Contradiction in Aristotle," trans. Vernon Wedin, *The Review of Metaphysics* 24 (1971): 508; emphasis is in the text.

See also Immanuel Kant, *Critique of Pure Reason* (trans. F. Max Müller [Garden City: Doubleday, 1966], p. 129) on the principle of contradiction as the highest principle of all analytic judgments: "The principle of contradiction is the general and altogether sufficient principle of all analytical knowledge, though beyond this its authority and utility, as a sufficient criterion of truth, must not be allowed to extend. For the fact that no knowledge can run counter to that principle, without destroying itself, makes it no doubt a *conditio sine qua non*, but never the determining reason of the truth of our knowledge."

32. Derrida, "White Mythology," especially pp. 28–31.
33. Richard Rorty has also recognized the operation of two modes of irony within the "increasingly ironist culture" of the West—namely, the "private irony" of metaphysical relativism (such as deconstruction and anti-foundationalism) and the "liberal irony" of public hope and human solidarity. See Rorty, *Contingency, Irony, and Solidarity* (Cambridge: Cambridge University Press, 1989), especially pp. 73–95.
34. Walker Percy, "Metaphor as Mistake," *The Sewanee Review* 66 (1958): 93, 98. This essay is reprinted without substantial change in Walker Percy, *The Message in the Bottle* (New York: Farrar, Straus and Giroux, 1975), pp. 64–82.
35. Ibid., pp. 81, 83.
36. Immediately following the sentences on the law of contradiction quoted in note 31, Kant declares the inapplicability of this law to synthetic *a priori* cognitions: "Now, as in our present enquiry we are chiefly concerned with the synthetical part of our knowledge, we must no doubt take great care never to offend against that inviolable principle [the law of contradiction], but we ought never to expect from it any help with regard to the truth of this kind of knowledge." Kant continues: "The determining reason of the truth of our knowledge" rests with "the synthetical part of our knowledge," and this form of knowledge cannot be probed or judged according to the principle of contradiction. This synthetical knowledge is given "objective reality" solely and necessarily by *"the possibility of experience."* However, Kant argues that experience "depends on the synthetical unity of phenomena"; and without this synthetical unity, experience "would not even be knowledge, but only a rhapsody of perceptions, which would never grow into a connected text according to the rules of an altogether coherent (possible) consciousness, nor into a transcendental and necessary unit of apperception" (Kant, pp. 129, 131–32; Kant's italics).
37. In "The Rhetoric of Blindness: Jacques Derrida's Reading of Rousseau" (*Blindness and Insight* [New York: Oxford University Press, 1971], pp. 102–41, Paul de Man argues that Rousseau was already aware of the "blind spots" or contradictions that Derrida finds in him. My point is not so much that an author is or is not conscious of contradictions as that his or her basic procedures with regard to poetic metaphor, in particular, and rhetoric, in general, necessitate contradiction. For a vigorous exposition of the thesis that contradiction is the constitutive principle of art, see chapters 5–10 of L. S. Vygotsky, *The Psychology of Art*, trans. Scripta Technica, Inc. (Cambridge: Massachusetts Institute of Technology Press, 1971), pp. 89–239. Vygotsky presents four chapters of analyses of aesthetic reaction to works, from fable to tragedy, and he reviews other theories and develops his own formula in the other two chapters. He concludes that "contradiction is the essential feature of artistic form and material" and that it is "the essential part of aesthetic response" (p. 217).

38. Research in the social anthropology of metaphor and rhetoric helps support materially and empirically this claim regarding the embeddedness and cognitive work of tropes in human cultures. See, for instance, the seven essays collected in J. David Sapir and J. Christopher Crocker, ed., *The Social Use of Metaphor: Essays on the Anthropology of Rhetoric* (Philadelphia: University of Pennsylvania Press, 1977) and James W. Fernandez, *Persuasions and Performances: The Play of Tropes in Culture* (Bloomington: Indiana University Press, 1986), especially pp. 28–70.
39. See George Lakoff and Mark Johnson, "Conceptual Metaphor in Everyday Language," *The Journal of Philosophy* 77 (1980): 453–86; *Metaphors We Live By* (Chicago: University of Chicago Press, 1980); and *More Than Cool Reason: A Field Guide to Poetic Metaphor* (Chicago: University of Chicago Press, 1989). See also Lakoff's *Women, Fire and Dangerous Things* (Chicago: University of Chicago Press, 1987).
40. I explore at length the positivist paradigm that Paul de Man's work assumes only in order to deconstruct it in two essays: "*Allegories of Reading:* Positing a Rhetoric of Romanticism: or, Paul de Man's Critique of Pure Figural Anteriority," *Pre/Text* 4, 1 (Spring 1983): 9–51; and "Recovering the Figure of J. L. Austin in Paul de Man's *Allegories of Reading*," in Hugh J. Silverman and Gary E. Aylesworth, ed., *The Textual Sublime: Deconstruction and Its Differences* (Albany: State University of New York Press, 1990), pp.139–46, 240–43.

# 7

# *Contradiction and Repression: Paradox in Fictional Narration*

## Richard Kuhns

*The firmest of all first principles is that it is impossible for the same thing to belong and not to belong to the same thing at the same time in the same respect.*
—Aristotle, Metaphysics B, 2 (996b, 26–30)

*. . . exemption from mutual contradiction is a characteristic of the system Ucs.*
—Sigmund Freud, "The Unconscious"

*Truth is like a thrashing-machine; tender sensibilities must keep out of the way.*
—Herman Melville, The Confidence Man

Contradiction and repression may seem concepts odd to be conjoined, yet they do belong to theories whose interconnection it will be worthwhile to study. One way to do that, I propose, is through the claims to truth made by fictional narrations. My procedure will be to examine contradiction and repression in their theoretical settings, and then to analyze the ways in which they underlie a set of paradoxes propounded by a fictional text, *The Confidence Man*, by Herman Melville. That strange story demonstrates how the two forces—for so they are in that setting, though one a property of sentences, the other a property of psychic conflict—interinanimate one another when they work in the shaping of sentences the truth or falsity of which we are challenged to determine. Although contradiction and repression conceptually belong to deeply differing theories about the logic of thought, the text I have chosen will help us to position the concepts toward one another, and the concepts, as they have received logical and psychological explication, will help us to understand the text in its demand for a determination of truth or falsity.

## I

A basic discovery in the logic of discourse was the familiar and traditional paradox of the liar. In its simplest form it is the assertion that 'All Cretans are liars' is a sentence which, when uttered by a Cretan, must be false if true and true if false. The undecidability of truth and falsehood as properties of the meanings of sentences has since the earliest recordings of logical disputes been seen as a puzzle and a tribulation. Its recurrent analysis in the history of philosophy establishes its importance, if perhaps also the impotence of philosophers. Whatever the underlying conditions for the persistence of this perplexity, it has received two recent treatments that continue to suggest means to a deeper understanding of the paradox.

Although the views offered by Bertrand Russell are no longer considered logically compelling, they do reveal beliefs about meaning in contexts that have a bearing on narrative texts. I therefore take his way of resolving paradox as insightful for purposes quite other than his, which many today consider somewhat lacking in logical sophistication. Yet one finds Russell's views still widely shared: that sentences carry tags of 'true' and 'false' and 'meaningless,' and if one knew enough and could be cleansed of confusion, one could utter only true sentences. If a person were to achieve such clarity, he would be transparently clear about a condition that is usually confused and often leads to uncontrollable paradox; the logical name given this condition Russell simply took over from the tradition, the paradox of the liar.

In his discussion of "object language" in Chapter 4 of *An Inquiry Into Meaning and Truth*,[1] Russell argued that in order to avoid the paradox of the liar, we must introduce into language the idea of a "hierarchy of languages," for without that we cannot understand how to use terms such as 'true' and 'false.' If we ask, "Are these sentences true or false?"—a question asked of particular assertions, claims, descriptions—we cannot understand the answer given in some cases unless we understand and use the structure of a hierarchy of languages. Thus, if I assert, "I am telling a lie of order $n$," I am telling a lie, to be sure, but a lie of order $n+1$. For me to say that a sentence I utter is a lie, I must be able to talk about that sentence with other sentences whose standing in the hierarchy of languages is 'above' the sentence I uttered. When I say, "I am lying," that sentence is really *about* the sentence I have already uttered. If the sentence I uttered is exactly the sentence, "I am lying," then I am generating the paradox of the liar, but at the same time resolving the paradox insofar as I understand that what I am doing is talking about sentences.

"The hierarchy," Russell wrote, "must extend upwards indefinitely, but not downwards, since if it did, language could never get started. There must, therefore, be a language of lowest type." Russell called this "the object language" or "the primary language."[2]

Problems arise when we think about Russell's "object language." For example, shall we hold that there is an identifiable object language in texts of narrative fiction? In stories such as *The Confidence Man*, just as in natural language of everyday speech and the logical languages of philosophical reflections on language, Russell's theory would say that there is a base from which the levels of language rise. But as soon as that is said, there is a problem that obtrudes: in both natural everyday language and literary narrative language, there seems to be an obverse hierarchy, or—if we can call it that—a hierarchy *downwards*. I am referring to the common idea that where there are presented sentences, there are very often hidden or latent meanings that are 'under' or 'below' the given sentences. Thus, as we view language in use, we might say that there are hierarchies in the service of truth-falsehood, the upward-moving hierarchies, and there are hierarchies in the service of meaning, the downward-moving hierarchies. It appears that we think about sentences and their meaning and their truth conditions in terms of a double pyramid with the apexes joined at the sentence in question. Thus, given any sentence, we can think of it as belonging to two hierarchies. Let us say tentatively that the upper pyramid is concerned with the danger of, and resolution of, contradiction; the lower pyramid is concerned with repression.

I introduce the notion of primary language with hierarchical extension upward and downward in order to compose a model for fictional narration. And because the resolution of paradox, such as the liar, solves only a limited problem, and because meaning in fictional narration involves us in many issues of understanding, the other issues have to be cared for. One persistent issue is the determination of inferred meanings that follow from interpretation of the text. Among those meanings are those that, in psychoanalytic terms, are 'repressed'—that is, they are held back from clear conscious articulation by a force that keeps them in the unconscious. What the reason for this is constitutes one of the psychoanalytic theoretical theses, and I shall return to it later.

The hierarchy upward that helps us determine the truth/falsity of statements and to avoid paradox, and the hierarchy downwards that helps us determine meanings are endowed by us as interpreters with an interesting common structure. Each begins with the assumption that the primary language possesses affirmative sentences, and that negation, when it occurs, is defined in terms of affirmation. Once again I turn to Russell for a statement of this condition as it is attributed to the primary language and the hierarchy upward. Although the conditions specified by Russell would be rejected today by many logicians, his way of construing denoting terms has peculiar and revealing affinities to psychological theories about meaning that were being developed about the same time as the theory of denoting was proposed. What I take to be revealing is a belief—actually psychological rather than logical in origin—about how we use language to describe the world. I shall read Russell as holding beliefs about sentences and events which reflect widely held assumptions about the function of negation in descriptions of reality.

In his analysis of denoting phrases, Russell argued that there is a logical and a psychological relationship among the three most common and important denoting terms, a relationship that must be brought into logical transparency if we are to advance our understanding of linguistic structure. Russell proposed that we take as basic a sentence the truth of which is affirmed, and one that implies there are no exceptions to its claim. Thus we begin our connection to the world with the basic denoting term 'everything.'

The terms 'nothing' and 'something' are then to be defined in terms of 'everything.' Russell offers the following definitions: the terms 'nothing' and 'something' are to be related to 'everything' in this way—that to be able to use the term 'nothing' correctly I must understand that " 'X is false' is always true." To use the denoting term 'something', I must understand that "It is false that 'X is false' is always true." I want to emphasize the psychological implications of these construals. The predicate "is true" is given logical primacy because of a psychological disposition that we stand to the world in a stance of affirmation, and although we may think it rather Pickwickian to translate all denoting terms into a version of 'everything', by so doing we achieve logical clarity in terms of psychological conditions that do dominate our language because of the affirmative assumptions we bring to the world.

Russell's way of dealing with denoting terms that introduce negation is curiously like Freud's way of dealing with negation. Psychoanalytic theory also argues for the affirmative form of sentences in the primary language. Freud, like Russell, believes that negation and the use of the predicate "is false" is parasitic upon affirmation and the use of the predicate "is true." On the basis of clinical practice, Freud observed that when we want to assign truth to sentences we often begin with a language higher up in the hierarchy than the primary language of immediate description. We say: "It is not such-and-such a thing I am referring to." Or, "I do not mean that . . ." where "that" is followed by an affirmative sentence. Freud further remarks that where negation is used, the person often intends affirmation. In some uses, especially in the clinical setting, negation is a symptom as well as a sign: where negation occurs, suspect repression. The use of negation is often the first bit of evidence that a repression is being lifted, for the use of negation permits the introduction of an affirmation in the form of the sentence following "I did not believe that . . . say that . . . intend that . . . know that . . .," and so on throughout all the various ways in which negation can be brought into linguistic communication.

Returning to Russell, there is a description of negation similar to that suggested by Freud. Russell wrote:

> Denial presupposes a form of words, and proceeds to state that this form of words is false. The word "not" is only significant when attached to a sentence, and therefore presupposes language. Consequently, if "p" is a sentence of the primary language, "not-p" is a sentence of the secondary language.[3]

This suggests a psychological mechanism that fits into the psychoanalytic conception of language. For although Russell believed he was cleaning up the messy linguistic reality of ordinary language—laying bare the underlying tidiness—his comments set before us a hierarchy in which 'not' appears as part of the secondary language. If we think of the secondary language as in effect the language spoken in the consulting clinic, then the psychoanalytic patient carries on discourse at a level one or more times removed from the primary level of assertion. In that sense, then, the introduction of negation (*Verneinung*) into the therapeutic conversation presupposes a more basic language in which negation does not occur. The psychoanalytic description of language, though from a vastly different operational viewpoint, matches Russell's description of language as hierarchy rising from a primary language. (It should be noted that Freud also relied upon the notion of 'primary' but in a way quite distinct from Russell's.)

Russell's preoccupation with laying bare the underlying tidiness of logical structures obscured the inescapable difficulties that our everyday use of language entails. A recent consideration of the paradox of the liar is more sensitive to these problems. Saul Kripke, in a paper entitled "Outline of A Theory of Truth,"[4] wrote, "*many, probably most, of our ordinary assertions about truth and falsity are liable, if the empirical facts are extremely unfavorable, to exhibit paradoxical features.*" Kripke's sensitivity to the unfavorable empirical facts leads him to suggest a developmental thesis in regard to the ways we learn to use language. Our capacity to use the predicates 'is true' and 'is false' matures slowly: "The sense in which we can say, in natural language, that a Liar sentence is not true must be thought of as associated with some later stage in the development of natural language, one in which speakers reflect on the generation process leading to the minimal fixed point." What Kripke means by this is that in every model we have of a natural language, there remains a limitation to this effect: "there are assertions we can make about the object language which we cannot make in the object language. For example, Liar sentences are *not true* in the object language, in the sense that the inductive process never makes them true; but we are precluded from saying this in the object language by our interpretation of negation and the truth predicate."[5]

That is a logical observation about the ways in which predicates can function in a certain model of natural languages. Kripke, like Russell, has a conception of a developmental process in the acquisition and use of language. The logical model relates to a developmental model, and bears strong resemblance to the developmental model of language use projected by the psychoanalytic model of psychic life. Kripke's description of learning to use the word *true* makes the point:

> Suppose we are explaining the word "true" to someone who does not understand it. We may say that we are entitled to assert (or deny) of any sentence that it is true precisely under the circumstances when we can assert (or deny) the sentence itself. Our interlocutor then can understand what it means, say, to attribute truth to "snow is white" but will still be puzzled about attributions of truth to sentences containing the word "true" itself. Since he did not understand these sentences initially, it will be equally nonexplanatory, initially, to explain to him that to call such a sentence "true" ("false") is tantamount to asserting (denying) the sentence itself.[6]

I am using Kripke's observations to emphasize the importance of an underlying developmental process that we presuppose when an initiate is inducted into the uses of language. As Kripke puts it: "In this manner, the subject will eventually be able to attribute truth to more and more statements involving the notion of truth itself."[7] That logical accomplishment is parallel to the psychological accomplishment which culminates in erasing negation and asserting sentences in the affirmative, for the meaning they represent is now conscious and intended.

I shall argue that the capacity to attribute truth to more and more statements involving the notion of truth itself is a basic capacity, that it shows a developmental profile, and that *it is intimately connected to our use of language in the telling and hearing of narrative fictions.* The "notion of truth itself" emerges first in the storytelling and story-revealed world of the child.

The developmental profile projected by Kripke in explaining the slow growth toward the ability to use "is true" and "is false" as parts of sentences is supplemented by the psychoanalytic model which introduces fantasy and wish-fulfillment as realities whose force affects the way affirmation and negation work on one another in the fictional world. Psychoanalytic theory gives an explanatory account of an initial inhibition and a slow growth toward the lifting of repression. Countering the force of repression also calls upon the capacity to use "true" and "false" as parts of sentences, only with the psychoanalytic observations the sense of 'capacity' has shifted. Logically, our 'capacity' is a function of intellectual acuity and a progressively more subtle understanding of how language relates to itself and to the world. Psychologically, 'capacity' is a function of access to unconscious thought. That capacity is actualized with the lifting of repression, and that occurs over the entire length of a person's life. Many forces help to counteract the force of repression; one of them, most often ignored, is experience with fictional narration. Our logical and psychological capacities are both tested and sharpened through language organized into story, because issues of truth and falsity as parts of sentences arise there in both explicit and hidden ways. One example of such a presentation and the demands it puts upon our logical and psychological capacities to use sentences in which "is true" and "is false" are at issue follows in sections III and IV.

## II

Freud's most interesting paper on the use of contradiction and negation in ordinary language is "Negation" (*Der Verneinung*).[8] The discovery Freud claims to have made is this: that in the language of the psychoanalytic exchange, "the content of a repressed image or idea can make its way into consciousness, on condition that it is *negated*. Negation is a way of taking cognizance of what is repressed; indeed it is already a lifting of the repression, though not, of course, an acceptance of what is repressed."[9] Since the concept of repression is basic to the model of psychic processes put forward by psychoanalytic theory, something of its meaning and function is presupposed by the observation on negation. If negation (the use of "not") is part of the lifting of repression, then the original condition under which it is claimed repression occurs must be examined.

Repression is one of the vicissitudes suffered by an instinctual impulse or demand: When that demand comes into conflict with others—either external or internal—it may be pushed out of consciousness or never allowed to enter consciousness. That is, the ideational representative of the instinct cannot be entertained consciously, but the instinct continues to exist as a force, a psychic reality, however much denied. Our use of language may on occasion reveal the presence and force of the instinctual through denying that something said or referred to is true, and this takes the form of negation: "I did *not* mean such-and-such"; "What I said does not refer to such a person, thought, wish, belief, etc." And as soon as that is said, there is some evidence for imputing to the utterer just the opposite of what is claimed. So we find ourselves in something like the liar's paradox: What I say is false if true, true if false, but—put more accurately in the psychological context—what I say is *both true and false*. Or, if you will, what I say violates the law of contradiction.

Now a new element enters, for violation of the law of contradiction has psychic as well as logical consequences. One part of the psychic function recognizes the violation: contradiction is not acceptable to what Freud had named "secondary process thought." A way must be found to overcome the conflict, even though the psychic function named "primary process thought" can accept the violation for it generates no conflict there.

The conflict itself (and its acceptability in one domain and unacceptability in another—both domains part of the thought process itself) generates the force of repression. When primary process thought and secondary process thought adhere to their norms, they cannot be coextensive in the descriptions they offer of the world.

One way to adjudicate the differences between primary and secondary thought processes is to shift into a new mode of declaration—that is, to shift into fictional narration as a mode of description. Storytelling has its rescue operation to perform: stories allow primary and secondary thought processes to coexist without repression being the consequence of conflict.

Telling stories allows the introduction of sentences that are properly speaking both true and false, sentences that do indeed violate the "firmest of all first principles," for fictional narration generates sentences representing primary thought through symbolic disguise. In that disguise, primary thought in which the logical operators do not function is represented by the sentences of secondary thought in which the logical operators do function. Fictional narration observes the logical commandments it uses as a disguise for the primary process it represents. That which we recognize as fiction in the linguistic arts is composed in part of primary process thought represented by secondary process sentences. In this way, repressed material is allowed into consciousness. We might refer to this through a loose application of the psychoanalytic concept of displacement. When Freud introduced the term *displacement* (*Verschiebung*), he referred to the possibility that repressed material could enter consciousness if the representation of the repressed material disguised it sufficiently so that it would not be recognized as a threat. If the representation of the primary process thought is far enough removed from the unconscious content, then the ego will allow it into consciousness. Freud's description of displacement points out the need for a certain distance from the original:

> Let us make it clear that it is not even correct to suppose that repression witholds from the conscious *all* the derivatives of what was primally repressed. If these derivatives have become sufficiently far removed from the repressed representative, whether owing to the adoption of distortions or by reason of the number of intermediate links inserted, they have free access to the conscious. It is as though the resistance of the conscious against them was a function of their distance from what was originally repressed.[10]

So one way to overcome contradiction psychologically is to insert a series of links between the repressed material and the remote mode of expression; then what is part of the consciousness is disguised and does not carry the threat of conflict in it.

To this end, the introduction of negation allows the idea entry into consciousness because a denial is put upon it: "No, that is *not* what I meant." But the sentence has been uttered. And so we have the liar's paradox again, but now in a pathological form: what I say is true only if false and is false only if true. The paradox now appears to possess a psychological importance and meaning we have not observed in it in its logical manifestations.

Psychologically, to speak paradoxically is to take the first step toward affirming a thought, toward allowing oneself to attach "is true" to a sentence. The psychological analysis of the liar's paradox, like the logical, focuses on the appearance of "is true" and "is false" as parts of the sentences themselves, but its solution to the paradox differs. Psychologically, to see through the confusion of sentences in which "is true" and "is false" are parts of the sentences themselves, we travel downward toward primary process thinking in which logical operators do not possess the force they possess in secondary process thinking. Logically, we are directed to introduce a hierarchy upward, for in that way we can separate out the "is true" and "is false" of the various language levels, and know when we are talking about a sentence and when we are talking about the world. Psychologically, we need to know when we are talking about a sentence to which the logical operators pertain, and when we are talking about thoughts whose sentential representations are disguises. The sources of contradiction are different from the logical and psychological points of view. Logically, contradictions result from confusion about how "is true" and "is false" function in sentences; psychologically, contradiction results from saying something that for a variety of reasons cannot be said and therefore substituting a negation for an affirmation.

Logicians and psychotherapists are not the only analysts of language disturbed by contradiction: Its presence in thought and utterance has posed for storytellers deep and intransigent problems. To the maker of fictional narrations, the logical and psychological solutions to paradox are themselves substance for further elaboration; the storyteller weaves those speculations into his fictions, as has happened in the following case.

## III

The opening chapter of Melville's *The Confidence Man* presents the reader with a disorienting paradox. Appearing suddenly in a crowd of Mississippi steamboat passengers, a man in "cream colors," referred to as wearing a "white fur" hat with "a long fleecy nap," writes upon a slate a set of sentences that turn out to be quotations from First Corinthians, Chapter 13. "Charity thinketh no evil," he writes, and "Charity suffereth long and is kind." And so on through the sentences that characterize charity as St. Paul so dramatically wrote of it to the congregation awaiting his visit. Upon reading the supposedly mute "evangelist's" message, we are solicited by the text to accept as sentences of itself these sentences taken from another text. The novel does not present the sentences as original but carefully gives each a separate line and supplies quotation marks.

Certainly every reader of the novel when it first appeared would have known the provenance of those sentences. Today, I find, few do, but once the origin of the message delivered at quayside is identified, we cannot avoid making the inference that the writer or "utterer" of the sentences (were he able to utter) has the dream of one in sheep's clothing, and therefore may be the false prophet we were warned against by Jesus in the Sermon on the Mount.[11] However, with that thought another occurs: the possibly false prophet might be described as the Lamb, and be therefore the long departed Christ, returned to preach the Gospel of Paul. Odd thought, but in the context of this perplexing action, altogether acceptable. We might ask, is this a wolf in sheep's clothing, or the Lamb? Is he come to redeem humankind, or to diddle the unwary?

If the man in cream colors is a false prophet, then what he writes on the slate is true if false, and false if true—and therefore the reader is entangled in the liar's paradox. However, to limit distortion as much as possible, we tell ourselves that this is a novel, so the truth conditions of all the sentences are in doubt. Novelists, we might think, are like Cretans; all novelists are liars, and in their rapacious way carry off sentences that don't belong to them. So if Melville usurps Paul, then the truth value of the Epistle cannot be settled in *this* setting. That simply compounds our problem, for as we move away from the source of the sentences, their truth conditions become attenuated. But however much we puzzle over the truth of sentences appearing in novels, this particular novel has guaranteed indeterminancy of truth value, because the paradox of the liar is further complicated by the paradoxes of character and plot.[12]

The sentences written on the slate generate the liar's paradox. Perhaps this perplexity of thought could be dealt with through turning to strategies of character identification (this character, we would say, utters sentences of indeterminate truth value) and through action (for the plot would direct us toward a kind of separating out), and thus we would distinguish reliable, ingenuous actions from misleading, disingenuous actions. Yet *The Confidence Man* allows us no such protection, no such defense. The novel complicates paradoxes of thought with paradoxes of character and paradoxes of plot. It can be said that this text compounds our difficulties, blocks almost completely, with a ruthless persistency, any assignation of truth to the central events. We are in a narrational world that resists, almost to the point of total indeterminancy, the application of the logical techniques employed to discover truth in paradoxical sentence structures.

Paradoxes of character are generated by representations that parallel paradoxes of sentences. The confidence man is, as his occupation implies, one character and several characters: his identity is indeterminate. Each presentation of a speaking, acting, narrating character embeds within it a set of other persons whom we suspect (though cannot know for sure) are the same person in different guises. Might we resolve the paradox of character by establishing a hierarchy of characters analogous to the hierarchy of languages with which we "resolved" paradoxes of thought?

Consider the difficulties. The confidence man appears over and over again; which of his manifestations shall be hierarchically dominant, which subordinate? In some sense we do establish a hierarchy, for when the confidence man relates a story told by himself in a previous disguise, or when he reports an action of 'himself' in an earlier appearance, we read the representations at each point as if in quotation marks, as a representation of an event already presented—analogous to a sentence in indirect discourse. A character can act in such a way that a previous act is re-presented just as a character can talk in quotation marks, repeating sentences previously uttered. In that respect, subsequent tellings and subsequent actions are like languages of a higher order commenting upon languages of a lower order.

Plot comments upon itself in somewhat analogous fashion, catching us up in a paradox of fictional narration. Plot does not go its usual linear way—beginning, middle, end—but consists of embedded stories whose relationship to one another poses delicate problems of interpretation. Reading the stories inside stories produces a giddiness, a feeling of falling into depths with no bottoms, yet we search for a footing. Might we find footing if we introduced a hierarchy of plots, so that one plot could be understood as being of higher order than another? Again, in some way we attempt that, for we try to read the novel as containing its own commentary on its parts.

One way in which self-criticism occurs is through another order of embeddedness: The text contains within it other texts, referred to and quoted. Quotation begins the narration, and quotation occurs frequently throughout the book. Biblical, secular philosophical, and apocryphal texts are commented upon and in turn make implied comments upon the characters and the plot. How shall we regard embedded texts? One way to look at them is this: because they are part of a fictional narration, in that context they have no more claim to truth than the fictional narration as a whole. Thus, embedded texts also generate a paradox: if true in their independence, they are indeterminate when subsumed under a fictional narration.

If all texts are indeterminate in the setting of *The Confidence Man*, then we might think of the sentences of the novel as claiming a right to truth as clearly defended as the right of any other text. Does that claim establish the sentences of the novel as the primary or object language from which the hierarchy of higher languages ascends? Immediately we are confronted again with the problem: which are the sentences of the novel? Can we as readers separate out within the text those sentences of the novel itself and distinguish them from sentences of other texts embedded in the novel? Since *The Confidence Man* embeds many sentences from other texts, it may contain within itself a hierarchy sufficient to allow resolution of at least the paradox of thought, though the paradoxes of character and plot remain unresolvable. Then we must decide which sentences make judgments upon the primary or object language sentences, and that seems almost impossible to do.

Setting aside for the moment the logical problems of the text, let us think of the text as a kind of action within which we can distinguish psychological strata, such as conscious and unconscious presentations in the maner of Freud's discussion of negation. If we think of character and plot as containing embedded episodes, then we might attribute to the embedded elements a function: they are repressed thoughts, wishes, and fantasies that if taken together achieve a coherence. The embedded characters (really the various disguises of the confidence man) and the embedded actions (the sequence of stories told by the apparently different characters) could be considered dreams—that is, they might be likened to what Freud called "dream thoughts," the latent content of dreams covered over by the manifest dream as remembered, so the embedded stories told by embedded characters could be considered latent content of the novel to be interpreted. Reading *The Confidence Man* is like listening to a novel tell its dreams. The teller of stories gives us the manifest content and we must penetrate through to the latent content. Indeed, there is evidence given at the end of the novel that the whole is a dream: the characters go into the dark. As the light goes out, we are left not with the novel but with the embedded stories.

The embedded stories are like symptoms. The novel 'behaves' with a duality of presentations: there are the everyday 'normal' actions and the bizarre psychopathic actions. The latter, the symptoms to be interpreted, can be likened to 'substitute formations' (*Ersatzbildung*), Freud's term for those aberrant psychic events that come to take the place of what a patient *really* means or intends. They are the manifest whose latent meaning is to be determined through the process of analysis. We can read the novel in that way: embedded stories are fictional events which function as substitute formations for hidden meanings that we are challenged to bring forth as we read. As substitute formations, the embedded stories represent events going on beneath the manifest level of narration, and they present themselves to us as representations of the latent. By interpreting the embedded stories, we create the hierarchy downward which leads to the repressed. Uncovering the repressed requires applying sentences to sentences, just as determining truth where paradox appears requires applying sentences to sentences. The difference is in the kinds of languages used to talk about the sentences of the text. Logically, to talk about sentences we introduce quotation marks. Psychologically, to talk about stories we introduce narrators, who function as narrational quotation marks—that is, they talk about stories, giving them the power to function as substitute formations, and thereby lead the reader to their hidden meanings.

Freud thought of substitute formations as functioning in two ways. Economically, they are to be regarded as symptoms which provide a substitute or replacement satisfaction for the unconscious. That is, they stand for, or stand in for, other more deeply repressed (we might novelistically say "more deeply embedded") thoughts, wishes, and fantasies. Indeed, novelistically the embedded present us with a hierarchy of substitute satisfactions reaching down into the most remote, hidden meanings of the text. The other sense of substitute formation that Freud saw is a symbolic function in which the replacement of one content by another occurs through a more or less complex chain of association.[13] My suggestion in reading *The Confidence Man* is that the substitute formations are arranged in the descending hierarchy so that as we move from one embedded story to another, we encounter interpretative commentary that is analogous to the levels of language introduced logically to solve the paradox of the liar. We might think of the paradox resolved through substitute formations as the paradox of fictional narration, a paradox generated by the nature itself of fictional sentences, which though parasitic upon everyday ordinary language sentences, still generate paradoxes when they start to talk about themselves. Just as paradox is generated by using the words *truth* and *falsity* as parts of sentences without distinguishing a hierarchy of languages, so in fictional narration the use of character and plot as part of themselves through embedding generates paradox unless we introduce the hierarchy downward. Once we do that, clarifications are available, though I believe that in the case of *The Confidence Man*, an indeterminacy of motive and meaning remains whatever effort we make to disentangle levels of substitute formations. The substitute formations do not clearly comment upon one another, yet if we think of the embedded material as related to the manifest content by a series of associations that we can uncover, a coherent set of narrational thoughts will clarify itself at least to this extent: we will come to know if determinacy of meaning is possible at all; and I will argue that the conclusion of the hierarchical repression for this novel is that determinacy cannot be achieved, and that paradox remains permanently embedded in all the texts referred to in *The Confidence Man*.

## IV

In Chapters 25 through 28, almost the exact middle of *The Confidence Man*, we are presented with the story of Colonel Moredock, the Indian-hater, a frontiersman who dedicated his life to killing Indians. One peculiarity of this story is its provenance: the original was heard from the lips of Judge James Hall, and the current teller has memorized it word for word. The whole story is a quotation embedded in the text, so we may regard it as in double quotation marks. But there is another peculiarity: within the story of John Moredock, Indian killer, is inserted a story, very brief, about the little colony of Wrights and Weavers, also told by Judge Hall. The point of this story is that an Indian chief, Mocmohoc, changed his demeanor. He seemed to have become benign when he had been perfidious. Once again we are confronted by paradox: All Indians are deceivers: when an Indian says, or acts as if, he is not a deceiver, he is lying. Analogous to the paradox of the Cretan, we are presented with the paradox of the Indian. That paradox is a paradox of action: We cannot know if an action is friendly or perfidious. It is as if we cannot assign a truth value to human behavior, as we cannot to human utterance.

The irony of the story is that Mocmohoc himself says only the frontiersman is to blame if he trusts an Indian. To trust an Indian is to enter into a contradiction, just as to believe what a Cretan says is to get caught up in a contradiction. But now we are at the lowest level of the descent into repression: the story of Mocmohoc occurs within the story of Colonel Moredock, which occurs within the story of the stories told by the confidence man, which themselves occur within *The Confidence Man*. And at that level of repression, the story of Mocmohoc is a substitute formation for lying in speech. The Indian does not talk, he acts. Paradoxes of action are more destructive than simple lying, for they end in death. The only way to overcome them is in a life devoted to eradication of the paradox—that is, kill all Indians. Clearly, that is a substitute formation for a judgment about all humankind, and a judgment about the life-sustaining texts we have taken to be truthful.

Turning to the tale of John Moredock, two central points are made about the character. First, although he was an Indian-hater and ruthless on the hunt, he still could not be deemed "an Indian-hater *par excellence*" (p. 160). And second, "Moredock was an example of something apparently self-contradicting, certainly curious, but, at the same time, undeniable: namely, that nearly all Indian-haters have at bottom loving hearts; at any rate, hearts, if anything, more generous than the average" (p. 162).[14]

Emphasized in the telling of the tale and in propounding the "metaphysics of Indian-hating" (Chapter 26) is the contradiction that though John Moredock hated Indians, killed Indians, and spent his life in the wilds tracking down Indians, there was within him a contradiction of feeling. He was a hater; he also loved. The listener to the story, the Cosmopolitan, is incredulous when the teller has finished. He asks, "If the man of hate, how could John Moredock be also the man of love?" The paradox of love-hate now takes its place beside the paradox of lying. Humans can be contradictory in affection. The man of love is, of course, Christ, and the text of love is the New Testament. Each has delivered to successive generations a paradox to be forever unresolved. Within the man of love is the man of hate, and within the text of love is the apocryphal swindle which casts doubt on every sentence we have endlessly rehearsed.

Although *The Confidence Man* proclaims its contradictory nature from the first page with the paradox of the mute "Lamb," it seeks to force upon us a deeper paradox. Its larger conceptual purpose, it seems to me, seeks to compel a comparison: persons are like texts, and texts are like persons. Both embed within themselves paradoxical assertions that deny the possibility of a determination of value. Neither truth nor falsity attaches to sentences and to actions. For within every text is another text, within every person is another person—and the embedded natures exist in contradiction to the encasing nature. We are not simply divided within ourselves; we are many selves. Books are not simply inconsistent; they are many texts rising in a hierarchy of commentary, falling in a hierarchy of interpretation.

The clearest representation of this situation occurs in Chapter 45. A priestlike man opens the Bible in such a way that the Old Testament falls on one side, the New Testament falls on the other side, and standing upright in the middle is the Apocrypha, the 'untrue' (or at best indeterminate) part of the text. (This way of printing the Bible was common in the nineteenth century.) The Bible itself is then displayed as a paradox-generating text: within it, as within human nature, is an indeterminate part that casts doubt on the sentences declared of the canon or 'true' part. By extension, every text that embeds other texts within it is like the Bible, of doubtful claim, full of contradiction. And by final application, *The Confidence Man* itself is such a text, for within it many other texts and stories occur, as within its characters many characters and within its plot many plots occur. Representations of truth, whether in assertion or in action do not deserve trust, for they are of indeterminate value.

Once we make the conceptual inference I have outlined, we find our footing at last. And if we can ever apply the value 'truth' to assertions in regard to this text, it is the truth of an assertion *about* the text, an assertion in a language that is not the language *of* the text. We can affirm the inescapability of paradox. To accept the whole text as true is to accept its indeterminacy of truth values. Our commitment to the inferences the text promotes then leads to a conclusion: texts, like persons, are indeterminate in their claims to be true, or to be false.

In addition, the comparative power with which we endow the text leads to another conclusion—that texts, like persons, secret within themselves a hidden inner that can, under the appropriate conditions, be revealed. Moving downward in the hierarchy of repression, we remove each covering of the hidden inner as we encounter negation. Where truth is denied, truth may be found. That paradoxical thought finds its textual declaration in a passage at the close of the book.

In the last chapter ("The Cosmopolitan Increases in Seriousness"), the following complex embeddedness occurs:

> "Can you, my aged friend, resolve me a doubt—a disturbing doubt?"
>
> "There are doubts, sir," replied the old man, with a changed countenance, "there are doubts, sir, which if man have them, it is not man that can solve them."
>
> "True; but look, now, what my doubt is. I am one who thinks well of man. I love man. I have confidence in man. But what was told me not a half-hour since? I was told that I would find it written—'Believe not his many words—an enemy speaketh sweetly with his lips'—and also I was told that I would find a good deal more to the same effect, and all in this book. I could not think it; and, coming here to look for myself, what do I read? Not only just what was quoted, but also, as was engaged, more to the same purpose, such as this: 'With much communication he will tempt thee; and speak thee fair and say What wantest thou? If thou be for his profit he will use thee; he will make thee bare, and will not be sorry for it. Observe and take good heed. When thou hearest these things, awake in thy sleep.' "[15]

Here the text steps downward several levels in the hierarchy of latent meaning, carrying us toward an affirmation which will say yes to the denial of the whole tradition upon which our beliefs in ultimate things are based.

*The Confidence Man* wreaks its vengeance upon the tradition that promised solacing belief and clarified argument, but in the end yielded only paradox. Assaulted too, the reader is stripped of the repressions that protected against doubt and contradiction. The text forces a negation from us, a negation of all that we have inherited as true belief, and thus pushes us towards the lifting of the repression that surrounds our response to once sacred and protected visions. Logically pessimistic, the tale denies a resolution of paradox. Psychologically realistic, the tale compels us to confront the anxiety of lifted repression.

As repression lifts, the disparity between manifest and latent comes clear, and the initial denial now yields to an affirmation of the latent content. But the affirmation forces a bitter acceptance, acceptance of the indeterminacy of the traditional texts that have been seen as sustaining pillars of our tradition. Affirming that they are as texts *indeterminant*—that is, in fact, the affirmation of *The Confidence Man*. Out of its paradox is born a relatively simple, perhaps terribly naive belief, a belief in the irresolvability of paradox, and indeterminacy of the truth of beliefs. Tender sensibilities can never tolerate such a conclusion. The thrashing machine of truth has indeed separated wheat and chaff of our sustenance, but it has left us no bread. The thrashing machine has worked with a vengeance, a vengeance as destructive to security in the tradition of revealed truth as that wreaked by the first preacher who brought 'good news.'[16]

## Notes

1. *An Inquiry Into Meaning and Truth* (London: George Allen and Unwin, 1940).
2. Ibid., p. 63.
3. *Inquiry*, Ch. 4.
4. *Journal of Philosophy* 72 (1975):691. Italics in text.
5. Ibid., p. 714.
6. Ibid., p. 701.
7. Ibid.
8. Standard Edition, Vol. 19, pp. 235ff.
9. Ibid., pp. 235–36. Italics in text.
10. "Repression," Std. Ed., Vol. 14, p. 149.
11. "Beware of false prophets, which come to you in sheep's clothing, but inwardly they are ravening wolves." *Matthew*, 7:15.
12. There is also a paradox of quotation marks, or at least an indeterminacy of quotation marks in this text. The mute writes on the slate; the quotation marks may appear as an orthographic convention because the text is reporting that the sentences are utterances, for which conventionally we use quotation marks. Or the use may be because the sentences are from First Corinthians. We don't know the writer's intention when he introduces quotation marks.
13. See J. LaPlanche and J.-B. Pontalis, *The Language of Psychoanalysis* (New York: W. W. Norton, 1973), p. 434.
14. All references are to The Signet, New American Library edition, (New York, 1964).
15. Quotations are from an apocryphal book, *Ecclesiasticus* 13, verses 11, 6, 4, 5, 13.
16. This essay appears in expanded form in my book, *Tragedy: Contradiction and Repression* (Chicago: University of Chicago Press, 1991).

# Index

Adam and Eve, 101-5, 107-11, 120 n. 28
  aloneness and companionship, 103-4, 107-8
  See also creation; deficiency; fall, freedom to; generation; sin; sufficiency (to stand)
adequation, 130, 131, 134, 140
  See also cancellation; zero
affirmation, 184-85, 197-98
  See also negation; truth; truth-claims
Alexander, Samuel, 105-6
alienation, 143
  See also money; negation
Al-Khowārazmi, Muhammad, 134, 143
Althusser, Louis, 153 n. 77, 154 n. 82
Altieri, Charles, 15, 18, 20-22, 23-24, 72 n. 3
Anaximander, 15
Anselm, 98
antinomy, 15
  See also contradiction; contrariety; opposition
*Apology* (Plato), 45, 55
Aquinas, St. Thomas, 15, 19, 24, 93, 95, 104, 123 n. 39, 123 n. 40, 130, 133, 146 n. 14, 148 n. 31
Aristotle, 15, 19, 82, 84, 87, 89, 94, 112, 119 n. 24, 122 n. 34, 148 n. 30, 156, 162, 171, 175 n. 5, 176 n. 9, 178 n. 31

*Aufhebung* (sublation), 25-26, 132-33, 134-40, 144, 145 n. 8, 146 n. 16, 148 n. 32, 153 n. 78
  and Absolute Spirit, 142
  and interest, 139-40, 150 n. 49, 150 n. 50
  and money, 134-40, 144, 149 n. 34
  See also adequation; cancellation; dialectic; Hegel; mediation
Austin, J. L., 175 n. 8
authority, 40-42
autoreferentiality, 10, 31 n. 11

Bach, Johann Sebastian, 10
Bacon, Francis, 45, 82, 118-19 n. 18
Bashō, 26, 160-62, 176 n. 14, 176 n. 15
Bede, 162
Benardete, Seth, 144-45 n. 1
Bickerton, Derek, 162, 175 n. 4, 176 n. 9, 177 n. 18
Biel, Gabriel, 112
Black, Max, 176 n. 11
Boehme, Jakob, 151 n. 52
*Book of the Dead* (Egyptian), 13
Boyle, Robert, 83, 119 n. 19
Bradley, F. H., 15
Bradwardine, Thomas, 91-92
Brahmagupta, 129, 143, 146 n. 10
Brokmeyer, Henry C., 139, 150 n. 46

## 200   Intimate Conflict

Brooke-Rose, Christine, 26, 156-58, 160, 162, 169, 174 n. 3, 174 n. 4, 175 n. 6, 177 n. 17
Brooks, Cleanth, 16
Burke, Kenneth, 42

Calvin, John, 83, 115 n. 7
cancellation (suppression), 25-26, 128-31, 134, 146 n. 13
  and monetary form, 128-29, 139
  and reciprocal exchange, 128, 131-32
  *See also* adequation; *Aufhebung*; dialectic; zero
Caputo, John D., 30 n. 6
Caraher, Brian G., 17, 18, 26-27, 174 n. 1, 180 n. 40
Carnap, Rudolph, 45, 158
Carroll, Lewis, 16
chance, 81
  and probability, 81, 118 n. 16
*Christian Doctrine, The* (Milton), 92, 95-96, 104, 117 n. 9, 117 n. 12, 117-18 n. 13, 119 n. 24, 121 n. 31
Cicero, 147 n. 28
circle, hermeneutic. *See* hermeneutic circle
Clark, Mili N., 15, 18, 22-24
coherence, 39, 41-45, 170-71
Colletti, Lucio, 145 n. 9
*Confidence Man, The* (Melville), 28-29, 181, 183, 190-98
conflict, 1, 5-8, 20, 22-23, 27-28, 99, 102, 188-89
  intimate, 2, 6-8, 11, 14, 29
contradiction, 1-6, 14-29, 35-37, 39, 40-41, 50-52, 57, 61, 71, 92-93, 94, 95-96, 99, 113-14, 115, 115 n. 2, 128, 166, 167-69, 170-73, 179 n. 37, 181, 183, 188, 190, 195-96
  binary model of, 19, 20, 25-27
  and contrary truth-claims, 15-16, 37
  and cultural frameworks, 42-45
  and human nature, 18, 23
  and irony, 17
  and metaphor, 166, 167-73
  and mythic structure of *Paradise Lost*, 76, 77-78, 80, 84, 99, 102, 103
  and painting, 7-14
  and repression, 181, 188, 190, 196-197
  and theology, 82-83, 92-98, 113-14, 119 n. 19, 122 n. 35, 122 n. 36, 123 n. 40, 123-24 n. 42, 125-26 n. 54
  self-contradiction, 23
  Socratic contradictions, 63-70
  ternary model of, 19, 23-24, 25
  *See also* antinomy; conflict; contrariety; experience, aesthetic; irony; mediation; negation; non-contradiction, principle of; paradox; opposition; rendering; strife
contrariety, 15-17, 18, 35
  *See also* antinomy, contradiction, opposition
conventions, 159
Copleston, Frederick, 96
cosmos, Milton's, 81, 83-84, 92, 105-6, 114
counterfeit, 141-42
creation, 22-23, 79-80, 95, 101-2, 105, 112
  mechanics of creation, 79, 112
  *See also* cosmos, Milton's; generation; God; Milton
Crusius, Timothy, 175 n. 6
Cudworth, Ralph, 120 n. 28
Culler, Jonathan, 176 n. 9

Curry, Walter Clyde, 123 n. 39, 124 n. 47
Cushman, Robert, 47
cyborgs, 24-25

deconstruction, 8, 17, 73 n. 11, 73 n. 13, 170-71, 173
  "pivot of deconstructibility," 41
deficiency, 76, 92, 100, 103, 104-5, 106-7, 109
  and authorship, 109-10
  structure of, in *Paradise Lost*, 109-12
  *See also* fall, freedom to; lack; sin
de Man, Paul, 170, 173, 179 n. 37, 180 n. 40
Derrida, Jacques, 4-5, 8, 17, 26, 30 n. 8, 51, 169-71, 173, 176 n. 9, 179 n. 37
Descartes, René, 18, 85-86, 89, 90, 119-20 n. 26, 132
desire (*eros*), 21-22, 39-40, 55-56, 58, 172
  and counter-transference, 40
dialectic, 24-26, 35, 46, 47, 56, 61, 62, 67, 72 n. 6, 74 n. 18, 127, 131, 143, 145 n. 9
  and dialectical hypotheses (Kant), 133
  and economic or monetary form, 127-28, 142-44
  Hegelian, 128, 133, 134, 139, 140, 142
  Marxian, 144
  Platonic, 127-28, 140
difference, 25, 131-32, 140
Dilman, Ilham, 50, 73 n. 9
discourse, 1-5, 41, 54, 158-59, 169, 170-71, 173
*Discourse on Method, A* (Descartes), 85
Donatus, Aelius, 162

*Dora* (Freud), 21, 39-42
drama, 44-47, 63-64

Eckstein, Jerome, 72 n. 5
Eco, Umberto, 175 n. 4
economics, 24-25, 128-29, 131, 134-40
  *See also* money
election, Reformation doctrine of, 77-79, 91-92, 115 n. 6
  and death penalty, 91-92
Eliade, Mircea, 32 n. 24
Eliot, T. S., 16
Empedocles, 15
Engels, Friedrich, 14, 17
Epimenides, 31 n. 10
Erasmus, Desiderius, 115, 117 n. 9
Escher, M. C., 2-4, 9-11
  Works: *Ascending and Descending*, 2-3, 10-11; *Waterfall*, 2, 4, 10-11
Esposito, Joseph L., 146-47 n. 21
*ethos*, 20-21, 41, 42, 44-45, 54
exemplification, 59-60
experience, aesthetic, 168, 171, 173
  and error, 171-73
  *See also* irony, aesthetic; literature; metaphor; rhetoric

fall, freedom to, 75-80, 92, 99, 110
Farnam, Henry W., 149 n. 37
Fichte, Johann Gottlieb, 131-32, 136-37, 144, 150 n. 47
Fish, Stanley, 47-48, 72 n. 6
foundationalism, 49-50
free will, 80-81, 114-15
  God's free will, 94-95, 96-97, 122-23 n. 37
Freud, Sigmund, 17, 19, 21, 27, 39-42, 44, 49, 184-85, 188, 189, 193-94

Frölich, Carl Wilhelm, 154 n. 75

generation (procreation), 82, 87,
    101-2, 104, 105, 120 n. 28
evolution of species according
    to Milton, 84-90
geometry, 2-3
Glück, Louise, 163-64
God, 82-83, 87, 91-98, 105, 123
    n. 40, 132
  God's Son (Christ), 99-101,
    105-7, 110, 125-26 n. 54
  Milton's God, 22-24, 75-81,
    84-87, 90-114, 122 n. 35
  St. Thomas Aquinas' God,
    92-94, 95, 122 n. 35
  *See also* contradiction and
    theology
Gödel, Kurt, 9
*Gödel, Escher, Bach* (Hofstadter),
    9-10
Goethe, Johann Wolfgang von,
    140, 150 n. 50, 153 n. 76
*Gorgias* (Plato), 21, 48, 50-55
Goux, Jean-Joseph, 153 n. 73
*Grammar of Metaphor, A*
    (Brooke-Rose), 156-67, 169,
    177 n. 17
Grattenhauer, Carl, 137

Habermas, Jürgen, 48, 71
*haiku*, 161, 176 n. 14
Harpham, Geoffrey Galt, 32 n. 19
Hartman, Charles O., 174 n. 2
Harvey, William, 82, 89-90, 120
    n. 28, 121 n. 32, 121 n. 33
Hegel, G. W. F., 14, 16, 17, 19,
    24-25, 46, 60, 62, 64, 72 n. 2,
    74 n. 18, 127, 128, 131-33,
    134, 136-42, 144, 146-47
    n. 21, 147 n. 26, 148 n. 31,
    149-50 n. 43, 151 n. 52, 152
    n. 64, 152 n. 66, 155
  Works: *The Difference Between
    Fichte's and Schelling's
    System of Philosophy*, 137;
    *Faith and Knowledge*, 132;
    *First Philosophy of Spirit*,
    144; *History of Philosophy*,
    131; *Logic*, 132, 140;
    *Phenomenology of Mind*,
    131, 140-42; *Philosophy of
    Right*, 142-43, 144; *System of
    Ethical Life*, 144
Heidegger, Martin, 5-9, 11, 13, 30
    n. 5, 30 n. 6
Heppe, Heinrich, 117 n. 11, 125
    n. 54
Heraclitus of Ephesus, 14, 16,
    151 n. 59
hermeneutic circle, 8-9, 30-31
    n. 9
Hesiod, 19, 20, 23, 35-37
  Works: *Theogony*, 20, 36-37
Hess, Moses, 143, 153 n. 71, 153
    n. 75
Hester, Marcus B., 175 n. 8
Hobbes, Thomas, 85
Hoeksema, Herman, 121-22 n. 34
Hofstadter, Douglas, 9-10, 16
Holkot, Robert, 105, 112-13
Homer, 36-37, 38 n. 7
Hufeland, Gottlieb, 137
Hume, David, 143
Hunter, William B., 119 n. 24,
    120 n. 27, 120 n. 29
Hus, Jan, 124 n. 42

Idea (the Platonic One), 127-28,
    130, 140, 142
  and monetary processes,
    127-28, 140, 145 n. 3
idealization, 21-22, 42, 44-46, 55,
    58, 59, 62-63, 70-71
ideology, 143
illusions, 170-71, 173
interaction (co-active exchange),
    26, 158-60, 162, 164-65

*See also* meaning; metaphor
interpretation, 124-25 n. 49
irony, 17-18, 19, 21, 27, 42, 55, 170-71, 173, 179 n. 33
  aesthetic, 27, 171-73
  deconstructive, 27, 170-71, 173

Jaeger, Hans, 30 n. 5
Jakobson, Roman, 169, 174-75 n. 4
Johnson, Mark, 173
Johnstone, Henry W., Jr., 15, 18, 20, 21, 23-24, 37 n. 2
Joyce, James, 30 n. 8
justice, 61-62, 64, 67, 68, 69-70, 81
justification, 90, 92, 116 n. 9, 125-26 n. 54

Kant, Immanuel, 15, 19, 24-25, 127, 128-33, 134, 136, 142, 144, 145 n. 3, 145 n. 9, 146 n. 13, 147 n. 25, 148 n. 30, 148 n. 31, 152 n. 66, 172, 178-79 n. 31, 179 n. 36
  Works: *The Concept of Negative Quantities*, 128-29, 131; *Critique of Pure Reason*, 130, 131, 132, 133, 178-79 n. 31; *Perpetual Peace*, 129
Kelley, Maurice, 117 n. 11, 124 n. 43
Kendrick, Christopher, 120-21 n. 31, 125 n. 49
Kierkegaard, Søren, 18
Kittay, Eva Feder, 174 n. 2
Klee, Paul, 12-14
  Works: *Child Consecrated to Suffering*, 12-14
Klein, Jakob, 144 n. 1
Kline, Morris, 146 n. 10
Kripke, Saul, 185-87
Kuhns, Richard, 17, 18, 27-29, 31 n. 10, 198 n. 16

lack, 59-61, 73 n. 15
Lakoff, George, 173
language, 182-87
  *See also* discourse; meaning; narration
Lazerowitz, Morris, 32 n. 22
Leaf, Walter, 38 n. 4
Lear, Edward, 164
Leibniz, G. W. von, 151 n. 52, 152 n. 64
Levin, Samuel R., 175 n. 5
Lewis, C. S., 119 n. 20
Lieb, Michael, 125-26 n. 54
literature, 1, 18, 19, 156, 170
logic, 1-4, 9-10, 15, 35-36, 37 n. 3, 96, 98, 130, 141, 182, 184, 189-90
  and money, 136-39, 141-42, 144, 151 n. 57
*logos*, 21, 41, 44
Lovejoy, Arthur O., 93, 95, 105, 122 n. 35, 122 n. 36
Lukács, Georg, 153 n. 75
Lukasiewicz, Jan, 178 n. 31
Luther, Martin, 78, 83, 115, 115 n. 7, 116-17 n. 9, 124 n. 42, 140, 150 n. 49
lying (falsehood), 28-29, 35-37, 195
  *See also* illusions; negation; paradox; repression; truth
Lyotard, Jean-François, 30 n. 6

Marx, Karl, 14, 17, 19, 24, 25, 142, 143-44, 145 n. 9, 151 n. 61, 153 n. 75, 153 n. 76, 153 n. 77
Massey, Irving, 174 n. 1, 177 n. 23
materialism, 84-90
  power of matter, 87-89, 119 n. 21, 119 n. 23
meaning, 158-59, 175-76 n. 9, 183, 184, 194

and context, 158, 159, 161, 175 n. 8, 182
and genre, 161
and over-determination, 159, 161
mechanism, 82-84, 91
mediation, 25-26, 133
  medieval system of, 96, 119 n. 20
  third entities, 24, 25, 75, 96, 99
Melville, Herman, 19, 27-29, 181, 191
  Works: *The Confidence Man*, 28-29, 181, 183, 190-98
Meninger, Karl, 149 n. 34
metaphor, 26-27, 155-73, 174 n. 3, 174-75 n. 4, 178 n. 27
  and context, 26, 156, 157-61, 178 n. 27
  and cognition, 167-69, 171-73, 180 n. 38
  epistemology of, 156, 165, 167-69
  formalist theory of, 164
  grammar of, 26, 156-60, 175 n. 6
  idealist theory of, 164
  metaphoric process, 161-62, 164-65, 169, 175 n. 4
  metaphoric tenor and vehicle, 160, 162, 164-65, 168, 176 n. 12
  poetic, 156, 162, 164-65, 168-69, 173
  *See also* interaction; meaning; rhetoric
metonymy, 157-58, 159, 169
Milton, John, 19, 22-24, 76-115, 115 n. 7, 116-17 n. 9, 117 n. 12, 117-18 n. 13, 119 n. 21, 120 n. 27, 120 n. 28, 120 n. 29, 121 n. 31, 121-22 n. 34, 123 n. 37, 123 n. 39, 124 n. 43, 124 n. 47, 125 n. 53, 126 n. 54
  Works: *Areopagitica*, 76; *Art of Logic*, 119 n. 24; *The Christian Doctrine*, 92, 95-96, 104, 117 n. 9, 117 n. 12, 117-18 n. 13, 119 n. 24, 121 n. 31; *Paradise Lost*, 22-24, 75-81, 84, 86-91, 94, 109, 116 n. 9, 118 n. 13, 120-21 n. 31, 124 n. 45, 125 n. 50
  *See also* cosmos (Milton's); God
Mirecourt, John of, 98, 122 n. 34
modernism, 45
*modus tollens*, 133, 141-42
  *See also Aufhebung*; cancellation; dialectic; money
money, 127, 130-31, 131-32, 134-40, 142-44, 152 n. 66
  and bookkeeping, 134, 137
  "money of the mind," 25, 144, 153 n. 76, 154 n. 82
  *See also* cancellation; dialectic; economics; *modus tollens*
Moran, Richard, 174 n. 2
More, Henry, 87, 99, 120 n. 28
Müller, Felix, 149 n. 34
mysticism, 5, 16

narration, 28-29, 187, 188-89, 193-94
  and language, 183-87, 192
natural neccesity, doctrine of, 93-94, 95, 100-101, 104, 106, 109, 114
negation (denial), 15-17, 27-29, 35, 47, 140-42, 184-86, 187, 188, 189-90, 197
  and repression, 188
  *See also* contradiction; lying;

repression; truth; truth-claims
Newton, Isaac, 152 n. 64
Nietzsche, Friedrich, 170
non-contradiction, principle of, 1, 20, 23, 27, 37, 92, 96
  and God, 96-101, 105-6, 107, 110-11, 113, 114
  Kant's law of contradiction, 170-71, 178-79 n. 31, 179 n. 36
  law of excluded middle, 1, 96
  See also contradiction; natural necessity, doctrine of
Nozick, Robert, 21, 43, 53, 63, 71, 72 n. 2
numbers, 130-31, 134, 146 n. 10

Ockham, William of, 96, 115 n. 7
Ogden, C. K., 15
opposition, 5-7, 15-16, 24-26, 128-30, 131, 134, 145 n. 9, 170
  coincidences of opposites, 16
  and formalist model of thought, 24-26, 131-32
  sublation of opposites, 25-26
  See also antinomy; cancellation; contrariety; contradiction

painting, 5-14
*Paradise Lost* (Milton), 22-24, 75-81, 84, 86-91, 116 n. 9, 118 n. 13, 120-21 n. 31, 124 n. 45, 125 n. 50
paradox, 9-10, 16-18, 23, 27-29, 31 n. 11, 98, 103, 189-90, 191-92, 194, 195-98
  liar's paradox, 27-29, 31 n. 10, 182-83, 185-86, 188, 189, 191
  "strange loops," 9-11, 31 n. 10
  See also contradiction

Pascal, Blaise, 18
pathetic fallacy, 176-77 n. 16
Patrides, C. A., 117 n. 12, 117-18 n. 13
Pegis, Anton C., 93, 95, 122 n. 36
Percy, Walker, 171-73
personification, 176 n. 16
perspective, 2-3, 10-11
*Phaedrus* (Plato), 21, 42, 43, 48, 50, 55-59, 61, 68, 73 n. 14
Phillips, Edward, 124 n. 43
philosopher-king, 67
philosophy, 1, 5, 15, 17, 18, 19, 20-22, 24-25, 44-46, 49, 50-52, 53-54, 55-56, 57, 67-68, 69, 73 n. 14, 128, 144, 155
  and economics, 136-40, 142-44, 154 n. 82
  medieval, 93, 96
*Philosophy of Rhetoric, The* (Richards), 155, 158-60, 176 n. 12
physics (Newtonian), 126, 131, 132
Piaget, Jean, 15
Plath, Sylvia, 163
Plato, 19, 20-22, 24, 41-42, 43-71, 72 n. 2, 72 n. 6, 73 n. 13, 73 n. 14, 74 n. 18, 76, 127-28, 129-30, 130-31, 140, 144-45 n. 1, 145 n. 4, 145 n. 9, 146 n. 14
  Works: *Apology*, 45, 55; *Gorgias*, 21, 48, 50-55; *Phaedrus*, 21, 42, 43, 48, 50, 55-59, 61, 68, 73 n. 14; *Republic*, 21, 42, 46, 50, 55, 61-71, 73 n. 12, 73 n. 14, 74 n. 18, 140, 145 n. 4; *Sophist*, 69; *Symposium*, 21, 50, 55, 56, 58, 59-61, 64, 73 n. 14, 73 n. 15
  See also Socrates

Platonists, Cambridge, 85, 86, 87, 89
Pletcher, Galen K., 32 n. 22
positivists, logical, 158, 173
Pound, Ezra, 165
preconceptions (presuppositions), 7-9, 11-12
*Problem of the Self, The* (Johnstone), 18, 20, 21, 37 n. 2
Protestantism, 83, 121 n. 31
psychoanalysis, 184-85, 186, 187
  and displacement, 189
  and dream thoughts, 193
  and substitute formations, 193-94, 195
  *See also* Freud, Sigmund; repression

Quine, W. V. O., 31 n. 11
Quintilian, Marcus Fabius, 162
quotation, 192, 193, 198 n. 12

Rand, Nicholas, 30 n. 6
Randall, John H., 72 n. 4
Rawls, John, 63, 68, 70, 71
Recorde, Robert, 152 n. 67
Reisch, Gregor, 149 n. 35
rendering, 7-9, 14, 31 n. 15
repetition, 115 n. 2
representation, 2-5, 11
repression, 28-29, 181, 183, 185, 187-89, 197
  and the repressed, 193
  *See also* negation; psychoanalysis
*Republic* (Plato), 21, 42, 46, 50, 55, 61-71, 73 n. 12, 73 n. 14, 74 n. 18, 140, 145 n. 4
Reyher, Andreas, 146 n. 16
rhetoric, 20-21, 42, 44-45, 47, 56, 162, 169-70, 173
Ricouer, Paul, 18, 162, 174 n. 2, 177 n. 17

Richards, I. A., 19, 26, 155, 158-60, 162, 164-65, 168, 176 n. 12
Robinson, Richard, 74 n. 18
Roget, Peter Mark, 15
Rorty, Richard, 48-49, 179 n. 33
Rosen, Stanley, 72 n. 5, 73-74 n. 16
Rosencranz, Karl, 149 n. 43
Ross, Stephen David, 174 n. 2
Rousseau, Jean-Jacques, 18, 143, 179 n. 37
Ruska, J., 146 n. 10
Ruskin, John, 176-77 n. 16
Russell, Bertrand, 9, 15, 19, 27, 31 n. 10, 182-83, 184-85

Said, Edward, 124 n. 45
St. Anselm. *See* Anselm
St. Augustine, 18, 123 n. 40
St. John of the Cross, 16
St. Paul, 78, 124 n. 42, 190-91
St. Peter, 124 n. 42
St. Thomas. *See* Aquinas, St. Thomas
Sallis, John, 47, 72 n. 5
Saner, Hans, 145 n. 7
Satan and Sin, 109-111, 124-25 n. 49
  *See also* Adam and Eve; deficiency; sin
Saussure, Ferdinand de, 158
Schapiro, Meyer, 8
Scheffler, Israel, 176 n. 10
Schelling, F. W. J. von, 131, 147 n. 21
Schiller, J. C. Friedrich von, 134, 140, 148 n. 32, 150 n. 50
Schopenhauer, Arthur, 127, 145 n. 2
Schulz, Wilhelm, 143
Searle, John, 175 n. 8
self (person), 18, 21-22, 42-45, 196

self-subsumption, 20-22, 24, 43-45, 63, 70-71, 72 n. 2
  *See also* autoreferentiality; self
Shakespeare, William, 134, 149 n. 37
Shell, Marc, 17, 24-26, 145 n. 1, 145 n. 5, 151 n. 59
Shell, Susan Meld, 145 n. 7
Simmel, Georg, 146 n. 18
sin, 77, 78-79, 81, 84, 89-90, 111-12, 121-22 n. 34
  *See also* deficiency; fall, freedom to
Smith, Adam, 129, 142, 152 n. 66
Socrates, 20-22, 24, 45, 46, 47, 48, 50, 51-67, 69-70, 72 n. 6, 73 n. 10, 73 n. 15, 127-28, 140, 145 n. 3, 146 n. 14
*Sophist* (Plato), 69
Sowernam, Ester, 125 n. 51
Spitzer, Adele, 73 n. 10
Stenzel, Julius, 62
Steuart, James, 142
Stewart, Susan, 31 n. 11
Storch, Heinrich (Henri), 143, 152 n. 68
Strauss, Leo, 47, 72 n. 5
strife, 5-6, 20, 23, 35-37, 38 n. 7
  *See also* contradiction
Stubbe, Hans, 118 n. 17
sublation. *See Aufhebung*
sufficiency (to stand), 75-80, 90-91, 92, 99
Sumner, Charles R., 119 n. 21, 119 n. 22, 119 n. 23
suppression. *See* cancellation
Svendsen, Kester, 125 n. 51
Swaim, Kathleen, 125 n. 50
*Symposium* (Plato), 21, 50, 55, 56, 58, 59-61, 64, 73 n. 14, 73 n. 15
synonymity, 157-58, 159, 169

systems, logico-mathematical, 9-11

Tarbet, David, 73 n. 15
tautology, 1, 84, 90, 96
Taylor, Charles, 147 n. 26
teleology, 49, 80
  and history, 80-81, 90-91
*Theogony* (Hesiod), 20, 36-37
theology (Christian), 84, 89-90, 91, 92-96, 105, 113, 116 n. 9, 121-22 n. 34, 123 n. 40
*Thesaurus of English Words and Phrases* (Roget), 15
Thomas, Dylan, 164
Todorov, Tzvetan, 174-75 n. 4
*Tractatus Logico-Philosophicus* (Wittgenstein), 2
tragedy, 39, 60-61, 111-12, 114
  tragic flaw (*hamartia*), 112
  *See also* deficiency; fall, freedom to; free will; lack
transference, 40
  *See also* desire
truth, 5-7, 8-9, 29, 140-42, 151 n. 52, 185-87, 191, 196-98
  *See also* lying; negation; truth-claims
truth-claims, 2-5, 15-16, 20, 23, 29, 37, 181-87, 191
  *See also* logic; lying; negation
*Truth in Painting, The* (Derrida), 8-9, 30 n. 8

values, 41-42, 44, 49-50, 63, 71
Van Gogh, Vincent, 5-9, 11, 13
Vlastos, Gregory, 72 n. 5, 146 n. 12
Voegelin, Eric, 74 n. 19
voice, 7-8
Vygotsky, L. S., 179 n. 37

Walch, Johann Georg, 145 n. 6
Warnock, Mary, 178 n. 28

Weber, Max, 121 n. 31
Westfall, Richard, 82-83
Wheelwright, Philip, 160
Whitehead, Alfred North, 9
Whitman, Walt, 50
Winterowd, W. Ross, 175 n. 6
Wittgenstein, Ludwig, 2-4, 14, 175 n. 8
Wollebius, Johannes, 124 n. 43
Woodhouse, A. S. P., 100
Woolf, Virginia, 30 n. 8
Wordsworth, William, 19, 26, 165-67
   Works: "The Old Cumberland Beggar," 165-68, 173; "Resolution and Independence," 165-68, 173
work of art, 5-9
writing, 56-57, 58-59

Yuasa, Nobuyuki, 176 n. 14, 176 n. 15

Zeno of Elea, 14, 16
Zeuthen, H. G., 145-46 n. 10
zero, 25-26, 128-31, 134, 142
   *See also* adequation; cancellation; number
Zilsel, Edgar, 152 n. 67